1968
WAR & DEMOCRACY

EUGENE J. MCCARTHY

1968
WAR & DEMOCRACY
by
Eugene J. McCarthy

© 2000 by Eugene J. McCarthy
ISBN 1-883477-37-9
Library of Congress CIP 99-068858

Published by LONE OAK PRESS

"From a political point of view, it would have to be called the year of the people. For it was the year in which the people, in so far as the system and the process would permit, asserted themselves..." Eugene McCarthy

The 1969 release title of this book, Year of the People, coupled with the author's name, carried a meaning to the reading pubic fit to that time. Thirty years later it would obscure the substance. Decisions about war and peace - how those decisions are made and by whom - are the essence of this book: not how improperly these were made at one time, but how these life and death decisions must only be made in a democracy.

Contents

Foreword

Opinions may divide as to whether Martin Scorsese's *Taxi Driver* is a great film about an American psycho, or a keen study of an American political campaign, or some subliminal combination of the two, but who can forget the moment when Albert Brooks mans the phones at the candidate's HQ?

> *"We asked for buttons saying 'We* Are *The People'. These buttons read 'We Are The People'...Oh, you don't think there's a difference? Well, we will not pay for the buttons.* We *will throw the buttons away..."*

The movie's Senator Palantine is a perfectly-confected phoney, and the cinema audiences of the mid-1970s had been pre-hardened by Watergate and Indochina to any number of insincere and indistinct appeals. ("Now more than ever", read the Nixon placards, and I still envy Renata Adler for noticing that this is the opening half of a line from Keat's beautiful *Ode To a Nightingale*: "Now more than ever seems it rich to die.") You couldn't decently try a title like "Year of the People" these days, not after "Putting People First" and all the rest of it. So the first point to make about Gene McCarthy's book is, simply, that it can be re-issued without embarrassment. This may not be as small an observation as it appears.

One day, I am sure, I will meet someone who recalls with pride the door-knocking that he or she did for Hubert Humphrey or Richard Nixon in that imperishable year. I mingle fairly freely, and have friends from the entire bestiary of American politics, but this anecdotal experience still lies in my future. On the other hand, I have met many people who claim to have busted their britches for "Gene" in 1968, and who almost certainly didn't. This must be one of the greatest-ever compliments paid by vice to virtue - like King Henry's prediction before Agincourt that the graying veteran would "remember, with advantages, what deeds he did that day."

I count it as a signal privilege that the Senator has asked me to contribute an introduction to the revival of the book, and may as

5

well say at once that I can't make any of the above claims. In 1968 I was aiding and abetting American draft-resisters in Oxford, and knew well the Leckford Road address where the most famous draft-*dodger* of all time was roosting among better men. I remember reading and even passing around a left-insurgent sheet, which had a satirical headline about "Clean Gene" and a list of his many betrayals of the working class, the civil rights movement and the cause in general. (In those days, some of us were not immune to the mantra of "No Friends On The Left.") One of the disquieting discoveries I made in this book is that that list, of the Senator's crimes against humanity, was lifted whole-cloth from a mendacious circular put out by Robert Kennedy's more "deniable" and less fastidious supporters. The lie, Mark Twain famously said, has gone round the world before truth can get its boots on. But to see a lie nailed, at any distance in time, is always a pleasure and an instruction and - in this case - a reproach.

When the Senator determined that someone would have to challenge the war policy of the Johnson administration, and also that that somebody would have to trust the people and call on the better angels of their nature, the reign of the lie was almost complete. The White House lied about Vietnam, lied about China, lied about the Gulf of Tonkin, lied about the motives of the dissidents, lied about the prospects of victory and - no small matter - lied about the possibility of fighting a colonial war and simultaneously redressing what Gene McCarthy rightly terms the "internal colonialism" under which dwelt the majority of black Americans. "All I have is a voice," wrote W. H. Auden in that other critical year of 1939, "to undo the folded lie." Anyone raising his own voice against the nexus and system of deception in 1968 had to count on being defamed and misrepresented in his turn.

Gene McCarthy had been defamed and misrepresented before. (He was one of the few Democrats willing to challenge his gruesome namesake from Wisconsin in the early years of the haunted Fifties.) But the difference this time was an essential one, because this time he was being slandered by the high-minded forces of Democratic liberalism. The campaign wasn't the usual abbreviated course in "lesser evils for the simple minded", but a morally and intellectually complex task of facing what one's own party had wrought. As he puts it here, with a nice dialectic:

" In 1964, we Democrats talked of peace. Promises were made of peace abroad and of progress at home. And similar promises were being made again in almost the same language as was used back in 1964. Most of us at Atlantic City [at the 1964 Democratic Convention] accepted and said through the

6

campaign that if our candidate was elected what has been happening in Vietnam would not have happened, and that if the other candidate was elected what is happening would have happened. "

The word for this is not so much accountability as responsibility. A necessary but not sufficient condition here is that of simply being observant:

"At a White House meeting on February 18 [1965], speaking to some twenty-five or thirty Senators, Secretary of State Dean Rusk advised us that the government in power in Vietnam - at that time under General Nguyen Khanh - was strongly supported, was stable, and gave every evidence that it would be effective for a long time to come. The Secretary gave us this assurance at about nine or ten o'clock that night. The morning papers gave us the news that the Khanh government had been overthrown. If one took into account the difference in time zones, the overthrow was being carried out at about the same time that the Secretary of State was speaking to the Senate group in the White House."

As Thoreau says, a trout found in the milk is not proof of what is going on, but proof that *something* is going on. To this day, I remember the jest that turned more sour than any milk - and that came to apply to other states in the Pax Americana - "If there was a general election, which general would you vote for?"

A person of average skepticism or even curiosity would have been alert no later than the Rusk briefing, and others like it. (From internal evidence, I deduce that Gene McCarthy sincerely wishes that he had joined Senators Morse and Gruening in voting against the Gulf of Tonkin resolution, and made a Horatian triumvirate with which to oppose a surreptitious and subversive non-declaration of a real war.) We are now accustomed to talk glibly of "the lessons of Vietnam", as if these formed part of a common heritage of common sense. But who else noticed, at the time of General Westmoreland's astonishing address to both Houses of Congress in April 1967, that he deliberately used the words "kill ratio" - a term that the Administration swore was a propaganda invention by men of ill-will? And who else observed so economically that an important constitutional threshold had also been surreptitiously passed?

"This was an act without precedent in that a field commander on active duty spoke on what were essentially the political aspects of the war rather than on the military aspects of it. But more significant was the fact that a field commander on active duty had been brought back to support not only the

*military program but also those political aspects of the war
which were subject to intense controversy."*

The lucidity of McCarthy's critique lay in this - the calm and
unanswerable way in which he connected the military destruction
of Vietnamese society to the militarist attack on American
democracy. It is this book's steady employment of Forster's
maxim - "Only Connect" - that justifies him in employing the
much-abused term "The People". Just as a populist may be a foe
of democracy even if he commands a temporary majority, so a
man taunted as "elitist" can be a man of the people if he argues for
popular and constitutional sovereignty. Just drink in, if you will,
the refreshment of this phrasing from three decades ago:

> *"If the issues are of major importance, poll taking is a
> waste of time and money. Certainly the issue of the
> Presidential campaign of 1968 was one of such consequence
> that one should not attempt to determine what he should do on
> the basis of what the polls might show."*

Does this mean indifference to the masses? On the contrary. In
state after state, beginning in Connecticut but building through
Pennsylvania, Michigan, New Mexico and California and
famously climaxing in Chicago, the McCarthy campaign became
a means by which popular choice and democratic procedure could
be asserted against Tammany rule. (The culminating instance is
the speech made by Julian Bond in Chicago, seconding the
McCarthy nomination but also picking up the banner of racial
integration from where it had been so shamefully dropped at the
Atlantic City convention of 1964.)

Understatement is part of the McCarthy style, and one seldom
wishes that this were otherwise. (What must Joseph Alsop have
thought, on re-reading the Senator's feline judgment that he was
"not running with the pack but running on his own track"? Even I,
who know damn well what that track was, *and* who laid it down,
was compelled to re-read the sentence twice.) In just the same
way, McCarthy deals graciously but annihilatingly with the many
low blows and sordid innuendoes that issued from the Robert
Kennedy camp. Read them and weep; they are not the kinds of
political slander that result from haste or misapprehension, and
the author courteously omits the outright racism and demagogy
that marred Kennedy's last debate with him. This may be out of
deference and consideration - Mr. Kennedy's assassination
followed hard upon - or it may be out of a generalised wish to
avoid sensation. (After all, the Senator refuses to tell in these
pages the many amusing moments in New Hampshire when he
was confused, to his own advantage, with Robert Kennedy's old
boss; the other McCarthy; the slobbering bigmouth who still helps

us to make the distinction between the crowd-pleaser and the democrat.) But how many politicians now could write so drily about a farm stop in rural Nebraska, where the Sibbersens were waiting and "the elder Mr. Sibbersen, who had retired from farming, had been a pioneer in land management and crop rotation. He was fully informed on the geological history of the entire area"?

It takes an effort of imagination as well as memory to recall the atmosphere of fantasy that lay over public affairs that year. Did people *really* believe that Chinese expansionism was being resisted in Vietnam, when all the time it was being resisted *by* Vietnam? And where did we find such men as Hale Boggs, chairman of the Platform Committee at the Chicago Convention? Congressman Boggs took it upon himself to tell the delegates that he had sought military advice, and been told by General Creighton Abrams that an unconditional bombing halt in Vietnam would lead to a fivefold increase in "Northern" presence in the "South". McCarthy's comment here is devastating. He coolly notes that such a statement, while irrelevant then, must have become relevant after the Administration's own decision to call a bombing halt. The pleasures of vindication, though rare enough, are almost Euclidian in comparison to those enjoyed by the Boggses of this world.

The disgraceful thuggery of the authorities, as flaunted at that same Convention, makes it plain without further emphasis that the battle against the war in Vietnam was, necessarily and inextricably, a battle not just to extend popular democracy at home but to preserve it from its enemies. (The difference between the two Georgia delegations at Chicago, one organised for racism and war by Governor Maddox, and one organised by Julian Bond for Gene McCarthy, makes the identical point in a similar way. Not even the complete stage management of the major party conventions can quite obscure the lasting changes that 1968 made to the American political tradition.)

I would be untrue to the spirit in which Senator McCarthy invited me to write this essay, if I did not mention my reservations and criticisms. I think he is somewhat condescending when he writes that his campaign caused people in Berkeley, for example, to abandon "the devices of the protest, the peace rally and the resistance march." Not only is this not true; it would not have been a good thing if it were true. I thought then and think now that the Senator was gravely mistaken in understating the importance of the August 1968 invasion of Czechoslovakia; immediately recognisable then as a hinge event. And I believe he is wrong, though in a different sense, to say that in 1968 "the division within the Democratic party was not one of personality."

We are of course accustomed to hear that we should concentrate on "issues" instead of personalities, and this distinction often sounds suitably serious. But experience teaches us that it can be a false one, or a distinction without a difference. Who would say that the personality of Lyndon Johnson or Robert Kennedy - perhaps especially the personality of the latter - was not a factor in prolonging the war? Who would argue that the personality of the Republican nominee of that year was not a political consideration on its own? Conversely or symmetrically - and here I make a point that the author is inhibited from making - can it really be said that Senator McCarthy's own nature and style were not powerful motivating forces on their own? I am writing this at a time when the Democratic and liberal cause has forced itself to pay an exorbitant price for overlooking what is now called "the character issue", but you will perhaps notice that the two words have lately become subtly and inescapably intertwined.

For a campaign or a candidate to get under way in these etiolated days, some backers must find a nominee or client, or else he must locate them, and then this nominee or client must take soundings to discover what his "issues" are, and then publicists may be recruited from the expired campaigns of any expired politician, and then the voters may be approached as if in some plebiscite or referendum, with the man or the manifesto already packaged, and with a law-firm or think-tank safety-net for the loser. In 1968, the "issues" - the divisions of principle and conviction, and the fight over democracy - had an effect of their own. The Senator's modesty is only appropriate to the extent that he concedes that the candidate was not the whole story.

Staunch fighter that he is, McCarthy has in many ways the character of a poet - reflective, ironic, and attendant on longer-term rhythms. We know from Gabriele D'Annunzio and Roy Campbell and Charles Baudelaire that there is nothing necessarily humane or democratic about the poetic vocation. Still, in these United States is has most often been a humane and democratic voice. More than any remotely comparable political memoir, *1968: Year of the People* relies on poetry to make its points and to mark its transitions. We hear from Robert Bly and Robert Lowell and Cecil Day-Lewis, and from the author himself, and also from young people who were moved to send him their own verses. (When I think of 1968 myself, I remember Robert Lowell saying that he feared, if the Movement failed, "a reign of piety and iron." He wasn't far afield in his intuition.)

10

So, in closing, I'd like to complete the beautiful monologue written by Auden in *September 1, 1939*. After confronting "the folded lie", which is also "the lie of authority", he closes by saying:

> *Defenseless under the night*
> > *Our world in stupor lies.*
> *Yet, dotted everywhere*
> > *Ironic points of light*
> *Shine out wherever the just*
> *Exchange their messages.*
> *May I, composed like them,*
> *Of Eros and of dust*
> *Beleaguered by the same*
> *Negation and despair,*
> *Show an affirming flame.*

The pulse of 1968 was supplied in large measure by the mutual recognition, through the speaking and hearing of truth, of disparate men and women who felt for the Vietnamese, and felt for their own country, and who laid aside the personal life in order to engage. No subsequent evocation of "points of light", by banal and stuttering professionals, has come near to matching this, let alone to surpassing it.

Christopher Hitchens
Washington, D.C. September, 2000

I, We, They

It is my hope that this book will be a testimonial to the many people, young and old, who practiced what came to be called the "New Politics" in the contest for the Democratic presidential nomination in the year 1968; that it will fill in some of the information gaps and clear up some of the misunderstandings that arose in the course of the campaign and prove to be a worthwhile commentary not only on the politics of 1968 but be a help in understanding and influencing American politics and government policies in the future.

Many difficulties arise as one undertakes to write a book about one's own campaign for the presidency, especially when that campaign is marked by both success and failure. The first to be met is deciding which pronoun one should use.

Should one speak of "my" campaign, while intending to include the efforts of everyone?

Would it be clearer to say that "we" did something, intending to include in it all who campaigned with or for the candidate?

Should one refer to the campaign as "our" campaign?

Should one attempt to make distinctions by saying "I" about something personal, by saying "we" about those things done by staff or organized campaigners?

Or should one include a third category of "they," which in the case of the 1968 campaign would be a very large one, to indicate those who acted quite independently and on their own initiative on behalf of the candidate and the cause which he represented?

There may have been campaigns in the past in which it was easy to make clear distinctions, crediting the candidate with nearly everything; other campaigns in which a "we" group was more important; perhaps, even some campaigns in which "they" did most of the work. In the case of my campaign of 1968, no such distinctions are possible. I will try to separate the more-or-less personal actions in the "I" category from those which were undertaken as a common or "we" effort, and also to recognize and

13

describe, in so far as I have knowledge of them, the great work carried on by persons or groups acting on their own initiative.

If one were to characterize the year 1968 in the way in which Chinese mark the years – the Year of the Horse and the Year of the Dragon – from a political point of view, 1968 would have to be called the Year of the People. For it was the year in which the people, in so far as the system and the process would permit, asserted themselves and demonstrated their willingness to make hard political judgments and to take full responsibility for those judgments. And in so doing they acted with more spirit and more commitment than did many political leaders.

The Call to Politics

On November 30, 1967, I announced that I would challenge President Lyndon Johnson for the nomination of the Democratic party.[1] This announcement was followed by a rather mixed reaction around the country. The early press reaction was one of surprise, and the political response, generally negative. Most commentators and editors looked upon this challenge as desperate if not altogether hopeless, and columnists and others rushed to explain my motivation. Some said I was acting out of frustration, others, out of anger or enmity; one writer reported that I had run because my daughter Mary had urged me to do so. My explanation is somewhat different.

For nearly twenty years, especially in talking to students, I had emphasized the need for a revived sense of profession and vocation in modern society, not in the traditional or formal way in which these two concepts were accepted in earlier times but in a modern context in which each person comes to an understanding of what his work is all about, what its social implications and consequences are; and on the basis of that understanding accepts those special responsibilities which rest upon all those in a given field of work.

I had suggested several times, over the years, that the list of professions should be greatly extended beyond medicine and law to include almost all work, especially that work which affects society directly, such as certified public accounting, newspaper reporting, investment counseling, and also, in a very special way, politics.

If there were a clear sense of vocation and profession in politics, both the practitioners and the public would have better standards for judging performance. The lack of any standards was clearly evident during the late years of the Truman administration and the early years of the Eisenhower administration when

---

[1] See Appendix 1.

15

charges of corruption were brought against party officials, officeholders, some of cabinet level, and some presidential aides. In almost every case, those who were called to account explained their actions as having been essentially the same as they would have been in the business or profession they pursued before taking political office.

The men revealed little evidence of understanding that what might be wholly acceptable behavior in a business office was not acceptable on the part of one who held public trust. One of the accused said in his defense that he had not done anything that his mother would not have approved.

I had been telling student and professional audiences through the years that acceptance of professional status carries special responsibilities and obligations, including the obligation to take risks. We expect doctors to take chances on being infected as they care for the sick. We expect lawyers to take certain cases – especially those involving crimes – that may bring public judgment against the lawyers themselves. We expect firemen to fight fires and policemen to take risks in the enforcement of the law. And we should also expect politicians, if the issue is important enough, to show a similar sense of profession and to understand the obligation to take political risks when necessary.

When 1968 began, I had been actively involved in politics for twenty-two years. I had been elected five times to the House of Representatives and twice to the United States Senate from the state of Minnesota. Minnesota politics, like its geography and its people, is very open. There was never an established class in our state. Nearly everyone of every nationality came in on essentially equal terms. The various immigrant groups established schools and colleges for the education of their young people. Never for any length of time were there uneducated minorities who could be controlled or manipulated by party leaders, and the spirit of political revolt has always been able to break out as it did in the Farmer-Labor party movement in the 1920's and 1930's. In the same way that the state was open to new political ideas and programs, it was also open to new personalities.

My first real participation in politics began almost by accident or default in 1946. As a college student in the Depression, I had not been indifferent to politics or government policies. When I became a teacher of social sciences and economics (both high school and college), I was attentive to current political problems and issues, and took clear positions on social problems and legislation. This was important in the years immediately following World War II when many students were veterans who had returned to college. American society had changed significantly in the years between 1938 and 1945. The United States had become an urban society; the great migration from country to city was taking place, and the movement of Negroes from the south into the northern cities was accelerating. In many cases the cultural differences between their old and their new environment was much greater for the Negroes than for the immigrants from foreign countries. Foreign immigrants received much more attention in becoming American citizens than any of the domestic migrants who moved during the thirties and forties.

Government policy to deal with social changes lagged behind. I believed that new federal legislation on housing, education, medical care, and civil rights was vitally necessary. Others did too; in fact, 1945 was a year of intensified political activity in Minnesota. Marshall Smelser, a colleague of mine on the faculty of St. Thomas College in St. Paul, became particularly interested in the reform of the Democratic-Farmer-Labor party – an effort being led by Hubert Humphrey, then mayor of Minneapolis. On Smelser's suggestion, a number of us on the faculty attended precinct meetings and the county convention in 1947. He nominated me to be county chairman; the nomination did not carry. Many years later in an article he wrote for *Harper's* magazine, he had a little fun with his unsuccessful nominee. "As an economics professor McCarthy was concerned more with the distribution of wealth than with its production or consumption," he wrote. "The effect on his students was mixed. After a semester of exposure to McCarthy's ideas of social justice, one young conservative protested, 'Professor, you're softening us up so we won't be able to go out of here and compete!'"

In 1948, Smelser left St. Paul for another teaching position, and I was left more or less to carry on the work he had initiated. The Ramsey County Democratic-Farmer-Labor party did not elect me as chairman in 1948, and in the course of the spring and early summer I decided to run for Congress.

Democrats had a good year in 1948. Running with Harry Truman, I was elected, and then re-elected for four additional terms.

During my early years in the House of Representatives, halting progress was made in establishing the social programs set out in the Truman campaign. It was particularly slow during the Eisenhower administration, a period of drift within the Democratic party; a period in which there was – especially after the second defeat of Adlai Stevenson – no strong voice to state policy or provide leadership, although Paul Butler, as national Democratic chairman, tried hard to establish a position for the party and to give it a liberal voice. His efforts were not successful, and gradually the focus of power within the Democratic party shifted to the Congress, and eventually to the Senate Majority Leader, Lyndon Johnson.

By 1957, Congressman Lee Metcalf of Montana and I agreed that it had become necessary for the liberal Democrats in the House to state their position on the important issues of the time. House members met in my office or in Metcalf's periodically for a month. We drafted a liberal program of action which included six vital areas for political action: civil rights, education, health, housing, foreign aid, and atomic policy. Eventually eighty members subscribed to this declaration.

Our purpose was to make the House of Representatives meet its constitutional responsibilities and to encourage members of the Democratic party in that body to fulfill their traditional party responsibilities, not only of legislating but of providing leadership and a program for the country as well. I have sometimes been accused of being more concerned with the process than with the substance of legislation or of congressional action. I am not disposed to make a defense of myself against these assertions, because the balance between the one and the other is often so delicate that it can be settled only by a subjective judgment. The process is often simply the operation of the institution. Our drafting of the liberal program, which was a proper operation of the institution, was construed in some quarters, of course, as irregular and as a challenge to the Democratic leadership.

In 1952, when Senator Joseph McCarthy of Wisconsin was a particularly strong force in Washington and the country because of his activities as chairman of the Permanent Sub-committee on Investigations of the Government Operations Committee and for his special campaign against communists – real or imagined – in the federal government, he was considered to be a politically dangerous opponent. I thought it necessary that someone challenge him, even though I was sure that one confrontation would not stop him. That was why I said "yes" when Theodore Granik, moderator and producer of the television program "American Forum of the Air," invited me to debate Senator McCarthy on his program. Granik told me he asked me to go on the program only after he had been turned down by other members of Congress.

I cannot claim that my debate with him was the beginning of his decline. Television commentators at the time described the debate as a draw. Harry MacArthur, a television critic for the Washington *Evening Star*, wrote on July 23, 1952: "The fallacy of Senator Joe McCarthy's invincibility in debate was exploded on Ted Granik's 'American Forum of the Air.' The technique for dealing with him in TV discussion – or maybe any other discussion for that matter – was demonstrated by another and different McCarthy, Representative Gene of Minnesota.

"Senator Joe McCarthy has always been a fearsome opponent. His manner aggravates many people, usually his foe in a debate more than any one else. The result is that he usually reaches the end of one of those broadcast sessions seeming a calm, reasonable and even persecuted man, while his opponent is reduced to incoherent rage.

"Senator McCarthy starts out with the friendly, disarming approach, full of affability and first-name calling. Preliminary debate gets under way and he just happens to have with him something bearing on that first point. From a voluminous briefcase he produces a thick document. It seems to be flowing with seals and ribbons as if notarized several times and is fearfully impressive.

"Representative Gene McCarthy seems to have found the formula, however. There probably was no true victor Sunday night; it is not likely that many McCarthy supporters were won over by any other McCarthy. Representative McCarthy emerged unruffled and unscarred, though. That is tantamount to victory in this league."

As the election of 1958 approached, I began to give thought to running for the Senate, even though the prospects of victory in the election at that time seemed uncertain. The Republican incumbent from Minnesota, Senator Edward Thye, had served two terms as governor and was finishing his second six-year term in the United States Senate. He was popular and respected and had a general liberal identification. I felt that the legislative programs proposed in the campaign of 1948 could be advanced more rapidly, however, and I believed that as a member of the Senate I would be in a better position to speak about these programs and of the nation's need for them. The foreign policy of this country had also become more and more important, and therefore the role of the Senate had become increasingly important.

I had positive views as to what I thought the Senate should be and as to what I would like to accomplish as a Senator. First, I was hopeful that I could advance the passage of delayed domestic legislation through influencing the public as well as by acting in the Senate. Second, as a member of the Senate which has some power over the federal court system, I hoped I could be helpful in establishing a truly national judiciary and move the country away from a regional system of justice which existed then and to some extent still exists today. Third, I wanted to do what I could to make the Senate a more effective force in determining foreign

19

policy, as the Constitution intended. The Minnesota voters endorsed my views and sent me to the Senate that fall with 53% of the vote.

Since coming to the Senate, I have been observed by at least one commentator to have been especially active in presidential years. There is truth to this observation. The process of choosing a new President is important not only because much power and influence attends the office, but also because the campaigning puts the issues before the people. The crucial points in the presidential election year are the national party conventions, and the most important action taken at them is the nomination of the candidates, although in some conventions, such as the 1948 Democratic convention in which civil rights was the central point of debate, an issue may become just as important, if not more important, than the candidates.

It is my opinion that members of the Senate particularly should be actively involved in national conventions and, as a general rule, be prepared to incur some risks to their political careers in order to influence the selection of party nominees and platforms. Their responsibility has taken on increased significance in recent years as the importance of foreign policy has come to outweigh the matters handled in the states by governors. Considering this shift, governors continue to be a stronger influence in national conventions than they should be.

My participation in presidential politics has reflected not only my beliefs, but also the fact that in three Democratic conventions before 1964 I was called upon as a Minnesotan and as one active in our political party to support various efforts and undertakings of Hubert Humphrey.

In 1952 at the Democratic convention in Chicago, I placed in nomination, as a favorite son, Senator Hubert Humphrey of my state of Minnesota.

In 1956, I was a supporter of Senator Humphrey in his bid for the vice-presidential nomination, which was thrown before the convention by the presidential nominee, Adlai Stevenson. My participation was very limited; the contest was principally between John Kennedy and Estes Kefauver. It was the first occasion, however, on which I found myself quite by accident and geography supporting the candidate opposed to John Kennedy.

In 1960, I was again, by virtue of essentially the same circumstances, made cochairman of the Humphrey for President campaign in the primaries. I participated in the campaign in Wisconsin and in West Virginia.

Senator Humphrey lost the primary election in Wisconsin and also in West Virginia, after which he withdrew from the contest for the nomination. The Minnesota delegation therefore went to the 1960 Democratic convention uninstructed and without a candidate. I was a member of that delegation and uncommitted to any candidate, having done little more after the primaries than attend a Washington, D.C. rally for Adlai Stevenson two weeks before the convention.

At the time of the convention's opening, I had reservations about the candidacy of Senator John Kennedy. I had no positive case against the candidacy, but it was my general opinion that he had not yet proved himself and was less well qualified to be President than either Lyndon Johnson or Adlai Stevenson. I had some reservations about the candidacy of Senator Johnson as well.

I was publicly announced for Senator Johnson at a press conference held by Senator Robert Kerr; however, the announcement was made without my clearance. I did not repudiate it altogether, but said that I thought that Senator Johnson would make a good prime minister – a remark which expressed my reservations about him as President, because a prime minister is much more subject to party limitations than is the President of the United States. I also said I thought that as President, Lyndon Johnson would have the capacity to get as much out of anything as was in it – the Congress, for example – but doubted his ability to move the nation to new and different achievements. I am of the opinion that had Lyndon Johnson come to the presidency through the normal way of first being nominated and then being elected, his leadership would have been strengthened and his presidency different.

During the presidential primaries of 1960, Adlai Stevenson had never publicly said that he was a candidate, nor had he said anything to me in private indicating his intentions. When his candidacy began to come alive – even in a very limited way – I joined in the efforts to advance it, attending a luncheon on July 11 during the convention at which Mrs. Eleanor Roosevelt spoke and a late night rally the same day at which I spoke in support of Stevenson.

On July 12, the Minnesota delegation leaders caucused until six o'clock in the morning on the question of who to support. Senator Humphrey was undecided, whereas Minnesota Governor Orville Freeman, who had been endorsed by our delegation for the vice presidency, argued for support of Kennedy on the first ballot. It had already been made public that he would nominate John Kennedy the next day. At the caucus, I announced my support of Stevenson.

21

Five hours later, about eleven o'clock on the morning of July 13, I was called by Senator A. M. (Mike) Monroney and asked whether I would nominate Governor Stevenson. I was surprised and asked for time to think it over. In about a half hour Adlai Stevenson called and asked me himself. I accepted and went on to prepare notes for the speech which, it was then thought, might have to be given by three o'clock that afternoon.

I was aware, of course, that the chances of a Stevenson nomination were remote and that it could be accomplished only if the Kennedy and Johnson forces deadlocked. But it seemed to me that the Democratic convention should, if Stevenson wished, consider him for nomination even though it might turn out to be no more than a tribute.

I asked the Democrats to accept Adlai Stevenson as a candidate for the third time,[2] and the response in votes turned out to be negligible: he obtained only 79 1/2 votes out of 1,521; Lyndon Johnson received 409; and John Kennedy won the nomination with 806 votes. But the demonstration following my speech for Stevenson was far more intense and enthusiastic than that given to any other candidate. There were those at the convention who were strongly for the nomination of Adlai Stevenson and they, of course, cheered. And there were those who had been for him in the past and responded to his nomination with cries of approval to make their change of loyalty easier. Finally, there were those who, in whatever category was left, cheered as a kind of testimonial to Adlai Stevenson as a man.

The speech was acclaimed an excellent nominating speech. Under the circumstances, I could not have given a bad one. I have suffered some at the hands of critics since that time – especially among those who heard that speech in 1960. People have expressed disappointment over subsequent speeches.

Rumors about my having received an offer of the vice presidency from Lyndon Johnson or from any other candidate at the 1960 convention were without substance. It was obvious that John Kennedy had he not been nominated for the presidency would have been the vice-presidential choice of either Stevenson or Johnson or of any other candidate who might have been nominated.

In the next presidential year, 1964, conservative strength seemed to be growing across the country. In anticipation of what I thought might be a confrontation, I wrote a book in 1963 entitled *The Liberal Answer to the Conservative Challenge*. With the nomination of Senator Barry Goldwater by the Republicans, the

---

[2] See Appendix 2.

need to defend the liberal position from the conservative attack was greatly reduced, however, since his positions generally were so extreme they offered little challenge.

Goldwater's year was also the year in which I was up for re-election to the Senate. On January 8, my campaign committee held a fund-raising dinner in Washington. Scheduled speakers included Adlai Stevenson and Senator Hubert Humphrey; President Johnson made a surprise appearance. The President's appearance was not the beginning of a vice-presidential boom, but it fit into a pattern of discussions which had begun to develop. There was never any direct or personal discussion of the office between the President and me, but persons then very close to him in the White House did give encouragement and requested that I maintain an apparent interest in the office. Since I was running for re-election to the Senate, the national publicity was helpful.

It was my opinion from the beginning that if the President were to make a personal choice freely, he would pick Hubert Humphrey who had been much closer to him for a longer time in the Senate than I had been and with whom he had worked politically.

Before leaving for the convention at Atlantic City, I had my staff check with the White House to make it clear to those with whom we had been speaking that I did not want to embarrass the President at the convention and would be glad to drop out. I was asked not to do so. We set up a limited headquarters, not at a convention hotel but at a motel on the edge of town, principally to keep in touch with the White House and to keep the candidacy alive.

We did bring down a campaign picture book about me that some columnists described as an elaborate book prepared to advance my vice-presidential candidacy. It was nothing of the kind. It had been prepared for my Senate campaign – and already had been distributed in barber shops, beauty shops, and other places in Minnesota.

The day before the vice-presidential nomination was to be made, President Johnson in a press conference listed some of the qualifications he was looking for in his running mate. It was my opinion that these qualifications fit Senator Humphrey much more closely than they fit me. It was also my opinion that, barring unforeseen developments, Senator Humphrey, with his support from labor, farm and liberal groups, was strong enough to insist he be given the vice presidency had he been moved to do so.

Since by the evening of that same day, I had heard nothing from the White House, and I was still satisfied that Hubert Humphrey would be chosen, I decided that it was best for me to take action to free myself. Therefore, I prepared a wire for transmission the next morning. It read:

DEAR MR. PRESIDENT: THE TIME FOR YOUR ANNOUNCEMENT OF YOUR CHOICE OF YOUR VICE PRESIDENTIAL RUNNING MATE IS VERY CLOSE. I HAVE, AS YOU KNOW, DURING THIS CONVENTION AND FOR SEVERAL WEEKS NOT BEEN INDIFFERENT TO THE CHOICE YOU MUST MAKE. THE ACTION THAT I HAVE TAKEN HAS BEEN TO THIS END AND TO THIS PURPOSE: THAT YOUR CHOICE WOULD BE A FREE ONE AND THAT THOSE WHOM YOU MIGHT CONSULT, OR WHO MIGHT MAKE RECOMMENDATIONS TO YOU, MIGHT BE WELL INFORMED. THE GREAT MAJORITY OF THE DELEGATES HERE ARE, AS YOU KNOW, READY TO SUPPORT YOUR CHOICE. IT IS MY OPINION THAT THE QUALIFICATIONS THAT YOU HAVE LISTED, OR WHICH YOU ARE SAID TO HAVE LISTED AS MOST DESIREABLE IN THE MAN WHO WOULD BE VICE PRESIDENT WITH YOU, WOULD BE MET MOST ADMIRABLE BY SEN. HUMPHREY. I WISH, THEREFORE, TO RECOMMEND FOR YOUR PRIMARY CONSIDERAT-ION, SEN. HUBERT H. HUMPHREY.

I instructed a staff man to send it and to call the White House at once to report that he had sent it. The White House spokesman even then urged that if we had not sent the wire, we not do so.

The President called me that afternoon to tell me of his decision, before making any public announcement with reference to Senator Humphrey and before flying him to Washington. He made a point in the telephone conversation to say that he had made the decision before he received my telegram. I think he had – perhaps several days before. Senator Thomas Dodd of Connecticut was asked to fly from Atlantic City to Washington on the same plane as Senator Humphrey. There were some who thought that had I not sent the telegram I might have been on the plane, serving much the same function as Senator Dodd served – to keep alive the illusion that there were other candidates for the vice presidency.

I was asked to nominate Senator Humphrey as Vice President. I did make the nominating speech.[3]

When the presidential year of 1968 arrived, no one who knew my record – theory and practice – should have been surprised by my concern over the campaign, nor by my decision to involve myself in it.

---

[3] See Appendix 3.

Just a Little More

It was in 1965 that the significant United States expansion of the war in Vietnam began. President Kennedy had increased the number of American military personnel from the approximately 900 men in Vietnam at the end of the Eisenhower administration to about 17,000. This increase was said to be purely quantitative, involving no change in military purpose or assignment. The rise in numbers was explained as necessary to provide protection for our military advisers who were already there to help the South Vietnamese in their effort to put down a revolution which was said to be directed from North Vietnam.

The fact is that an increase from 900 to 17,000 men, because of its magnitude, does assume a qualitative character. An advisory group of 800 or 900 men can be moved out of a country rather quickly, in four or five aircraft. When the number reaches 17,000 or 18,000, the movement takes on a massive character, and any removal under stress, whatever it may be called, comes very close to being an evacuation. Throughout most of 1965, the reports of both the State Department and the Defense Department were optimistic, although there was a lessening of enthusiasm toward the end of that year. The early reports seemed to sustain the White House statement of October 2, 1963, in which Secretary of Defense Robert McNamara and General Maxwell Taylor "reported their judgment that the major part of the U.S. military task can be completed by the end of 1965, although there may be a continuing requirement for a limited number of U.S. training personnel."

By the end of 1965. McNamara had become a little more cautious, although he still looked on the bright side. On his return from a trip to Vietnam on November 30, 1965, he told the nation, "The most vital impression I'm bringing back is that we have stopped losing the war."

I had had some doubts about the accuracy of the Administration's reports about conditions in Vietnam almost from the beginning of our involvement in that country. These doubts reached a critical point in early 1965 when at a White House meeting on February 18, speaking to some twenty-five or thirty Senators, Secretary of State Dean Rusk advised us that the government in power in Vietnam – at that time under General Nguyen Khanh – was strong supported, was stable, and gave every evidence that it would be effective for a long time to come. The Secretary gave us this assurance at about nine or ten o'clock at night. The morning papers gave us the news that the Khanh government had been overthrown.

If one took into the account the difference in time zones, the overthrow was being carried out at about the time that the Secretary of State was speaking to the Senate group in the White House.

As 1965 moved along, I began to look more seriously and deeply into American involvement in Vietnam. Along with other members of the Foreign Relations Committee, I met with men whom we considered to be objective reporters or analysts, including Bernard Fall, a professor at Howard University and author of several books on Vietnam; Jean Lacouture, a French journalist with long experience in Vietnam; Harrison Salisbury, of the New York *Times*, who had just returned from a visit to North Vietnam, and others.

I reread *The Centurions* by Jean Lartéguy, a novel which I had read several years earlier and which dealt with the problems of the French in Algeria and in Vietnam. A particular image, which I recall, was that of a French officer being brought before a Vietnamese officer to surrender. Glatigny, the French officer, sees his opposite number, a bareheaded, barefooted, foul-tobacco-smoking, squatting man, as looking like a peasant – a "peasant from the paddy fields who had beaten him, Glatigny, the descendant of one of the great military dynasties of the West, for whom war was a profession..."

The message and the moral, it seemed to me, was that all the calculators and all the computers could not in any way measure the power and the strength and the willingness to die in a cause. I thought that the failure on the part of Secretary McNamara, experienced in the statistics of the automobile industry of Detroit – an industry in which the president of one of the big three could not, by the very nature of the industry itself, ever fail – to understand this reality moved him from one misjudgment to another.

As the year moved along, it became clear to me, as it did to others, that the essential nature of the conflict in Vietnam was very different from that being presented by Administration spokesmen. The United States was, in fact, making a massive commitment on one side of a civil war, or, to state the matter more exactly, a rebellion within one-half of a divided country, abetted by the other half, against a government which had so little ability to inspire either the loyalty of its people or the fighting spirit of its large and well-equipped army that it was on the verge of collapse when the United States came to its rescue.

I had not opposed the Korean war, which appeared to me a relatively clear case of aggression against a people who were willing to defend themselves with our support and that of other members of the United Nations.

I could not accept the argument of Administration spokesmen that there was no difference between the issue in Vietnam and the issues in Greece in 1947 or in Czechoslovakia in 1939 or in Ethiopia in 1936, or the argument that the credibility of the American commitment under our mutual defense treaties or our national security or our national interest or our honor were at stake in Vietnam.

Yet for a few months, I refrained from a public break with Administration policy. I hoped that my views, offered privately, might carry more weight.

Other members of the Senate were also forming judgments at that time. One of these was Senator Mike Mansfield, the majority leader of the Senate. In late 1965, Senator Mansfield, accompanied by Senators Aiken, Muskie, Boggs, and Inouye, visited Europe and Asia, including Vietnam. Upon their return to the United States, Senator Mansfield reported his findings to the President, and on January 8, 1966, the mission's report to the Foreign Relations Committee, "The Vietnam Conflict: The Substance and the Shadow," was filed.

The report noted that total Viet Cong strength appeared to be increasing despite their serious losses, and it concluded that "the question is not only of applying increased U.S. pressure to a defined military situation but rather of pressing on in a military situation which is, in effect, open ended...

"All of mainland southeast Asia, at least," it said, "cannot be ruled out as a potential battlefield." It noted that the Vietnamese government could not be expected in the near future to carry much more of the burden than it then assumed for it was only "at the beginning of a beginning in dealing with the problems of popular mobilization in support of the Government. They were starting, moreover, from a point considerably behind that which prevailed at the time of President Diem's assassination." The Mansfield report warned that the enormous increase in military participation by the United States might tend to drain the war of any purpose relevant to the Vietnamese people. It also cautioned against any false hope of assistance for our effort from other nations. Rather, it warned that as the war expanded in scope, our relations with our allies both in Europe and in the Far East would become increasingly strained.

At the time Senator Mansfield filed this report, a suspension of the United States bombing of North Vietnam, inaugurated as part of a holiday truce, was in effect. There was hope that if the bombing halt could be prolonged, it might be possible to begin negotiations.

On January 19, 1966, the President sent to Congress a request for an additional $13.1 billion for supplemental appropriations to meet Vietnam costs, and the full amount was approved in March. This was his third request for funds specifically for Vietnam in addition to the regular military budget. He had previously sought and been granted $700 million in supplemental funds for 1965 and $1.7 billion in fiscal 1966 appropriations. On January 24, the budget for fiscal year 1967 was submitted. Included in it were requests for $9.1 billion of new obligational authority for Vietnam expenses which were estimated at $10.5 billion.

On January 24, Secretary of State Dean Rusk appeared in closed session before the Senate Foreign Relations Committee. His presentation was a reiteration of old arguments in support of the Administration's course in Vietnam. He did not appear to be disturbed by the seriousness of the breach that was growing between the executive branch and the Foreign Relations Committee not only on the Vietnam issue but, because of it, on other issues of American foreign policy.

It became clear about this time that the bombing of North Vietnam was soon to be resumed. I did not believe that North Vietnam could be bombed to the conference table, and believed that the resumption of the bombing would result in further escalation of the war and that it would postpone the beginning of negotiations.

Therefore, I joined on January 27 with fourteen other Democratic Senators in signing a public letter to the President urging him not to resume bombing. The letter stated:

As members of the Senate, we take this occasion to express our general agreement with recent statements of the majority leader, Mr. Mansfield; the senior member of the Republican party, Mr. Aiken; and the chairman of the Committee on Foreign Relations, Mr. Fulbright, which relate to whether the national interest of the United States would be served by renewal of the bombing of North Vietnam at this time.

Senator Fulbright said on January 24 that he was opposed to the resumption of the bombing of North Vietnam by United States forces for the foreseeable future; Senator Mansfield said that there should be an indefinite suspension of these bombings; and Senator Aiken endorsed the foregoing views by stating bombing should be suspended until it becomes perfectly clear that the Communist nations intend to fight the war to the finish.

We understand in some small degree the agony you must suffer when called upon by our constitutional system to make judgments which may involve war or peace. We believe you should have our collective judgment before you when you make your decision.[4]

On that same date, January 27, 1966, I made my first formal statement in the Senate in opposition to the Administration's Vietnam policy. I felt that the debate over our involvement in Vietnam, occasioned by the prospect of renewed bombing of the North, was "a proper point for the beginning of a much deeper and much more extensive discussion not only of Vietnam but also of the whole role of America in this second half of the twentieth century."

When the decision was made to resume the bombing, it had been argued that bombing would accomplish a military purpose and a political purpose. The Defense Department had not been able to show that the previous bombing had achieved any significant military effect nor had the State Department been able to prove that it had had any kind of beneficial political or diplomatic effect. I thought it likely, on the basis of information available to us, that if bombing was resumed there would be a substantial increase in ground forces by the North Vietnamese.

The serious problem was that we were called upon to make a moral commitment to an objective or to a set of purposes that we did not clearly understand. I did not believe then, or now, that this imbalance between our comprehension of the objective and the

---

[4] The letter was signed by Senators E. L. Bartlett of Alaska, Lee Metcalf of Montana, Vance Hartke of Indiana, Maurine Neuberger of Oregon, Frank Church of Idaho, Quentin Burdick of North Dakota, William Proxmire of Wisconsin, Stephen Young of Ohio, Ernest Gruening of Alaska, Joseph Clark of Pennsylvania, Wayne Morse of Oregon, Gaylord Nelson of Wisconsin, George McGovern of South Dakota, Harrison Williams of New Jersey, and by me. Senators Church, Clark, Morse, and I were members of the Foreign Relations Committee. Senator Frank Moss of Utah, who had participated in drawing up the letter, was out of the country when it was sent to the President but subscribed to it.

moral commitment we had been called upon to make could be resolved or restored only by Senate debate. The problem clearly demanded the attention and judgment of the entire nation.

The letter to the President did not reflect the full measure of anti-bombing sentiment in the Senate at that time. Republican Senators were not asked to sign because we saw the statement as a Democratic responsibility. But several Republicans, including Senator John Sherman Cooper of Kentucky, who spoke out publicly, opposed the resumption of bombing. In addition, on the Democratic side, Senator Jennings Randolph urged the President not to resume the bombing, and Senators Philip Hart, Albert Gore, and Claiborne Pell, the latter two members of the Foreign Relations Committee, made speeches in opposition to the bombing.

On January 26, 1996, Senator Randolph stated in the Senate:

I hope that our efforts to achieve a basis for negotiations will continue. And, as a part of these efforts, I trust that we will continue to refrain from bombing North Vietnam unless there is a clear indication that such a policy unnecessarily jeopardizes American and allied forces in South Vietnam.

On the same day, Senator Cooper told the Senate:

...bombing should not be resumed now. If bombings are resumed we will lose, at least for the present, the chance to negotiate, however slim it is.

On January 31, 1966, Senator Gore said:

This is a serious hour in the United States and in the world. I know there will be those who will be critical of the Senate in conducting what may appear to some to be a divisive debate in this hour. Senators have made errors of judgment, but so have three Presidents. So have the heads of our armed services. Unfortunately, there has been a plethora of mistakes, and in that all of us have shared.

In my judgment, at that time about one-third of the full Senate, a substantial percentage, and probably a majority of the Foreign Relations Committee, opposed resumption of the bombing. If only one-third were speaking out, I sensed that perhaps another third shared our position.

The purpose of the letter and the other expressions of opinion had been to bring to the attention of the President the growing concern in the Senate. Those who spoke out did so with a sense of responsibility as members of the Senate to participate as the Constitution intended in determining the direction of foreign policy. Most thought the President would welcome their views and that it would be helpful to him (the President) to know how we felt.

The President did not respond to our letter of January 27 as expected. His reply on the next day referred to the Tonkin Gulf Resolution and to a copy of his recent letter to members of the House. In that letter he said:

January 22, 1966
Dear Mr. Congressman:
I am responding to you as the first in alphabetical order of the Members of the House who have written to me under date of January 21 on the search for peace in Vietnam. I hope you will share this answer with your co-signers.

I am grateful for your strong support of our effort to move the war in Vietnam to the conference table. This support is a real encouragement, coupled as it is with the equally strong support of our determination to meet our commitments in Vietnam.

I share your interest in effective action through the United Nations, and I want you to know that there is no part of this whole problem to which we give closer attention. I have reviewed this matter many times with Ambassador Goldberg, and we have repeatedly considered the suggestion you offer. You can be assured that he and I are firmly determined to make every possible use of the United Nations in moving toward peace, and toward an effective ceasefire as part of that purpose.

Unfortunately, you are correct in your statement that the response from the other side has not been encouraging. The evidence available to this government indicates only continuing hostility and aggressiveness in Hanoi and an insistence on the abandonment of South Vietnam to Communist takeover. We are making no hasty assumptions of any sort, but it is quite another matter to close our eyes to the heavy weight of evidence which has accumulated during the last month.

I can give you categorical assurance that there will be no abandonment of our peace efforts. Even though it is increasingly clear that we have had only a hostile response to the present pause in bombing North Vietnam, you can be sure that our unflagging pursuit of peace will continue. As I said this week in a letter to Speaker McCormack, "Whether the present effort is successful or not, our purpose of peace will be constant; we will continue to press on every door."

31

*And at the same time, I am confident that as elected
representatives of the American people, you will share my
determination that our fighting forces in Vietnam shall be
sustained and supported "by every dollar and every gun and
every decision" that they must have – "whatever the cost and
whatever the challenge." For a month we have held our hand
in an important area of military action. But the infiltration of
the aggressor's forces has continued, and so have his attacks
on our allies and on our own men. I am sure you will agree
that we have a heavy obligation not to add lightly to the
dangers our troops must face. We must give them the support
they need in fulfillment of the commitment so accurately stated
in your letter – "the determination of our Government to resist
the terror and aggression which deny the people of South
Vietnam the right freely to determine their own future."*
    Sincerely,
    LYNDON B. JOHNSON
*Letter sent to the Honorable Brock Adams, House of
Representatives, Washington, D.C.*

Members of the Senate were offended on two counts: one, the
use of the Tonkin Gulf Resolution as an answer to their serious
questioning; and second, the use of a letter to the House of
Representatives as an answer to the Senate challenge, since this
reflected upon the constitutional responsibility for foreign policy
which is quite specifically vested in the Senate.

During the next few days there was much discussion of the
matter in the corridors and cloakrooms. The signers of the letter
met and were joined by other Senators who had not signed but
who were sympathetic; no agreement was reached on action,
however.

The Administration moved to defend its position and tried to
quiet the criticism. On January 27, with other Senators, I visited
Ambassador Averell Harriman who, at the request of the
President, attempted to clarify the Administration's position. A
few days later, McGeorge Bundy, the President's Assistant for
National Security Affairs, and General Maxwell Taylor, former
Ambassador to South Vietnam, made personal visits to the offices
of some Senators, including mine, to explain the Administration's
position. And there were other messengers and spokesmen.

Secretary Dean Rusk appeared again before the Foreign
Relations Committee at a public hearing on January 28, 1966. A
week later, Secretary of Defense Robert McNamara declined on
grounds of security to appear publicly before the committee, and
the President backed up his refusal.

The Foreign Relations Committee hearings went on. General Taylor appeared before the committee in an unofficial appearance to support Administration policy, even though it was known he was acting in an informal advisory capacity at the White House. Retired General James Gavin and former Ambassador George Kennan also came to the hearings. Both spoke strongly against the Administration policy. George Kennan stated his opinion that:

...If we were not already involved as we are today in Vietnam, I would know of no reason why we should wish to become so involved, and I could think of several reasons why we should wish not to.

Vietnam is not a region of major military and industrial importance. It is difficult to believe that any decisive developments of the world situation would be determined in normal circumstances by what happens on that territory. If it were not for the considerations of prestige that arise precisely out of our present involvement, even a situation in which South Vietnam was controlled exclusively by the Vietcong, while regrettable, and no doubt morally unwarranted, would not, in my opinion, present dangers great enough to justify our direct military intervention.

General Gavin proposed what became known as the enclave theory:

Today we have sufficient force in South Vietnam to hold several enclaves on the coast, where sea and air power can be made fully effective. By enclaves I suggest Camranh Bay, Danang, and similar areas where American bases are being established. However, we are stretching these resources beyond reason in our endeavors to secure the entire country of South Vietnam from the Vietcong penetration...

The Gavin proposal, it appeared to me, contained the seeds of the policy the Administration ought to be following: that we ought to hold the strong points in Vietnam to indicate to the Vietcong and Hanoi that we could be just as patient as they could. This would be a kind of limited commitment, with a limited number of troops and involving a manageable drain on our economy.

As public attention to the committee hearings heightened, the President flew to a meeting with the South Vietnamese leaders in Honolulu. At the conclusion of the conference, "The Pledge of Honolulu," essentially a statement of American and South Vietnamese war aims, was issued. The "common commitment" of the South Vietnamese and American governments was stated to be a pledge:

to defense against aggression,

to the work of social revolution,
to the goal of free self-government,
to the attack on hunger, ignorance, and disease,
and to the unending quest for peace.

The statement made at Honolulu went far beyond any declaration of policy for South Vietnam that the Administration had made in the past, and certainly beyond anything that the Congress itself had in any formal way been committed to. This declaration, together with the attitudes of the Secretary of State and the Secretary of Defense and a number of minor incidents, had the effect of making 1966 a year of virtual stalemate between the executive branch of the government and the Foreign Relations Committee of the Senate.

The power and the role of the Foreign Relations Committee as an agency of the Senate in the determination of the foreign policy of the country is generally not understood.

There are two congressional functions in which the responsibility is rather clearly defined in the Constitution: one is that of the House of Representatives to initiate revenue measures – a responsibility which is very clearly comprehended and not only comprehended but carried out by the Ways and Means Committee then under the chairmanship of Congressman Wilbur Mills of Arkansas. The second is that of the Senate to participate in the determination of foreign policy. This is a responsibility which is somewhat more difficult to define and to execute than the revenue responsibility but nonetheless is one which is not only recognized but claimed by the Senate, and sometimes even carried out.

After the Senate had been told by Administration witnesses that the regular authorization of foreign aid funds for South Vietnam constituted part of our "commitment," sentiment began to build up against foreign aid generally. The committee, convinced that it was being denied its role in the process of determining the direction of foreign policy, resorted to sniping at policy from the edges; for example, it restricted foreign-aid authorization to one year although it was plain that longer term authorizations provide a better basis for planning, particularly for economic development. The feeling that, if it could do nothing else to influence the direction of our foreign commitments, the committee at least ought to have an opportunity for annual review of our policy, was overriding.

The statements made by Secretary Rusk in the early months of 1969, after his retirement from office, expressed great concern over the growing isolationism in the country. This was characteristic of the inaccuracy and the obscurantism of statements by the Secretary. What he called isolationism in 1969 was not the isolationism of the twenties and the thirties or of the fifties and the sixties, but something quite different and not in any way subject to being classified under the term isolationism. It was, rather, a new and different approach to international responsibility. It should have been clear to him that this new approach to international responsibility had begun to show as long ago as 1966, largely as a reaction to his own and the Administration's assertions that with economic aid went the almost total and open-ended commitment which he repeated declared the United States had made to Vietnam.

Rusk, despite his image, was not a true internationalist but rather a person with a concept of an American or Rusk plan for the reorganization of the world or, if not for reorganization, the direction of the world as then organized. He was a most effective spokesman for a Senate Department which is the only established national religion in America.

Another project that was also a victim of the committee's resentment was the attempt to revise the Charter of the Organization of American States to include the Alliance for Progress. This resulted in a broadly phrased resolution of support for our Latin-American foreign policy so heavily rewritten in the Senate that the Administration decided it would be better to have no resolution at all.[5]

Meanwhile, escalation of the war had continued through 1966, and unrest grew within South Vietnam. On March 9, American planes carried out the heaviest bombardment of the war. United Nations Secretary General U Thant called for cessation of the bombing, a reduction of military activities, and for participation of

---

[5] The OAS Foreign Ministers had met in late 1965 to lay down guidelines for a negotiating session to be held in Panama in March 1966. During the Panama negotiations, State Department officials met with members of the committee to discuss drafts that were being drawn up in Panama. The Latin-American subcommittee indicated that if revisions of the charter were drawn up on the basis of the drafts they had been shown, the committee would refuse to approve ratification. Members of the committee were concerned that in spite of Administration assurances to the contrary, the revisions would represent a considerable extension of American commitments. Satisfactory revisions were eventually worked out.

Later, in the spring of 1967, when the President was preparing for the Punta del Este conference, a broad foreign-policy support resolution dealing with Latin America was sent up to the Foreign Relations Committee. While the House passed the resolution in the form the President wanted, it was so thoroughly rewritten in the Senate committee that the Administration decided against any resolution.

the National Liberation Front in any peace settlement. Demonstrations against the military government in Saigon began in several large cities in South Vietnam. Some of these demonstrations took on an anti-American character.

By April 1966, B-52s from Guam were bombing North Vietnam, and the Defense Department had acknowledged that the civilian unrest in South Vietnam was hampering military operations. On April 26, the State Department stated that it was our policy to follow the doctrine of hot pursuit of enemy aircraft into China if necessary.

Near the end of April, infiltration of North Vietnamese into South Vietnam was officially set at 5,500 men per month, and Secretary McNamara was predicting a further increase in U.S. combat troop strength. The infiltration was estimated as between 5,500 and 7,000 per month. This was approximately a 20 to 50% increase over the estimate made early in the year when Secretary McNamara said that they had the capacity to infiltrate "up to" 4,500 men a month.

When asked about this statement on May 11, 1966, McNamara said that "up to" did not mean a ceiling, that the number they could infiltrate is "less than x, x being quite a bit in excess of 4,500; but, in any event, there is some ceiling that would result from the bombing of the lines of communications." He never did say what x was.

Certainly in my mind, and in the minds of other Senators, this explanation by the Secretary of Defense of what the words meant to him, contrasted with what they meant to us, added to the growing doubt as to whether one could rely upon him either as an observer of the war or as a witness concerning the progress of the war.

It was experiences of this kind on the part of the committee that led to a growing distrust of the testimony of the Secretary of Defense and to a feeling that he was not really responsive to the questions which were being asked. Often he included facts which were either irrelevant or which distracted from the point which was being raised. For example, in testimony before the committee on April 20, 1966, when the Secretary was asked by Senator Wayne Morse about military equipment in Latin America, he said that "the total number of combat aircraft in Latin America was 547, which is fewer than the combat aircraft of North Korea." He never explained the relationship, if any, between the number of combat aircraft in North Korea and the number in Latin America, since the two situations were completely unrelated. In the same testimony he said that the total number of tanks in Latin America was 974. "That," he said, "is 60% as many as a single country –

Bulgaria – has." On May 11, when the Secretary appeared before the Foreign Relations Committee again, I asked him for an explanation of his statement concerning the number of tanks in Latin America in relation to the number of tanks in Bulgaria. When I said to him, "Is there a kind of Bulgarian absolute?" McNamara replied, "If there were, I would be happy to give it to you. I don't know what it is here."

Oil installations in the areas of Hanoi and Haiphong were being bombed by the end of June, and in July the South Vietnamese Chief of State was saying that the North would be invaded if necessary. Bombing continued over infiltration routes in Laos, and at the end of July, troop concentrations in and around the demilitarized zone separating the two Vietnams were being bombed by B-52s.

In the fall, after the Manila Conference, the President paid a surprise visit to Vietnam where he exhorted the troops to bring home the coonskin. McNamara was saying the number of U.S. troops would continue to increase in 1967.

Progress reports on the war were still being made in terms of "kill ratios"; that is, how many North Vietnamese were killed to every American killed, and some reports went so far as to see what was considered an acceptable ratio – acceptable in the sense that if more than four or five of the enemy were being killed to every American or South Vietnamese, this was a mark of progress.

As the end of 1966 approached, the press was reporting that United States advisers were taking an active part in operations in Thailand, and American troops were being moved into the Mekong Delta area of South Vietnam, where operations previously had been conducted solely by the South Vietnamese army.

In early December, American bombers staged heavy raids on truck depots, railroad yards, and fuel dumps in the immediate vicinity of Hanoi, and there were reports that residential areas as well were being hit. Attacks on civilian areas were said to be incidental to attempts to destroy military targets.

George Orwell, in an essay, "*Politics and the English Language*," in 1946, wrote:

> *In our time, political speech and writing are largely the defense of the indefensible. Things like the continuance of British rule in India, the Russian purges and deportations, the dropping of atom bombs on Japan, can indeed be defended, but only by arguments which are too brutal for most people to face, and which do not square with the professed aims of political parties. Thus political language has to consist largely*

of euphemism, question-begging and sheer cloudy vagueness. Defenseless villages are bombarded from the air, the inhabitants driven out into the countryside, the cattle machine-gunned, the huts set on fire with incendiary bullets: this is called pacification. *Millions of peasants are robbed of their farms and sent trudging along the roads with no more than they can carry: this is called* transfer of population *or* rectification of frontiers. *People are imprisoned for years without trial, or shot in the back of the neck or sent to die of scurvy in Arctic lumber camps: this is called* elimination of unreliable elements...*

The inflated style is itself a kind of euphemism. A mass of Latin words falls upon the facts like soft snow, blurring the outlines and covering up all the details. The great enemy of clear language is insincerity. When there is a gap between one's real and one's declared aims, one turns as it were instinctively to long words and exhausted idioms, like a cuttlefish squirting out ink.

In the Vietnam war the key Latin word became *escalation*, which gave to the war the character of a continuum: that is, a movement without interruption, not subject to outside influence or direction but growing out of itself and not allowing any point at which one might say: "Here we will stop and go no further."

Count the Bodies

As the year 1966 wore on and criticism of the war mounted, the Administration became more defensive and the language of its response more violent.

The motives of those who spoke out were questioned. Critics of the war were called "nervous Nellie" and "special pleaders." At a Medal of Honor ceremony in December 1966, the President had a word for dissenters:

[The war] is a cause which deserves not only the bravery of our soldiers, but the patience and fortitude of all of our citizens.

And all of these we have in good supply.

It far outweighs the reluctance of men who exercise so well the right of dissent, but let others fight to protect them from those whose very philosophy is to do away with the right of dissent.

In February 1966, a White House spokesman referred to members of the National Council of Churches who had criticized the war as "alleged churchmen." Such a reference to churchmen had not been used by a leading public official since the days of Senator Joseph McCarthy of Wisconsin.

In March, a racist theme was injected when Vice President Humphrey said:

You can't get yourself labeled that the only people you want to die for are the whites...Are we saying that we're unable to keep our commitments for the brown and the yellow people – and can keep them only for the whites?

Those who suggested that our interest in Europe and in other parts of the world were being neglected in the preoccupation with the war in Southeast Asia were labeled "crypto-pacifist isolationists" by columnist William S. White.

At another White House Medal of Honor ceremony in May 1967, critics of the war were again warned by the President that:

The debate will go on, and it will have its price. It is a price our democracy must be prepared to pay, and that the angriest voices of dissent should be prepared to acknowledge.

Senate critics and the public were frequently reminded that other Presidents had borne heavy burdens of criticism for their war policies but had "stuck it out" and eventually had been vindicated by history. Lincoln, in particular, was cited.

At the same time, reassuring and optimistic reports on the war itself continued to be issued, much as they had been in 1966.

In January 1967, our Ambassador to Vietnam, Henry Cabot Lodge, had predicted "sensational" military gains in 1967. He added that open peace negotiations would probably never take place; rather, the enemy would merely fade away.

On April 28, 1967, the Commanding General, William C. Westmoreland, at the request of the Administration, appeared before a joint meeting of the Congress. Much of General Westmoreland's statement dealt with his estimate of the military situation and his anticipation of the enemy's possible future strategy. He said that our forces and those of the other free world allies had grown in strength and profited from experience.

Of the South Vietnamese army, he asserted:

What I see now in Vietnam is a military force that performs with growing professional skill. During the last six months, Vietnamese troops have scored repeated successes against some of the best Vietcong and North Vietnamese army units.

We were fighting a war with no front lines, he pointed out, and we could not measure progress by lines on a map. We had to use other means to chart progress. As examples of progress:

Two years ago...there were three jet-capable runways in South Vietnam. Today there are fourteen...Then there was one deep-water port for sea-going ships. Now there are seven...

During 1965 the Republic of Vietnam Armed Forces and its allies killed 36,000 of the enemy at a cost of approximately 12,000 friendly killed, and 90% of these were Vietnamese. During recent months this 3 to 1 ratio in favor of the allies has risen significantly and in some weeks has been as high as 10 or 20 to 1 in our favor.

The Westmoreland statement did not move the critics of the war. The escalation continued through 1967: the bombing was expanded steadily; casualties, both civilian and military, continued to mount.

In January and February of 1967, our military forces in Vietnam conducted "Operation Cedar Falls" and "Operation Junction City," uprooting large numbers of Vietnamese from their homes and lands and removing them to resettlement villages surrounded by barbed wire. American artillery in South Vietnam began shelling North Vietnam, and we started to mine North Vietnamese rivers. By April, we were bombing power plants inside Haiphong, and we attacked North Vietnamese MIG bases for the first time.

We moved troops into the demilitarized zone and bombed a power plant a mile north of the center of Hanoi. Twice we accidentally struck Soviet ships in North Vietnamese ports. In June, our troop strength in Vietnam reached 463,000.

In August, United States planes destroyed Vietnam's most important railway bridge linking Hanoi with Haiphong and China. We admitted we had been bombing in Laos since 1964. Also in August, a "maximum limit" of 525,000 American troops were authorized for Vietnam.

In his address to the Congress, Westmoreland had cited the help of our allies:

It is also worthy of note that 30 other nations are providing noncombat support ... Their exploits deserve recognition, not only for their direct contribution to the overall effort, but for their symbolic reminder that the whole of free Asia opposes communist expansion.

Westmoreland neglected to mention that, with the exception of a few nations such as Korea for whose assistance we are paying, assistance to Vietnam by most governments is largely of a humanitarian nature, aimed at relieving the suffering and rebuilding the war damage.

Two things in his statement were of particular interest and also of concern. One was his use of the term "kill ratio." A year before, the Foreign Relations Committee had been told that there was no such thing as a kill ratio, that it was something dreamed up by the press, and that our effort in Vietnam was directed to doing the job with the least possible loss of life, both Vietnamese and American. Now General Westmoreland was admitting that we were engaged in a war of attrition, a war of matching American lives against Asian lives on the Asian mainland, a course our most eminent generals had warned against.

The second was the obvious political character of his remarks. He said that he had seen "no evidence that this is an internal insurrection" but "that it is aggression from the North."

This was an act without precedent in that a field commander on active duty spoke on what were essentially the political aspects of the war rather than on the military aspects of it.

But more significant was the fact that a field commander on active duty had been brought back to support not only the military

41

program but also those political issues of the war which were subject to intense controversy.

On September 18, 1967, Secretary of Defense Robert McNamara announced that the United States would begin deployment of a "Chinese oriented" anti-ballistic missile system, while warning of the danger that "pressures will develop to expand it." As we moved into October, the Administration began to put greater and greater emphasis on the Chinese threat to America. This was an escalation of objectives to go along with the escalation of our military efforts.

Vice President Hubert Humphrey spoke most forcefully of the Chinese threat on October 15. He said that American security was at stake in Asia and that "the threat to world peace is militant, aggressive Asian communism, with its headquarters in Peking, China."

This followed a press conference by Secretary of State Dean Rusk on October 12, in which he made reference to a "a billion Chinese." Rusk restated his old position about our obligations growing out of the SEATO treaty; he cited the Tonkin Gulf Resolution again; reported that thing were moving ahead in South Vietnam; and then, in answer to a question relating to whether or not our national security was really at stake in Vietnam, stated: "Within the next decade or two, there will be a billion Chinese on the mainland, armed with nuclear weapons, with no certainty about what their attitude toward the rest of Asia will be." He then talked about the importance of strengthening the other nations of Asia and concluded with this sentence: "So we have a tremendous stake in the ability of the free nations of Asia to live in peace; and to turn the interest of people in mainland China to the pragmatic requirements of their own people and away from a doctrinaire and ideological adventurism abroad."

This move – to enlarge the Vietnam war into a war against China – caused me great concern and injected both new political and moral considerations into the controversy over the war in Vietnam. It demonstrated the rule that when one thinks defensively, the threat always rises to the level of the deterrent and then surpasses it. On October 16, 1967, I took my case to the floor of the Senate.

I spoke of Rusk's press conference. He had opened with a statement which was marked by some editors and commentators as "significant" – already they were not clear or in agreement as to just what the significance was. His remarks had been labeled "bold and clarifying." They did not seem to me to be any bolder or any clearer than his previous statements, the style and language being his own. But the Secretary had not spoken of bringing the

Great Society to Southeast Asia, nor of honoring the pledges of four Presidents, nor did he suggest that we could not improve life in our own cities unless we made improvements first in Vietnam. He had said, instead, "Our commitment is clear and our national interest is real."

I did not intend, at that point, to reopen the question of whether or not our commitment was as clear as all that, especially since it had been subject to strenuous debate and challenge by citizens and officials for nearly a year and a half. He had suggested that there was "no significant body of American opinion which would have us withdraw from Vietnam" and "no serious opinion among us which wishes to transform this struggle into a general war," a statement which was quite irrelevant because the debate fell between the two extremes.

Secretary Rusk spoke of the fate which Asian communism planned for Southeast Asia. Asian communism, and for that matter world communism, undoubtedly had a fate planned for all the world. But the fact that it had such plans did not mean that the plans were possible of realization or that we had to respond as if the total plan were in operation and were likely to be realized.

Secretary Rusk had not shown himself to be the most accurate judge of Chinese intentions or of their potential. Or of the other forces running within the world. To demonstrate I gave a short review of his predictions and analyses:

In his May 18, 1951, speech before the China Institute in New York, he described the "greedy hands" of Russia stretching out to dismember China. China, he said, was being "sacrificed to the ambitions of the communist conspiracy. China has been driven by foreign masters into an adventure of foreign aggression..." (Korea)

"The Peiping regime may be a colonial Russian government – a Slavic Manchukuo on a larger scale. It is not the government of China. It does not pass the first test. It is not Chinese."

He said of the Nationalist Chinese government: "We believe it more authentically represents the views of the great body of the people of China, particularly their historical demand for independence from foreign control."

But the principal point to be made against Rusk was that the growing debate on Vietnam was not, as he tried to put it, a debate over procedures for carrying out policies on which the nation was united; it was a debate of great substance over policies about which the nation was deeply divided.

I could not accept his assessment that there were "problems about going through an exercise of futility ... to satisfy some

43

critics among our own people." The members of the Senate have a constitutional responsibility to be concerned over foreign policy (a responsibility which in the case of the Secretary of State exists only by delegation). As a matter of a fact, much of what was being done in Vietnam could well have been an exercise in futility. The Secretary of Defense not long before had admitted that the bombing of the North, for example, had failed to reduce significantly the supply of arms and men to the South, and the publicized program of "pacification" (more commonly labeled "revolutionary development"), an attempt to graft onto Asian society Western values and institutions, had not progressed very far.

The one thing that did come through clearly was Rusk's belief that the United States had to maintain an anti-Communist bastion in South Vietnam, as a part of the overall strategy of containing China by encirclement, and that all of this bore directly on our national interest if not our survival. This was a continuing application of the John Foster Dulles strategic theory, and was a new reflection of the ancient fear of the "yellow peril." Rusk's statement that within the next "decade or two" there would be a billion Chinese on the mainland, armed with nuclear weapons, did not help one to understand how, if this was the specter haunting Asia, an improbable and total victory in South Vietnam would rid Asia of it.

The Secretary seemed to be accepting the Chinese Communist's belief that their doctrine of world revolution was applicable to the entire underdeveloped world. It must have been encouraging to Chinese propagandists to see a basic tenet of their philosophy accepted and endorsed by the American Secretary of State.

What is the measure of the Chinese threat? I asked. What was its record?

The Chinese experience, with the one exception of Vietnam, had almost no relevance outside China. Mao was able to gain control of China because he gained the leadership of the Chinese nationalist movement and led it against a foreign invader in World War II. Ho Chi Minh was the only Communist leader in the underdeveloped world to do the same. Chinese attempts to promote their style of revolution elsewhere had met with failure. China continued to talk a world-power game, but her great internal difficulties, particularly in food and population, might only be a dress rehearsal for what would come after Mao passed from the scene.

Few of us expected in 1945 that twenty years later we would have 225,000 troops in Europe. We still had, in 1967, 55,000

44

troops in South Korea, fourteen years after the end of the fighting. At the height of the Korean conflict we never had as many troops committed as we have in Vietnam. We had to ask ourselves therefore, it seemed to me, whether we were prepared to maintain from 100,000 to 200,000 troops in South Vietnam for fifteen or twenty years after the fighting ended. If we were not prepared to do so, then the process of involvement had to be reversed before a temporary commitment assumed the character of a permanent establishment.

"With regret," I said, in commenting on Rusk's China speech, "I must conclude that the Secretary has added nothing constructive ... by way of new facts, new policies, strategy, or understanding." Rather, because of a posture and the careless or intentional abuse of language, he had served only to obscure issues and to cause further frustration and division within the country, and between Congress and the executive branch of government.

That year, 1967, was, for me and for many, a year of growing anxiety about the morality, as well as the practicality, of what we were doing in Vietnam. Perhaps the first significant expression of a widening new judgment had occurred at the conference of Clergy and Laymen Concerned About Vietnam. These men met in Washington early in February of 1967.

This was not a conference of the standard or traditional opponents of the war, but one which was made up of the more or less regular clergy of almost every denomination. They could hardly be described as "alleged churchmen" or peaceniks or pacifists. Many had come very conservative churches or synagogues, and they came from all over the country. The organization was a coalition of some of the leading figures in the religious community of the United States. It included such men as Dr. John C. Bennett of the Union Theological Seminary of America, Philip Scharper of the Catholic publishers Sheed & Ward, the Reverend Eugene Carson Blake of the World Council of Churches, Father Joseph Mulligan of Fordam University, Dr. Robert McAfee Brown, professor of religion at Stanford University, Bishop John Wesley Lord, United Methodist Bishop of the Washington area, and others.

Senator Morse, Senator Gruening, and I spoke at the conference. Wayne Morse said that the war was immoral, illegal, unjustifiable, and needlessly prolonged. Ernest Gruening said, "There is no justification for our being in Vietnam and no good will come of it. Any way out would be an improvement over what we are doing."

Discussion during the conference often fell between the two extreme views of the place of religious and moral judgment on government policy and political action. The first holds that there is a kind of direct, one-to-one relationship, that every political decision can be subjected to a clear and precise moral judgment. This view is manifest in the theory that if you have good men in government they come up with the right decisions. It is reflected also in such laws as the one requiring the words "In God We Trust" to be printed on American money, and in such proposed constitutional amendments as the Dirksen Amendment that would overrule the Supreme Court decisions prohibiting prayer in public schools.

The other extreme position is the one which takes the pragmatic tack that morality and religious judgment have little place in domestic politics and no place whatsoever in the conduct of foreign affairs. According to this point of view, foreign policy and the methods by which we conduct it are beyond criticism; morality stops at the water's edge or at the entrance of the Central Intelligence Agency.

At the conference, I set out three questions bearing upon the justice or injustice of our presence in the war in Vietnam. These were:

First, the purposes and objectives;

Second, the methods and means;

And third, the proportion: that is, even if we accepted the idea that the purposes were good and the methods justifiable, we still had to question whether the evil and destruction required to win the war were proportionate to the good that might be achieved.

For the first time in this century, we as a nation were called upon to question deeply the justification or provocation for our involvement in a war.

In World War I, our participation was certainly morally defensible, and in World War II even more clearly so. In each of these wars, a reasonably good case could be made for the methods and the instruments of war which we used. The great exception, of course, was the use of the atomic bomb on Hiroshima and Nagasaki.

Of special concern to me was the burden which was being placed on the consciences of young men who were called to face the hard moral question of fighting or not fighting in Vietnam.

This meeting of clergy and laymen and what followed contributed more than anything else, I believe, to exploring the moral issues. Following the conference the clergymen returned to their own states and cities and held conferences. And the press began to deal more intensively with the moral issues they had raised.

Publications such as *Christianity and Crisis* and *Commonweal*, journals that express the view on public affairs of some Protestant and Catholic clergy and laymen, printed articles condemning the war and called on their readers to respond.

Women too became concerned. The Women's International League for Peace and Freedom increased its membership and its activities because of the war in Vietnam. New groups were organized, and established groups such as Church Women United took a strong position on the war.

In some respects the best presentation of the moral anguish of the war was presented not in speeches about the war, not in articles, but in poetic works of men like Robert Lowell, Robert Bly, and John Haag. One of Robert Bly's poems made clear, I think, that the measure of "success" had been a measure of the dead. He titles it "Counting Small-Boned Bodies."

> *Let's count bodies over again.*
>
> *If we could only make the bodies smaller,*
> *The size of skulls,*
> *We could make a whole plain white with*
> *Skulls in the moonlight!*
>
> *If we could only make the bodies smaller,*
> *Maybe we could get*
> *A whole year's kill in front of us on a desk!*
>
> *If we could only make the bodies smaller*
> *We could fit*
> *A body into a finger-ring, for a keepsake forever.*

A second poem, "Kilroy," by John Haag, is of a different nature but has the same final effect – if one remembers the slogan of World War II, "Kilroy was here."

> *Kilroy, mustered out at last, stepped*
> *down from his long vigil on the walls*
> *about the whole damned world's*
> *urinals –*
> *and wept. Old Adam Kilroy, the first man*
> *anywhere, hero to us all and saint*
> *to combat soldiers, has packed it in,*
> *refusing to negate his magnificent*

career in defense of the just state
by serving in Viet Nam.

And from a non-American point of view, one poem by Thich Nhat Hanh, a Vietnamese poet, "Our Green Garden":

I say farewell to the blazing, blackening place
where I was born.
Here is my breast! Aim you gun at it, brother, shoot!
I offer my body, the body our mother bore and nurtured.
Destroy it if you will,

* * *

Destroy me if you will
And build my carrion whatever it is that you are
dreaming of.

Who will be left to celebrate a victory made of
blood and fire?

By late October 1967, nearly everything that had to be considered for making a judgment on the war in Vietnam had become quite apparent to me. The military difficulties of the war were evident. The political problems and difficulties had become exposed, and the moral aspects of our involvement had taken on overwhelming importance.

As the year of 1968 approached, so did the time for considering the practical means by which not just an opinion, but a judgment leading to action on the war might be registered. Nearly every method short of the open political challenge of elections had been tried. The President had been advised and urged privately. The device of a resolution signed by a number of Senators had been used in the hope that that would bring about a change in policy. The Senate Committee on Foreign Relations had made public the case against the war, and many people outside of politics had used whatever means they had available to make their position known.

There remained the test of the campaign of 1968. I believed the people of the country had the right to be given the opportunity to make an intellectual and moral determination on the war in Vietnam.

48

Come As You Are

Before making any announcement of political intentions for 1968, I tried as best I could to determine the plans of Senator Robert Kennedy of New York. As early as March 1967, I told James Wechsler of the New York *Post* that I thought Senator Kennedy would be the strongest candidate in a challenge to President Johnson and that I was prepared to support him if he did run.

I still believed in late 1967 that Senator Kennedy could make the strongest challenge, but I believed that if he were to come into the campaign later, after I had committed myself, the whole effort to change policies would be weakened by conflict and division. I therefore continued to be concerned about what his plans might be.

I concluded in late 1967 that he was not going to enter the primaries. This conclusion was based upon his public statements – that he would not challenge the President and that he could not foresee any circumstances under which he might run. In private conversation he said the same things to me. I was assured by friends of his, including Richard Goodwin, that he had made a final decision not to run in the primaries of 1968. I did know, of course, that there was sharp division among his friends and political advisers on the question of whether he should run or not run. Dick Goodwin, who had worked for the Kennedys as a writer, met with me in Washington on February 10 and volunteered to work in my campaign. He made this offer, of course, because he believed that Senator Kennedy would not be a candidate.

On February 10, Arthur Schlesinger, Jr., a close adviser to the Kennedy group, was one of the strongest voices raised at an Americans for Democratic Action meeting urging that organization to endorse my candidacy. The New York *Times* story the next day reported that Schlesinger strongly backed the move to endorse me. He said that he had backed the "draft Eisenhower"

49

move in 1948 and said "that was the greatest mistake I ever made. But this is different today. At that time, we were going with a man whose views on issues we didn't know. Here, we know how McCarthy stands on the issues." I accepted this Schlesinger action as confirming evidence that Senator Kennedy would not enter the primaries.

Kennedy had pledged his support to President Johnson, the article pointed out, even though he had been highly critical of the President's Vietnam policy and some of his domestic policies.

And later in an interview on the BBC, reported in *The Listener* of March 14, 1968, Senator Kennedy said in answer to a question as to what factors made him decide not to seek the presidential nomination that "if I did make the effort, it would cause a deep division within the Democratic party. It would lead to the defeat of many fine Democrats who are running around the country, who happen to have the same opinion as I do."

In late October 1967, I made the decision that I would challenge President Johnson in 1968. Most of November and December was spent in preparing for a campaign, the limits of which had not yet been defined.

There were problems. How could I be most effective and where?

What was necessary to build at least a skeleton campaign staff and establish a rudimentary organization?

How would we raise the necessary money for the campaign?

Many of the principal Senate opponents of the Vietnam policy were up for re-election in 1968: Senator Fulbright in Arkansas, Senator Gruening in Alaska, Senator Morse in Oregon, Senator Clark in Pennsylvania, Senator McGovern in South Dakota, Senator Gaylord Nelson in Wisconsin, and Senator Church in Idaho. I was especially concerned that a challenge to the President – although I felt the need for it – might prove politically dangerous to Senators who were running for re-election in states (Oregon, Wisconsin, South Dakota, and Pennsylvania) where primaries were scheduled. Some Senators had come out against the war but not against President Johnson directly. My challenge would leave them no choice, for how could one then be anti-war but pro-Johnson?

I talked with Senator George McGovern about the situation in South Dakota, deferring to his judgment as to what would be best for him. The South Dakota primary was scheduled for June 4 – the same day as the California primary – and consequently it could have little effect on the national contest. He talked about the possibility of his running as a favorite son[6] or, as an alternative, of having an uninstructed delegation which would be satisfactory to the various factions – if they could be called that – within the South Dakota Democratic party.

Vance Hartke, at this time, also was reported giving some attention to becoming a favorite son in Indiana.

I realized that many things could happen in the course of the six months of primary campaigning following my announcement, that there would be a shifting and changing of position.

In the meantime, I continued to carry out my speaking schedule. This included three speeches on college campuses in November: one at Macalester College in St. Paul, Minnesota, one at the University of Michigan in Ann Arbor, one at Fairleigh Dickinson University in Rutherford, New Jersey, and a speech to the College Young Democrats' National Convention dinner in Cambridge, Massachusetts.

Meeting with these students re-enforced my belief that it was vitally important that the young people be given a chance to participate in the politics of 1968. This, I felt, would not be the more-or-less traditional student participation. If given a chance, their activities would be of a much higher political order. The great body of students on the campuses I visited were deeply concerned over the two great issues facing the country: the war in Vietnam and racial inequities and injustices in the United States.

On November 12, 1967, I spoke in Chicago at the National Labor Leadership Assembly for Peace. This meeting was called by a group of trade union leaders from all parts of the country who were opposed to the Administration's conduct of the war in Vietnam. Victor Reuther of the UAW, Frank Rosenblum of the Amalgamated Clothing Workers, Harold Gibbons of the Teamsters, and others were there. This was the first and only organized labor challenge to the policies of the national labor organizations which were on record as supporting the President's policies in Vietnam.

A luncheon at the Harvard Club in Boston was proposed in mid-October by Jerome Grossman, a Boston businessman, who had urged me to become a candidate in order to provide a focus

---

[6] Favorite son: a candidate for the presidency proposed at a national convention whose support is exclusively or largely from his home state's delegation. Often the state will delegate a governor or a senator as an honorary gesture, although sometimes the favorite son is proposed as a serious candidate. Usually, however, the term implies that the candidate is not likely to receive the nomination of the convention or the party. The *Crescent Dictionary of American Politics* by Eugene J. McCarthy, The Macmillan Company, 1962, p. 58.

and a forum for the orderly expression of dissent. He had proposed a small meeting of about twenty professors, clergymen, financiers, and businessmen who might become the nucleus of a citizens committee in Massachusetts. The luncheon was finally limited to sixty-five guests, and it included a number of faculty members from Harvard and other universities and colleges, as well as businessmen and bankers from the Boston area.

In the discussion which followed my talk, a number of those present acknowledged the validity of the moral judgments I had called for, but moved immediately to practical political questions about my "style" and about peripheral political techniques which are supposed to be of primary concern to what are called rank-and-file voters. One participant said later that the politicians there sounded like philosophers and the philosophers tried to sound like tough politicians. He commented that those he regarded as the most impractical people gave what they thought was most practical advice.

The meeting did produce such practical results as the Massachusetts Citizens Committee for McCarthy and the beginning of the National Scientists and Engineers Committee – later to number 10,000 members – as well as contributors and dedicated workers.

Within days the Massachusetts group opened headquarters, hired a full-time staff, and organized volunteer activities at a pace that surprised the old-line professionals, as well as those who feared that the entire endeavor was impractical.

Massachusetts State Representative Irving Fishman was named temporary chairman of the McCarthy for President Committee, and State Representative Michael Harrington named vice-chairman. They and Jerome Grossman suggested an early meeting with Democratic members of the state legislature to seek advice and support for the Massachusetts primary. About thirty legislators, together with local elected officials, got together for breakfast at the Statler Hilton Hotel on December 18. Earlier, I had met with the Massachusetts State Democratic Chairman, Lester Hyman, on November 11 while I was in Boston to speak at the Young Democrats National Convention.

These first signs and then the whole Massachusetts response led me to believe that an effective organization could be built in other states.

Convinced that an organization could be built, we set out to build it. The next weeks were a series of meetings, breakfasts, talks, phone calls. I saw people from the academic community, including especially John Kenneth Galbraith. In my very first talk with Galbraith on the question of a campaign, he pointed out his continuing loyalty to the Kennedy family, going back to the campaign of 1960 and even before that. He also made reference to his appointment by President John Kennedy as Ambassador to India. He set up the reservation that he might transfer to Senator Robert Kennedy if the Senator should decide to enter the campaign.

Professor Galbraith was one of the first to speak of the possibility that President Johnson would not be nominated by the Democratic convention, and at the meeting of the National Board of the Americans for Democratic Action in February 1968, he offered the resolution endorsing my candidacy. This action was vigorously opposed by some of the labor members of the ADA Board. My endorsement brought on the resignation of a number of labor members and also that of John Roche who, at that time, was Special Consultant to the President. Under these circumstances, his resignation was not surprising.

During this period, I asked a number of persons to take various posts in my campaign group. I was disappointed in some who refused, since I knew how they stood on the issues and felt they should have been somewhat more willing to take personal chances through commitment. Women I found to be more ready than men, and wives more committed than husbands. We did at one time propose the organization of something called the Nicodemus Society – a reference to the New Testament character Nicodemus who supported the cause only between sundown and sunrise – and always left for the day. All the classical excuses were given: family obligations, professional commitments, etc. One individual said he had just joined a law firm and too much depended on his being in the firm. Another used the argument of his general financial business interests, and some, that they had received political favors of one kind or another from the Johnson administration.

Gerald Hill, chairman of the California Democratic Council (CDC), had written to me in late July asking me to speak at their convention. It was not possible to accept, but I suggested that we meet in October. At breakfast in the Ambassador Hotel, Los Angeles, on October 23, 1967, we discussed a slate of delegates to be put forward by the CDC for the California primary election the next summer, committed to an unnamed "peace candidate." Hill, a very realistic politician, was optimistic about the potential support for my candidacy in California. His position was that the challenge to the Administration's Vietnam policy could be made effectively in California and within the structure of the Democratic party itself. At that meeting I repeated my hope that others would also raise the war issue.

When I decided to announce my candidacy, I telephoned Hill, then also cochairman of the Concerned Democrats, who urged that the announcement be made in Washington rather than at a December Conference of Concerned Democrats scheduled in Chicago. We agreed that the California Democratic Council slate in California would serve as a nucleus for the campaign committee in that state and that the California organization would have primary responsibility in the conduct of the state campaign. Discussions of a working arrangement with a projected national organization were premature, since there was no national organization.

At about the same I met with Allard Lowenstein, cochairman of the Conference of Concerned Democrats, and Curtis Gans, national coordinator of the same organization. My next public appearance was at their conference in Chicago on December 2.

I had made the announcement of my candidacy two days earlier in Washington. The reason was that I did not wish to be represented as the candidate of any one special group or organization, and also because I had some reservations about the tone and the criticism of the Administration by some of the Concerned Democrats. Allard Lowenstein had said, for example, "When a President is both wrong and unpopular, to refuse to oppose him is both a moral abdication and a political stupidity." And, "If a man cheats you once, shame on him. But if he cheats you twice, shame on you!"

There were two stories of significance out of the Chicago meeting: one was the reaction to my speech. It was generally criticized as not having been inspiring and as not having "turned on" the audience. I thought as I prepared it that it was rather a good speech and on rereading it after the criticism was still of the same opinion. As to the tone in which it was delivered, probably no one understood at the time but, first, it followed the speech of Al Lowenstein, which I thought was an overstatement of the case against Lyndon Johnson and which was not in the spirit of the campaign which I intended to wage. And second, the people gathered there did not need to be inflamed or exhorted. They were pretty well turned on before arriving in Chicago and were ready to hold the election immediately. They needed, I thought, a speech of some restraint if they were to be prepared for the long and difficult campaign, which I knew lay ahead. It was not a time for storming the walls, but for beginning a long march.

That Chicago speech, together with my announcement two days earlier, laid out the basic reasons for my campaign and the basic case I intended to make.[7]

The second news story out of the conference was the announcement that I would enter the Massachusetts primary. At the outset, I had not included Massachusetts as one of the primaries in which I would run. I delayed this announcement following a conversation on November 28, 1967, with Senator Edward Kennedy of Massachusetts. In the course of that conversation, I had agreed to hold off announcing a run in Massachusetts in the hope that either a satisfactory favorite-son candidate might be entered or that a delegation representing with balance and fairness the various groups from the state would be entered in the primary. If these things could be settled, it was my hope that any confrontation between Senator Edward Kennedy and me and among the various groups in Massachusetts could be avoided. He seemed to agree with this approach and indicated that he hoped such a balance might be achieved.

But on the day that I spoke in Chicago to the Concerned Democrats, the State Democratic Committee of Massachusetts met and voted 44 to 4 to support President Johnson. This was not the kind of balance I had thought could be achieved. Edward Kennedy was reported as not supporting the pro-Johnson resolution. In any case, Massachusetts delegates at the meeting in Chicago asked me to permit them to announce publicly that I would enter the Massachusetts primary. The announcement was made.

Despite difficulties, delays, and some disappointments, a campaign staff, made up of John Safer, a Washington businessman, Tom Page, former director of public information for the Peace Corps, and June Degnan of California, was set up. Blair Clark, a friend of mine, – a former vice-president of CBS News and former associate publisher of the New York *Post*, visited me at the Blackstone Hotel in Chicago on December 2, offering to help. On the 10th of December I asked him to become my general campaign manger. He accepted and began the work of obtaining office space and of expanding the basic campaign staff.

Seymour Hersh, an Associated Press reporter who had covered the Pentagon, was taken on as our first press secretary, and Peter Barnes, a *Newsweek* reporter, took a leave of absence to do research and writing. Curtis Gans closed the national office of the Concerned Democrats in Washington, and became a kind of assistant campaign manager, coordinating the work of the

---

[7] See Appendix 5.

Concerned Democrats with the other efforts which were being made. Sam Brown, a Harvard divinity student and former officer of the National Student Association, whose name, I believe, was first suggested by my daughter Mary, became the national coordinator of the students.

It was both the strength and the weakness of my campaign that there was no inner circle of special consultants and advisers. This made for some inefficiency, but on the other hand it encouraged initiative and individual and separate group efforts. As books and articles have come out on the campaign, I have found that there were a number of people who thought there was an inner circle or at least thought there should have been one and that they should have been included in it.

My first conception was of a limited campaign. I intended to concentrate on four critical primaries: Massachusetts, in the Northeast, as representative of that area; Wisconsin, which would give us a test of the Midwest; a third in Oregon, in part because it was a Northwestern state but also because historically it had been a highly significant primary; and California, as a final test of issues and personalities.

Our overall budget estimate then ran to about $1 million, which was to be spent in support of a minimal national organization, to help co-ordinate state efforts, and to pay for a very limited national advertising program. The prevailing notion was that a candidate had to be a rich man, or be richly backed, to run. We believed that with limited funds we could test the political system in a few states, and test the press, national publications, plus radio and television, as a means of informing people and moving them to action. Later, this test I had intended to make became obscured by the expansion of our campaign and by a return to at least some of the traditional methods of political competition.

New Hampshire was not included in our early considerations because it came before Massachusetts, and it was our opinion that the Massachusetts test would be a critical one. Also, it came early and we thought we would not have time to campaign there and make all the other plans and preparations for the national effort.

On the 14th of December, I went to Bedford, New Hampshire, to participate in the Sidore Lecture Series, a commitment I had made before any consideration of a possible presidential campaign. I spoke, as agreed, on the housing problems of the country. The press found it impossible to disassociate this speech from the campaign itself, even though at the time I had not made any decision to enter the New Hampshire primary.

After the lecture, I was invited by David Hoeh, associate director of the Public Affairs Center at Dartmouth, to meet with a few friends at the home of Mr. And Mrs. Philip Chaplain. There were about fifty people present. In a large living room, and over coffee and cookies, we discussed my possible candidacy in the New Hampshire primary. At an earlier meeting in Chicago during the Conference of Concerned Democrats, I had assured the New Hampshire delegation that I would consider such a contest if it were possible or consistent with the effort then planned for Massachusetts.

These were men and women, so sincere and so concerned, that although I did not agree to run, I listened carefully. Nearly everyone at the meeting, including elected public and party officials, spoke with deep feeling of their desire to challenge the President on the issues, but they spoke also of the difficulty of challenging the party organization in New Hampshire. Most of them believed that an active campaign on my part would be necessary to overcome the routine workings of the party machinery. They were considering a write-in or a stand-in if I did not run.

Despite its rural and small-town image, New Hampshire is a highly industrialized state with a large percentage of military and military-related industries. The Democratic party is the minority party, but a minority with the kind of discipline required to have elected a Democratic governor and a Democratic Senator, both of whom were supporting President Johnson. The President had polled 63.9% of the state's vote in the 1964 general election.

At the time it seemed as though there was little reason to go to New Hampshire except in response to the enthusiasm and spirit of the people there. At this first meeting, one of those present suggested that they would take a poll if that would influence my decision. I said that I did not think they should take one, that it might be too discouraging.

This was consistent with the position I had taken in my earlier campaigns for the Senate, which was that if the issues are of major importance, poll taking is a waste of time and money. Certainly the issue of the presidential campaign of 1968 – the issue as I saw it, that is primarily the war in Vietnam – was one of such consequence that one should not attempt to determine what he should do on the basis of what the polls might show. I have no serious objection to poll taking as a method of determining what issues are important in the minds of the electorate if there is uncertainty as to what these issues are, but there was no need for polls to determine what the main issues were in 1968. And I have no objection to polls taken which deal with secondary or with less important aspects of a campaign, or the more generalized polls about the acceptability or unacceptability, the general strength or general weakness of a candidate, although I think there ought to be some limits upon the publication of such polls immediately before an election. I also believe that the voting projections made on Election Night, especially by the networks, which have proved to be at times accurate and possibly influential in late voting, should be discouraged.

The arguments against going to New Hampshire were strong, but all of them were within the limits of what is called conventional political wisdom. It was argued that running, even winning New Hampshire would be irrelevant to the national effort; that the press attention given to the New Hampshire primary was out of all proportion to its significance; that winners of the New Hampshire primary were often losers at the conventions (Senator Estes Kefauver in 1952 and again in 1956, Ambassador Henry Cabot Lodge in 1964). Charles McDowell, Jr., writing in the December 1967 *Atlantic*, quoted Republican Senator Norris Cotton as saying, when asked why the people of New Hampshire enjoyed their primary, "For commercial reasons mainly. It's a heyday in the off-season between skiing and the summer camping. Then there's all this national publicity. Here come the politicians and the television crews and the busloads of reporters spending money and filling up motels, and the people just love it. I tell you." McDowell also wrote that the people of New Hampshire were mischievous. This latter characteristic, I thought, might help my campaign.

In mid-November, before my announcement as a candidate, and before my first New Hampshire appearance, Governor John W. King was already organizing a slate of delegates for President Johnson. Both he and Senator Thomas McIntyre publicly expressed their view that any effort in New Hampshire on my part would be futile. They were joined by all ten of New Hampshire's Democratic county chairmen in reaffirming their support of the President. This display of unity, five months before the primary, was apparently meant to discourage me and my potential supporters in the state.

Spokesmen for the Democratic party in New Hampshire were saying that I would probably not get more than 11% of the vote or 3,000 to 5,000 votes if I entered. Similar estimates and predictions made it somewhat easier to decide to enter, since I was sure that any reasonably competent candidate could get 3,000 to 5,000 votes, and that the 11 to 12% estimate was far too low. At the same time, the Administration was encouraged by the polls that were being taken and began to issue public, if unofficial, statements relating to New Hampshire.

One of the most interesting news articles of the whole campaign was an unsigned story in the Washington *Post* of December 15. The headline heralded that the White House was opening its campaign against my challenge. The article expressed an Administration official's opinion that they would not only defeat me but that at the same time the President's position for the general election campaign would be strengthened. The anonymous official, quoted in the unsigned article, said that everyone in the Administration would campaign against me and that there would be a massive organizational effort by Democratic state officials coordinated through the Democratic National committee. The plan, the story said, had already been put into effect in New Hampshire, Wisconsin, Nebraska, and California. The same official added that the lineup of strength for the President in New Hampshire, Wisconsin, Nebraska, and California made it virtually certain that my campaign would fail. If I were to run in New Hampshire, he went on to say, my "only allies would be two or three guys who hadn't made it to the party." The same official expressed the hope that Senator Robert Kennedy would endorse President Johnson for re-nomination.

Set against these threatening assertions were genuine considerations of importance.

First, among those who were concerned about the issues of 1968, a kind of moral and political pressure was developing for an early test.

Second, was the enthusiasm and spirit of the people of New Hampshire who were urging me to run.

And third, with Massachusetts beginning to fade as a significant primary site, to enter New Hampshire was consistent with my early announcement that I wished to test the issues in major areas across the country, and I considered New Hampshire as the alternative to Massachusetts for the Northeast. Moreover, I did not believe that polls were accurate or that the New Hampshire people were as controlled by the Democratic party as some party leaders and commentators said they were, or that they would automatically vote for the war, as a number of analysts argued, because of the defense and military establishments which were so important to the economy of the state.

And so, on January 3, I decided to enter the New Hampshire primary.

Spring Came Early

New Hampshire

Just specimens is all New Hampshire has,
One each of everything as in a show-case
Which naturally she doesn't care to sell.

...New Hampshire has
One real reformer who would change the world
So it would be accepted by two classes,
Artists the minute they set up as artists,
Before, that is, they are themselves accepted,
And boys the minute they get out of college.
I can't help thinking those are tests to go by.

* * *

She's one of the two best states in the Union.
Vermont's the other. And the two have been
Yoke-fellows in the sap-yoke from of old
In many Marches...

The campaign in New Hampshire began in January and ended in March. It was, in Robert Frost's phrase, the first of "many Marches."[8] The state was covered with snow; all the tress, excepting the evergreens, were lifeless and black. Most houses had storm windows and storm doors; long underwear flapped frozen on the wash lines.

The early response was rather slow. Yet, after a few days of campaigning, I was sure that I would do better than the expert political analysts had predicted. The reports, which said that the people of New Hampshire were taciturn and unfriendly, that they would be generally indifferent because of previous presidential primaries, were not accurate. The reception on the streets was warm and friendly and even enthusiastic. The most common

---

[8] Frost published the poem above in 1930.

response, when I introduced myself, was "Good luck!" and "I am glad to see you here." If I had been evaluating the campaign as one for the Senate in my own state, I would have had to say, after campaigning on streets and in the factories, that it was going well.

New Hampshire tested many things. It was a major test of the young people of America in the political campaigns of 1968. It tested my adult support in that state. It tested my candidacy and my campaign organization. It tested the character of some politicians, not necessarily making them honest but certainly more truthful. It also tested the American press and commentators and other forms of public information and communication.

Most significant was the response of students and young people. I detected early that my campaign was giving a sense of purpose to young people. The students came into New Hampshire like early spring. The older people were glad to see them, too. Some remarked that they had not talked to their own children in years as they talked with the young workers in my campaign. I had expected student help in somewhat the same measure and manner as students had been active in other campaigns – in my campaigns for the Senate, for example, and in the presidential campaigns of Adlai Stevenson. There were two significant differences, however, in student help in New Hampshire.

The first was quantitative – the sheer numbers that responded. And they came from all over the country. There have been estimates that as many as 2,000 students were campaigning full time in New Hampshire in the ten days before the election and that as many as 5,000 joined the effort on weekends. They came not only from Yale, Harvard, Radcliffe, Smith, and Columbia in the East, but from campuses as far as Michigan, Wisconsin, Ohio, and even California. A good half of them were old enough to vote, and graduate students put their disciplines to work in ways that the college catalogues never described. Busloads of high school students took over the routine campaign chores of the local headquarters on weekends while the more experienced students pushed the door-to-door and ward-to-ward canvass.

The second difference was qualitative and was reflected in the way they participated in the campaign itself. We did not distinguish between an adult or a youth movement. There was a general sharing of responsibility, unrelated to the age of a participant or to his or her experience. The young people did everything from the most menial kind of campaign work to performing in the most demanding administrative offices.

It would be impossible to list all of those who campaigned, but here are just a few who illustrate the kind of inspired volunteers there were and the importance of the work performed:

Ann Hart, aged twenty; assumed responsibility for handling the influx of volunteers, for organizing them, and assigning them for campaign duty. She continued to do the same work in other primary states.

Parker Donham, aged twenty-three; a Harvard student who joined the campaign in New Hampshire and stayed with it. Along the way, he performed a variety of services, principally dealing with the press. When my press secretary left the campaign in July, Donham became traveling press secretary for the rest of the campaign.

Tom Saltonstall, aged twenty-one; another Harvard student, who became a master of the tape recorder. Tom and Jane Taffinder, twenty-three, became so effective that he could record a speech and she could transcribe it and have it in the hands of the press within a few hours after it was given – a technique that I found much more satisfactory than giving out advance texts, which I might change either before a speech was given or in the course of its delivery.

Steve Cohen, aged twenty-three; an Amherst graduate who became the general utility man of the campaign. He worked at organizing students, writing speeches, as an advance man, and as a crowd gatherer.

Joshua Leinsdorf, aged twenty-four; became the master of transportation: of airline schedules and charter plane availability, of busses and automobiles, of all the special transports of a campaign.

There was Win Rockwell, twenty-one, the most intelligent baggage handler of all time, and Jeff Lynford, twenty, who assisted in arrangements at the Chicago convention and other loyal and capable student workers whose names are one of the sounds of the campaign: Cindy Samuels, twenty-one, Mary Davis, twenty, Marge Sklencar, twenty-one, Chris Howells, nineteen, Alice Krakauer, twenty-three, Nancy Perlman, twenty-four, Kathy Anderson, twenty-one, Eric Schnapper, twenty-four, Sarah Elston, twenty-one – and, not least, not last, but my daughter Mary, nineteen.

The two members of my family who were most openly active in the campaign were Mary and my wife, Abigail. My wife's efforts were directed largely to working with women's groups, informally with those who were non-political and more formally with those who were organized specifically for my campaign. She was most effective in these efforts and also in her public appearances – both in interviews and in speeches. Mary took a leave of absence from Radcliffe when the campaign began and was active in the campaign from New Hampshire through

Chicago. By design, she stayed outside of the student and youth organizations and acted as a kind of free agent – quite freely presenting her own views along with those she knew to be mine. The three other children, Ellen, Margaret, and Michael, continued in school. They did participate in the campaign but not on a formal or continuing basis. I attempted to keep family involvement beyond New Hampshire at a minimum as I foresaw the campaign would certainly be long, and with the entrance of Senator Kennedy more complicated than I had anticipated before going into New Hampshire.

The New Hampshire campaign was more than a student or youth movement. The adult organization, made up principally of New Hampshire people, was also very effective.[9]

I campaigned vigorously in New Hampshire and my campaigning there had some effect upon the results. I was criticized for not stirring up the people. That was not my style in the first place, but if it had been, I would not have used it, as there was no need to stir the people in the state of New Hampshire. First, because the issues of war and of our domestic problems were stirring enough. Second, because New Hampshire was not the sort of state in which shouting would be very well received in January or February or March, if at any other time.

I visited more factories in New Hampshire in approximately six weeks of campaigning than I had in all of my campaigns for the House and Senate in my own state. Most were shoe factories or textile factories, although we did visit one greeting-card factory, which in January of 1968 was turning out Merry Christmas wishes for eleven months hence. One sweater manufacturer was disturbed when Robert Lowell, the poet, who was with me for several days in New Hampshire, pointed out that people working in shoe factories were happier than those who worked in sweater factories. The manufacturer of sweaters considered himself to be an enlightened and advanced employer. He announced that he was going to set out to discover if it were true and if so, why. I have no idea as to what he discovered. He was dealing with the kind of distinction only a poet might see, and such appraisals are not subject to management analysis.

---

[9] Again, I cannot or should not list all, but there was David Hoeh, of the Public Affairs Center at Dartmouth, and his wife, Sandy; Gerry Studds, a master at St. Paul's School, Concord, and our state campaign manager; Dr. David Underwood and his wife, Barbara; State Representative Jean Wallin of Nashua; John Holland, our campaign treasurer in New Hampshire; and Joe Welton, Nashua city Democratic chairman, among others.

During the early stages of the New Hampshire campaign, George Romney was a candidate on the Republican ticket. Governor Romney emphasized physical fitness by jogging, by appearing at bowling alleys, and by skiing. I responded to his challenge in some degree, by riding a snowmobile, by bowling, and finally by participating in what was called an old timers hockey game in Concord. I was a little bit taken aback when I arrived at the rink to note the ages of the old timers who were warming up at the arena. The New Hampshire man who had arranged for me to play said, when I mentioned that the average age of the old timers seemed to be about twenty-five, that the standards for old timer eligibility were that (a) you were too old for the juveniles and (b) you had never played for the Boston Bruins. I think our side won.

Three or four developments we had not planned on were helpful in New Hampshire. The ineptness of those who were making the case for a Johnson write-in vote was important. Serial-numbered pledge cards were distributed to registered Democrats by the regular Democratic organization. Each card had three sections, all bearing the serial number. One was a pledge of support for President Johnson in the primary. It noted parenthetically that "as expression of your support this card will be forwarded to the White House, Washington, D.C." Another section of the card was to be returned to the party organization. The third section was to be retained by the voter. Thus the party regulars would know who had which card and who had failed to sign up. This use of "pledge cards" came close to denying people a basic American right: the right of secret ballots. The effect was to discredit the state organization.

Then late in the campaign, when the polls began to show that I was running strongly, New Hampshire Governor John L. King and Senator Thomas McIntyre threw themselves into the fight against me – I suspect with some urging from the White House. The Governor, in public statements, said that a significant vote for me would be greeted by cheers in Hanoi. He added:

> *Shall we continue to resist naked communist aggression with all the resources at our command or will we say the price is too high, the going is too rough, and we are ready to negotiate on terms laid down by Ho Chi Minh? That is why the people most interested in the results of this election are Ho Chi Minh and his communist friends. They will be scrutinizing the returns for signs of a breaking of the American will.*

And about the same time, the regular Democrats in New Hampshire were running this advertisement:

65

*The communists in Vietnam are watching the New
Hampshire primary...They are hoping for a divided America.
Don't vote for fuzzy thinking and surrendering. Support our
fighting men...by writing the name of President Johnson.*

The second form of attack was used by Senator McIntyre. On
the Monday morning before election, New Hampshire stations
broadcast a commercial quoting McIntyre. He said that I had
proposed laws to let "American draft dodgers...return home scot
free without punishment." He added:

*To honor draft dodgers and deserters will destroy the very
fabric of our national devotion. This is fuzzy thinking about
principles that have made our nation great. Support the loyal
men who do serve this country by writing the name of
President Johnson on your ballot.*

I think our response to both of these charges was an effective
one and that the result of the exchange was an increase in my
vote.

The Governor King charge required no specific response since
the whole thrust of my campaign was a challenge to our policy in
Vietnam, and my concern was with the American response rather
than any response in Hanoi or Saigon. Senator McIntyre's charge
required a somewhat more special response since it was a gross
misrepresentation of my position. What I had advocated in the
campaign was a program for selective objection to the draft on
non-religious grounds, with provision that those whose objections
were honored would be required to accept alternate service in
some civilian agency like the Peace Corps as well as a long period
of obligation in military reserve. I had also said that in so far as
the case of young men who had left the country was concerned, a
similar offer – with somewhat harsher terms – should be made as
a condition of their being allowed to return home.

Outside the state of New Hampshire, the most helpful political
occurrence was a negative one: the failure of the Democrats in
Massachusetts to file anyone against me. This was useful in
several ways: it gave the appearance of strength on my part; it left
us free to campaign more vigorously in New Hampshire; and it
showed the weakness and confusion of the opposition as well as
the strength of our organization in Massachusetts.

The Massachusetts McCarthy for President committee had
been formed at the beginning of December 1967, shortly after the
Conference of Concerned Democrats meeting in Chicago, at
which I had said I would enter the Massachusetts primary in
April. In the course of gathering signatures to put my name on the

ballot in that state, committees were formed in about two hundred cities and towns (out of 351 municipalities). The McCarthy people decided to try to gather as many signature as possible. (Statewide, 2,500 were required.) They collected nearly 100,000 signatures before the certification date of February 27, 1968.

There were two ways to win a primary in Massachusetts. One was for the candidate to attract the biggest vote when the citizens expressed their presidential preference. The other was to capture the delegates to the national political convention who would be elected simultaneously. A Massachusetts law passed in 1966 required that all delegates elected in the primary were bound to vote on the first ballot at the convention for the presidential candidate who had received the highest number of votes in the primary.

Massachusetts' 72 convention votes were to be cast by delegates of two kinds – 24 district delegates (2 to be elected from each congressional district) and 40 "at-large" delegates. The at-large slate was put together by the State Democratic party chairman, and his list was composed of prominent Massachusetts Democrats – all high, elected officials, as well as many former officeholders. (He could also put in nomination for the presidential preference vote any name he chose.) But at-large delegates could also be nominated by petition.

Our people debated: Should they contest for delegates in the districts or for the at-large delegates? Or for both – in addition to supporting me in the presidential preference aspect the contest?

It was assumed that President Johnson would be a candidate for re-election and therefore the crucial ballot at the national convention would be the first ballot. They also assumed that Johnson's name would be on the April 30 Massachusetts primary ballot. They had to decide which procedure would give us a better chance to obtain all 72 votes on the first ballot: running a slate of McCarthy delegates-at-large, thereby challenging all the powerful Massachusetts Democrats who would be on the official slate; or concentrating on the presidential preference vote, which could assure me of the 72 votes on the first ballot.

They eventually decided to follow the latter course. Challenging the local politicians would force them to work to get out the vote and any additional votes in response to *organization* pressure were likely to be votes for President Johnson rather than for me. By permitting the regular organization's candidates

67

election by default, it was felt we would have a better chance of winning the preference vote binding all the delegates.[10]

March 5, the filing deadline at the State House, produced a dramatic moment. There had been much conjecture as to whether President Johnson would permit his name to be placed on the ballot or whether he would select a strong local figure as a stand-in. While we understood that Senator Edward Kennedy would not act as a stand-in, the names of House Speaker John McCormack and Maurice Donohue, the Massachusetts Senate President, were being considered. At the 5 p.m. deadline, after the McCarthy signatures had been filed, the state committee chairman appeared. He announced that he would not place any name on the ballot for the presidential preference vote. President Johnson had conceded us Massachusetts and its 72 convention votes. A week before the New Hampshire primary, we had our first delegates – and a substantial bloc.

The best explanation for the failure to file anyone was that it was a case of a kind of mutual mistrust between the Administration and the Massachusetts Democrats. The President and his spokesmen had been urging the regular Democrats in Massachusetts to pick a candidate, so that in case of failure to win, they would be held responsible. The Massachusetts Democrats asked the President to pick a man, in which case a loss could be blamed on the Administration.[11]

The concession of Massachusetts was important for our gathering strength. But it was important in another way – as the first overt indication we had that the campaign might affect the President's future course of action.

Our Massachusetts people still worked hard to get out a record vote in the April 30 primary, although mine was the only name printed on the ballot. Their effort was particularly important after March 16, 1968 – when Senator Robert Kennedy announced his candidacy.

---

[10] This strategy was not applied to the congressional district delegates. The decision was to make a fight in four of the twelve districts, and our people won in those four they contested.

[11] The second outside achievement, which had a good effect in New Hampshire, was the showing made by my supporters in the caucuses in Minnesota, where an effort, organized without my personal participation, elected delegates in the three metropolitan congressional districts, containing one-half of the population of the state. In addition, they carried the major cities of the state and claimed to be within 100 to 150 votes of controlling the state convention.

New Hampshire was also a time for the testing of the role of the press. I am not sure that the national press had any significant effect on the outcome in New Hampshire itself. The leading local paper in New Hampshire was the Manchester *Union-Leader*, described accurately as being archconservative. The *Union Leader* in its editorials vigorously attacked my position, and on one or two occasions called me a "skunk." It was, at the same time, very fair in its news coverage of what I said and what I did in the state of New Hampshire. This, I think, is the important test of the integrity of a newspaper. By contrast, the Indianapolis *Star*, which is also conservative, practically ignored me in its "news" coverage when I campaigned in Indianapolis and other parts of Indiana.

The response of the national press seemed at first to be one of curiosity rather than of political concern. There were articles saying that the crowds were small. (Crowds in a small state like New Hampshire are generally small.) The theme, begun even before I went into New Hampshire, was that my campaign was too low key and that I was putting people to sleep. There was the regular searching out at almost every stop of someone who was prepared to say he was for me because I was the only candidate. There was usually a graduate student available on a college campus willing to say I was a nice person but that I did not understand the problems of politics.

Gerald Moore, writing in *Life* magazine of January 19, 1968, made the rather interesting, intuitive observation that I was "laps behind Lyndon" in the campaign. He pointed out that my campaign had not taken off after a speech in New York. I never quite knew what the evidence of a take-off would have been. Moore also said I "fiercely" adored Sir Thomas More and that I was quoting him at length.

I do not know Moore's feelings about More, but I do know mine. Veneration would have been closer than adoration. In any case, I recall quoting Thomas More only once in the campaign.

At the same time, the press in general saw signs of defeat in New Hampshire. While some columnists saw me being taken over by the New Left, others were pointing out that I had disappointed the Left and was being rejected by them. Joseph Alsop, as usual not running with the pack but running on his own track, reported in a column of January 28 that President Johnson was doing very well in West Virginia. He also referred to what he called "soundings" taken in Wisconsin by the *Wall Street Journal*, which, he said, showed there was little enthusiasm for my candidacy and much evidence of real respect, if not affection, for President Johnson.

The best general newspaper coverage, beginning in New Hampshire and continuing through the campaign, was that of the Boston *Globe*. It was detached and objective and not concerned with proving anything in particular about me or about its previous stands. Possibly the *Globe's* reporters, aware of the strength of my Massachusetts organization,[12] and sensitive, as most Massachusetts political writers are, to political movements, concluded that if I had that kind of strength in Massachusetts it was at least possible that I would have similar strength in neighboring New Hampshire and elsewhere in the country.

Paul Wieck of the *New Republic* also was objective and highly accurate in his evaluation of the campaign and in his projections of how it was going. He wrote in March, well before Election Day:

> *New Hampshire is still "Nixon country." The former vice president, aware that he has the nation's first presidential primary pretty well nailed down if he can avoid a major slip, is playing a cautious game. It is like presenting the people of the Granite State with a beautifully wrapped package with a tag reading "do not open until Christmas."*
>
> *In contrast, the Democratic race is wide open. To suggest at this point, that McCarthy could win would be on the daring side of the ledger. But it no longer seems impossible...*
>
> *It would be inaccurate to say the votes for Senator McCarthy were there in mid-February. He might be lucky to get 30 or 35% of the vote. But the write-in votes weren't there for LBJ either. On the whole, the press appears ready to award McCarthy a major psychological victory if he gets 40% of the vote, which is very possible.*

It was a relief through the campaign to have Haynes Johnson of the Washington *Evening Star* in the press corps. I could look forward to straight, objective reporting of what had happened and what I had said.

I was always glad to have Harry Kelley of the Associated Press on board – partly because of what he wrote, but mostly because he was such good company.

Of all the papers that I read regularly during the campaign, the Washington *Post*, day in and day out, was the least accurate in reporting the campaign and in interpreting it.

Throughout the campaign, I found the reporting by foreign correspondents – particularly by British reporters – more accurate than the work of the American press. Reporters from other countries seem to be freer of many clichés of American politics

---

[12] Headed by Paul Counihan.

70

and especially of the preliminary judgments which condition the writings of American reporters. (I must make an exception in the case of Alistair Cooke, who perhaps has been affected by the fact that he has spent so much time in America with the American press.) I do not mean to fault the press generally, although in some individual cases the reporting was inexcusable. Nor do I mean to imply that the result of the campaign would have been any different – or not significantly different in any case – if the response of the press had been other than it was.

Much of the difficulty of our political press was well described by Anthony Howard, the Washington correspondent for *The Observer* of London.

The relationship between Government and the press in the nation's capital is so intimate as to be almost incestuous. Where newspapers in other parts of the world see it as their responsibility to lay a mine field for authority to walk through, the pundits and bureau chiefs of Washington's press corps often seem to regard it as their business instead to lay out a red carpet.

The trouble inevitably is – and it could not have been more clearly demonstrated than it has been this year – that editors and even political reports soon acquire their own vested interest in the unperturbed working of the system as they themselves have always understood it to operate: for it is explaining and expounding the working of that system that provides them with their own stock-in-trade. They may of course criticize it from time to time; they may even occasionally call for reform – but they do both in the same assured, reasonable tones and with the same sense of moral rectitude that they share in common with those who rule this nation.

It is not, I hope, uncharitable to comment that I shall always remain convinced that one reason the press and the TV media came so belatedly and reluctantly to recognize the significance of Senator Eugene McCarthy's campaign lay in the fact that from the beginning his candidacy had been mounted entirely outside their own terms of reference. The power of Senator McCarthy's appeal represented an attack on the assumptions of political writer David Broder just as much as it did on those of politician John Bailey; an undermining of the reputations of pollsters like Oliver Quayle just as much as of politicians like Governor John W. King or Senator Thomas J. McIntyre of New Hampshire; a stool hurled at the studios of the networks just as much as a stone pitched through the White House windows.

71

It is difficult to evaluate the quality of the radio and television reporting either early in the campaign or later, because I saw little of it. In New Hampshire we did use local radio stations scattered throughout the state, assuming that people stay inside during the winter and that the radio is often their companion. When we came to a little station, we would stop in and were always welcomed ("Well, look who's here...").

Among the television correspondents who covered my campaign at various times throughout the year, David Schoumacher of CBS, in my judgment, had the most creative view of the way in which television should be used to present the story of a political campaign. This was true of his straight news reporting and also of his interviews during the campaign, when the substance and sequence of his questions were expert. Schoumacher was a hard questioner, but in the context of the campaign and related to the important issues. The two interviews by him that I remember most clearly were the one on the night of the New Hampshire primary, in which the point he emphasized was not the near victory in New Hampshire but the political significance of what had happened in that state, and then later, the interview in Green Bay, Wisconsin, following the announcement by Senator Robert Kennedy of his candidacy.

Herb Kaplow of NBC was with my campaign for a short time. On the basis of what I saw of his reporting of other candidates in the course of the campaign, I was sorry he had left my campaign. It was my impression that he, too, was using the television medium in a professional way. His great confrontation in New Hampshire was with the president of the Claremont Rotary Club. In an effort persuade the club president to allow television crews to be set up at a Rotary luncheon at which I was speaking, Kaplow argued from the Constitution of the United States and particularly the First Amendment and freedom of press. He was put down by the president, who used as a basis for his refusal the constitution of the Rotary Clubs of America.

In the course of the New Hampshire campaign, some of the perennial difficulties of every campaign began to show. One of these is the relationship of the candidate to his speech writers. This relationship is especially sensitive if the speech writers themselves have reputations as writers, if they are talented both in the substance of what they write and in their style. The relationship is further complicated when a speech writer has had no real political experience or has the more or less standard view as to how a campaign should be conducted.

My principal speech and press-release writers were Jeremy Larner and Paul Gorman. I know they were unhappy many times during the campaign. I fear that unhappiness is generally the role of speech writers. If a candidate does not use their material, they are disappointed. If he does use it, they are also likely to be somewhat disappointed at not getting credit.

In New Hampshire we had somewhat similar difficulties with the talented advertising agency people who came to assist in the campaign. The friction started either because of a lack of experience in political campaigning or the disposition to use advertising for my campaign of the same sort used in previous political wars.

My objection to the traditional advertising was twofold: One was that it did not reflect the kind of campaign that I was carrying on, which was essentially an educational one in which I was not interested in moving people to respond to slogans and symbols. The second objection was a practical one. I believed that slogans would not be effective anyway if the issues distinguishing candidates were complex or if a candidate did not represent primarily a party position.

During the campaign it was necessary to have a showdown with three or four agencies. In most cases the confrontation had good results. Six volunteers from Doyle, Dane and Bernbach prepared exceptional ads. One of the ads in the New York *Times* on March 24 showed me greeting a crowd of young people. The picture had been taken at a rally at the University of Wisconsin in Madison in February. Under the picture was the statement "Our Children Have Come Home," and this text:

> *Suddenly there's hope among our young people.*
> *Suddenly they've come back into the mainstream of*
> *American life. And it's a different country.*
> *Suddenly the kids have thrown themselves into politics,*
> *with all their fabulous intelligence and energy. And it's a new*
> *election.*

Another which appeared on Sunday, April 14, carried the headline, "A Breath of Fresh Air." Under it was a picture of me taken as I got off a plane. I do not know how much of a breath of fresh air the ad proved, but the photograph certainly demonstrated that I was wind-blown.

Another was headed "Man vs. Machine."

> *We are the volunteers, and the mercenaries are no match*
> *for us.*
> *We are the contributors of the ten and twenty dollar bills,*
> *and together we are bigger than the big money.*

We are the asphalt, and we are conquering the steamroller.

Perhaps the best of all was one run in the Sunday New York *Times* of May 26. "McCarthy's Machine Needs Money," it read, and there was a picture of a group of young people with coats over their arms, labeled "The Machine." Excerpts from the copy:

> *Senator McCarthy is backed by the most improbable political machine in American history.*
>
> *It works for nothing, runs on peanut butter sandwiches and soft drinks, and spends the night in sleeping bags or empty warehouses.*
>
> *You can't buy a machine like this, even with the offer of money...*
>
> *And you can't con them either, with a lot of overblown promises.*
>
> *They're looking for a new kind of leadership for our country and they believe that Senator McCarthy is the only one who can provide it.*
>
> *That's why they went out and rang every doorbell in the state of New Hampshire for him.*
>
> *And why they did the same in Wisconsin.*
>
> *And why, now, when the Senator is preparing for his biggest battles of all, they're ready to go into Oregon and California to do it all over again...*
>
> *But unless you help, they'll never get there...*
>
> *They can't fight big business and personal fortunes on an empty stomach.*
>
> *Please don't let them down.*

They were, I think, the best ads of my campaign and possibly the best ads run in any political campaign in recent history. The authors won the Andy Award in 1969 for political advertising for their effort in my campaign.[13]

In the course of the New Hampshire primary we were able to organize a finance committee and satisfy ourselves that we could raise enough money to conduct a strong campaign in other primaries and beyond the primaries.[14]

---

[13] My concept of what ads should contain was well presented and also well defended by Bill Nee, a partner in a Minneapolis advertising agency, and his wife, Kay, who together worked on advertising in my Minnesota campaigns, and also by Arthur Michelson, my former press secretary, who had served in my 1964 campaign for Senate.

[14] Most active and effective in New Hampshire and beyond were Howard Stein, president of Dreyfus Fund, Incorporated, New York, who became chairman of my national finance committee; Arnold Hiatt, president of Green Shoe Manufacturing Company, Boston, who became

As the campaign in New Hampshire drew to an end, I was convinced that the early estimates were far off. Those estimates gave me only 11% of the vote. Even the later estimates which were raised considerably above that were also on the low side. We went so far as to believe that if the process of writing was not so difficult or if crossing over was not so difficult, that we might get more votes in the state than President Johnson was likely to get.

The increased tempo of the war in Vietnam – the Tet Offensive – and the continued hearings being held by the Senate Foreign Relations Committee also influenced the vote in New Hampshire.

The results in New Hampshire were very satisfying and encouraging, especially to the students and to the people to whom politics was new. I had won 42% of the vote in the Democratic primary, and when the write-in votes for President Johnson and for me were counted, I had come within 230 votes of defeating him.

the treasurer; Martin Peretz, member of the Committee on Degrees in Social Studies, Harvard; Stewart Mott, New York philanthropist; Blair Clark, who was also chairman of the campaign; Mrs. June Oppen Degnan, a California businesswoman; and Stephen T. Quigley, former Commissioner of Administration of the state of Minnesota, who acted as comptroller.

The President Drops Out

On March 13, the Wednesday morning after the New Hampshire election, I returned to Washington and was met at the airport by the press asking for comments on reports that Senator Robert Kennedy was about to announce his entrance into the campaign. I declined comment since it was still only a matter of rumor, but rumor that was beginning to take on substance.

Senator Kennedy had called my Senate office in Washington several times that morning asking to see me when I arrived in Washington. I did not receive the request until I reached my office around two o'clock, and I then arranged to see Senator Kennedy in his brother Edward Kennedy's office at 4:30 p.m.

Reporters were already gathered in the halls of the Senate Office building. In order to be free of them, I went to the Senate gymnasium from which reporters are excluded – about the only place in the Capitol from which they are – and left the gymnasium by another door to join Senator Robert Kennedy in his brother's office. Senator Edward Kennedy was present at the meeting.

Earlier that day, Robert Kennedy had told a group of reporters gathered outside a Senate hearing room, "I am reassessing my position as to whether I'll run against President Johnson. I think that the election in New Hampshire has indicated a good deal of concern in the Democratic party about the direction our country is going." When he and I met in his brother's office, it was this statement we talked about. We talked for ten or fifteen minutes. There were some periods of silence, but not the long silences and coldness that a number of reporters, who were not present, later described. What was not said at the meeting was more important than what was said. I said that it did not appear likely that I could get the nomination, but in case it did work out I wanted him to know that I was interested only in one term. This was consistent with my effort to depersonalize the presidency. However, I did not ask Senator Kennedy for his support in return for my stepping aside in 1972, nor did I promise to support him in 1972. I simply said I was interested only in one term. He did not specifically state his intention, but I got the definite impression that he was going to run.

I returned by way of the back door of the gymnasium and then met with the waiting reporters and told them only that I had seen Senator Kennedy.

The next day, the 14th, in response to requests of people who had been asking me to enter primaries in their states, I agreed to get into both Indiana and South Dakota. The timing of this announcement was not unrelated to the announcement which I anticipated Senator Kennedy would make within a few days. I then went on into Wisconsin to begin the final drive of the primary there.

In our preliminary speculation and planning, we had counted on Wisconsin for our first and perhaps most certain victory. We considered a win most likely there for a number of reasons: first, because of the independent tradition of the state itself; second, because it was a state in which I was relatively well known and in which the politics, especially in the progressive tradition, was very similar to that of the Farmer-Labor party in my own state; and third, because even before I announced that I would be a candidate, there was the beginning of a strong anti-war and anti-President Johnson movement among both Democrats and Republicans in Wisconsin.

We anticipated, also, that my candidacy would have the support of two or three major newspapers with the possibility of formal endorsement from at least two. The Madison *Capital Times* issue of December 1 was encouraging; it said I might be surprised at the turn that politics could take in the state of Wisconsin. We were also counting on the long-time influence of *The Progressive*, a monthly magazine founded in 1909 by Robert M. La Follette, Sr., which has a national reputation for responsible editorial judgment on political and social issues.

There was yet another advantage in Wisconsin – a potential which had not existed in New Hampshire – and that was the ease with which Republicans could cross over and vote in the Democratic primary. The possibility of this crossover was greatly improved when, on March 21, Governor Nelson A. Rockefeller announced his decision not to enter the race for the Republican nomination, leaving the liberal Republicans without a candidate and with no way to express opposition to the policies of Vietnam in their own party.

Despite the built-in advantages in Wisconsin, the judgment of the national press at the beginning of the year was that my chances were not much better than they were in New Hampshire.

The *Wall Street Journal* reported on January 19 that the going might be even tougher than I expected. I never knew how they could know how tough I expected the going in Wisconsin would be, especially since I thought the going would be quite good. Their reporter had interviewed, "scores of people," he said. One of his observations was that many of my supporters were not old enough to vote. (This is the kind of observation we had to live with throughout the campaign.)

CBS commentators and some of the papers, including the *Christian Science Monitor*, were still referring to me as the Senator from Wisconsin. And the Gallup poll released on January 6 showed I could get 12% of the vote in the national election. The popular estimate was that in Wisconsin I would get about 19% of the vote. The press did point out, however, that this would be a somewhat more serious contest. It was expected that not only the President himself, whose name was on the ballot, but also the Vice President and members of the Cabinet would come in to campaign for the President.[15]

I had a good organization in Wisconsin. It had been established quite independently without any help from my national campaign organization and was competently run by such people as Mrs. Ed Miller of Madison, Mrs. Keith Downey of Green Bay, Don Peterson of Eau Claire, Mr. and Mrs. Hayden Jamieson, Mr. and Mrs. Arthur Buck, Arnold Serwer, associate editor of the *Progressive* magazine, all of Madison, Jay Sykes and Ted Warshafsky of Milwaukee, and many others. The organization was ready and waiting when the student movement began to take on force and volume. It absorbed the students and used them most effectively. Before my arrival in mid-March, it had prepared a heavy speaking schedule.

On my first day out, after a luncheon speech at the Executive Inn in Sheboygan, Wisconsin, I received a message from my campaign headquarters in Washington that Senator Edward Kennedy wanted to make an unpublicized trip to Wisconsin that night to meet with me. My wife was speaking in Green Bay, and I had planned to fly there in a small plane in the late evening, leaving the reporters behind.

---

[15] Wisconsin law had been changed, prior to the 1968 primary, to provide that if only one Democrat or Republican was listed on the ballot, a voter who did not want to vote for him could vote no by checking a box on the ballot marked "none of the names shown." Democrats presumed that the Republican legislature enacted this option to embarrass President Johnson. It is quite possible that the no vote for president would have carried if I had not entered the primary.

Arriving in Green Bay after nine o'clock in the evening, I was told that Senator Kennedy and members of my staff traveling with him had left Washington too late to make airline connections in Chicago and were attempting to charter a private jet to Green Bay. As late as eleven o'clock the Green Bay airport reported no flight plan for a charter aircraft and so, assuming that Senator Kennedy would not arrive until morning, I went to bed and to sleep.

I was awakened some time after one o'clock and told that Senator Kennedy was arriving at the Holiday Inn, and I suggested that he come to our suite at the Northland Hotel. Because several reporters had arrived from Sheboygan and were in the hotel, the manager offered the use of a back entrance and freight elevator to bring the Senator to my suite.

In no time the suite was crowded with people. I was somewhat surprised at the number. There were, in addition to Senator Kennedy, Curtis Gans and Blair Clark of my staff who accompanied him from Washington, Richard Goodwin who was traveling with me, my wife and daughter, and others. It was like a family gathering for a matchmaking, some of them hoping an engagement would take place, others not.

Like the walrus and the carpenter, Senator Kennedy and I talked about many things. We talked about the campaign and the way it was developing, the public opposition to the Administration's policy, his recent trip to South Vietnam to investigate corruption in the civil government, and about the St. Patrick's Day parade in Boston in which we were both scheduled to march. Finally, he indicated that his brother would announce his candidacy the following day. I said that the announcement could make no significant change in my announced purposes and objectives. Had anything more happened, there would at least have been plenty of witnesses.

It was after three o'clock when Senator Kennedy left the suite. Both of us, without previous agreement, referred to the visit as a courtesy call. The reports of the meeting were generally quite accurate except for the question of who requested the meeting. I decided after reading reports of what Senator Edward Kennedy had to say that he believed the initiative was mine, and I had been led to believe the initiative was his. My only conclusion is that somehow it was suggested to each of us by someone that the other wanted a meeting.

On the morning of March 16, Senator Robert Kennedy announced that he would enter a number of primaries, and that afternoon, I held a press conference. Prior to the conference I was interviewed by David Schoumacher of CBS for about twenty minutes. I thought the interview was most helpful in laying out my response to Senator Robert Kennedy, and it was also an effective use of television as a medium of information and education. There was nothing very surprising in what I said following the announcement, as my position remained unchanged and my earlier commitment remained firm. In response to a question from Schoumacher, I said that I was not in any way reassessing my position or making any deals with reference to my campaign or to my candidacy. I said I would run as hard as I could in every primary and stand as firm as I could at the convention. Would I trade delegates? I said I did not have any delegates whom I could trade. I also rejected the offer of help from Senator Kennedy in Wisconsin. I did not need his money or his organization, I said. All I needed was running room.

Near the end of the interview, Schoumacher said a lot of people expected me to fold under the new threat. My answer was that I did not know how many, but I thought the people who knew me well did not expect me to. Vice President Hubert Humphrey, for example, I said has given no indication publicly, and I am quite sure that he has given no indication to the President privately that once I got into this I would fold under White House pressure or any other pressure.

It was clearly the view of some of Senator Kennedy's followers that many of my supporters would immediately go over to the Kennedy campaign. This was a view accepted not only by those active in the Kennedy campaign but by rather detached observers like Richard Rovere who, In *The New Yorker* article on March 23, said that my support came not because of any personal attachment to me on the part of the voters but rather because of hostility toward Lyndon Johnson, and that the young people who had been drawn to me were intelligent enough not to let their loyalty to me stand in the way of their switching to Senator Kennedy if it appeared that I could not win.

I suppose one should not be too severe in criticizing magazine writers like Rovere, although I think there is less excuse for rash judgments in magazine articles than there is in the articles of columnists who have to be profound on short notice three to five times a week. There certainly is cause to protest what Rovere wrote, as he did in this article, that my record on domestic affairs was to the right of the Administration and that I had never been identified with the civil rights movement. He concluded that it was almost inevitable that I would have to share my New Hampshire victory with Senator Kennedy and, in all probability, "deliver its fruits to him." I use the example of Rovere only because I had considered his judgment generally more objective and detached than that of some other columnists and as an example of how he and others misread both the nature of my campaign and the commitment of many of my supporters. This is the kind of writing one might expect of Jack Newfield of *The Village Voice*, but we have a right to expect better of Rovere.

The immediate response to the entrance of Senator Kennedy was most encouraging to me. A few hours after his announcement I spoke to a group of students and citizens at St. Norbert's College in Green Bay, Wisconsin, and later the same day I spoke in Indianapolis to an overflow crowd at a meeting of the Hoosiers for a Democratic Alternative. The enthusiasm of the crowds was greater than it had been before his announcement, and within a week, both the number of volunteers and unsolicited contributions increased greatly – most noticeably in $5 and $10 bills, many of which were addressed simply to "Senator McCarthy, Washington, D.C."

About the time that Senator Kennedy announced his candidacy, the national press reported that he had offered to stay out of the race if President Johnson would name a commission to redirect the nation's Vietnam policy. There is some confusion as to whether the idea of a presidential commission originated with Senator Kennedy, with Theodore Sorensen, or with Mayor Richard Daley of Chicago. Senator Kennedy's statement on the matter, which appeared in the New York *Times* on March 18, 1968, indicates that he would not have sought the nomination in 1968 had it become evident that a change in Vietnam policy was forthcoming. The President's rejection of the commission proposal made it clear to him, Senator Kennedy stated, "that so long as Lyndon B. Johnson was President our Vietnam policy would consist of only more war, more troops, more killing and more senseless destruction of the country we were supposedly there to save."

It was difficult for me to conceive of Senator Kennedy's having made such an offer, and even more difficult to understand how President Johnson, or any President of the United States, could consider such a proposal, if he did consider it even for a day as reported. A commission cannot make foreign policy, nor can a President delegate this authority to others. These two actions taken together, if they were as reported, and I had to accept that they were, underscored my concern over the personalization of the office of the presidency which had taken place in both the Johnson and Kennedy administrations, and my concern over a growing disregard of constitutional lines of authority, especially the involvement of the Senate in determining our foreign policy.

The Wisconsin campaign differed from the one in New Hampshire. Although the student support was there and was very effective, the overall campaign was somewhat more traditional. It was possible to raise other issues – some of them related to the war in Vietnam and some standing separately. Despite what was said about ours being a one-issue campaign, in New Hampshire we had in fact, raised a number of basic issues. For some reason these statements of the issues were not accepted or identified by the press. In Wisconsin, with the larger audiences and the university campuses as platforms, it was easier to show that more than Vietnam was involved in the campaign of 1968.

A distinctive characteristic of politics in Wisconsin is, of course, the importance of the University of Wisconsin as a political and cultural force. It may be because it is situated in the capital city of Madison and because there are good newspapers there. At any rate, there is no other state in the country in which one university is so strong an influence and so much a matter of concern to its people.

The campaign in Wisconsin proceeded much as we hoped it would. Never in recent presidential elections did so many cabinet members come into one state on a non-partisan basis as they did into Wisconsin in the weeks just preceding the primary. Vice President Humphrey came twice, and although he was most restrained in his criticism of me, he did, of course, present his stand on the war.

The Secretary of Agriculture, Orville Freeman, appeared at least twice and was somewhat less restrained. During his first appearance he was subjected to severe heckling, which caused us some concern. The second time, because we had time to mobilize our students to exert their influence over potential hecklers, he was received without serious protest. The Secretary came in to defend farm policy which, at least in so far as Wisconsin was concerned, made it somewhat easier for me to criticize the program. One positive result of the campaign in Wisconsin was the increase in the price supports for milk products. On March 20, a few days before the Wisconsin primary election, Secretary Freeman announced that dairy price supports would be set at 90% of parity. This action raised the price support from $4.00 per hundredweight to $4.28 per hundredweight.

In March, Robert Weaver, the Secretary of Housing and Urban Development, was brought in to tour federally aided projects. Although his visit was also billed as non-partisan, it was arranged by local party officials. It made it easier for me to draw the contrast between what the Administration had declared to be the needs of the cities and its failure to establish a program to meet them, and also dramatized the importance of setting priorities for America. Sending the Attorney General, Ramsey Clark, to speak at the University of Wisconsin Law School helped to make the case that the Administration did not have a clear sense of the special institutional functions of certain offices of the government.

The high point of the Wisconsin campaign was the rally at the Dane County Memorial Coliseum in Madison on March 25. This was the day I received the endorsement of the Madison *Capital Times*. Some 18,000 persons jammed the auditorium, 5,000 more than it was designed to hold. I felt the spirit of the campaign as I had never felt it before, and I quoted Walt Whitman's poem:

> *I hear America singing, the varied carols I hear;*
> *Those of mechanics – each one singing his, as it should be,*
> *blithe and strong;*
> *The carpenter singing his, as he measures his plank or*
> *beam,*
> *The mason singing his, as he makes ready for work, or*
> *leaves off work;*
> *The boatman singing what belongs to him in his boat – the*
> *deck-hand singing on the steamboat deck;*
> *The shoemaker singing as he sits on his bench – the hatter*
> *singing as he stands;*
> *The wood-cutter's song – the ploughboy's on his way in the*
> *morning, or at the noon intermission, or at sundown;*
> *The delicious singing of the mother – or of the young wife*
> *at work – or of the girl sewing or washing;*
> *Each singing what belongs to him or her, and to none else;*
> ** * **
> *Poets to come! Orators, singers, musicians to come!*
> *Not to-day is to justify me, and answer what I am for;*
> *But you, a new brood, native, athletic, continental, greater*
> *than before known.*
> *Arouse! Arouse – for you must justify me – you must*
> *answer.*

At this rally I presented my conception of the role of the presidency.[16] Any man who offers himself for the presidency, I said, must meet three conditions of character, experience, and understanding. The President of the United States must be able to interpret and read with reasonable judgment the needs and aspirations of the people of this nation.

He must know the limitations of power and influence, particularly since there is no greater political power or influence than that entrusted by the people to their President. Because the

---

[16] See Appendix 6.

84

potential for leadership exists in every American, the President must be prepared to be a channel for the desires and aspirations of the people. He must guide the nation to the goals it seeks – and never impose the office upon the people.

Finally, the office of the presidency of the United States, I said, must never be a personal office. The President should not speak of "my country" but of "our country," not of "my cabinet" but of "the cabinet," not of "my Supreme Court" but of "the Supreme Court."

The role of presidency at all times, but especially in 1968, I felt, must be one of uniting this nation, not one of adding it up in some way, not of putting it together of bits and pieces, and not one even of organizing it. The need of America is not a need for organization, but a need to develop a sense of national character, with common purposes and shared ideals.

Three incidental events had a slight bearing on the campaign in the closing days of the Wisconsin primary. One was a so-called long march through Negro and Polish neighborhoods in central Milwaukee. The march, like others, was at odds with the press charge that we had not been going into ghetto areas (New Hampshire, the only other state in which I had thus far been involved, did not even have a ghetto). The charge was to persist throughout the campaign and beyond, despite the fact that I visited ghetto areas in Chicago, Indianapolis, Gary, Newark, New York, Pittsburgh, Philadelphia, Omaha, Atlanta, Louisville, Los Angeles, and San Francisco.

In nearly every one of those stops, I talked to the leaders of minority groups. My campaign staff and organization included a number of very able Negro advisers. I did not use them as a separate corps or for exhibit purposes, but they were included as a part of the overall organization. Among them were Herbert Reid, professor of law at Howard University, and Morrison Hansborough – both of Washington, D.C. From New York I had Clarence Jones and Ivanhoe Donaldson, and from Boston, Marvin Harrell. In addition, there were Bruce Gordon and Louis Lomax in California, and others.

During our five-mile walk in Milwaukee on the evening of March 30, I shook hands and talked with people and looked over the run-down buildings in which they lived.

The second incident was what was described as a great upheaval in my campaign organization, revolving around the departure of a press secretary. A press secretary is always a matter of great concern to the traveling reporters and columnists, and I concluded that one should anticipate sacrificing one or two as a kind of ritualistic offering to the press in each campaign.

Presidential press aides often suffer the same fate. Sy Hersh, who had been my press secretary, was not dismissed but resigned, with no breach of friendship between him and me. Robert Lowell, who was traveling with me then, observed that Hersh had given great service to the press but little respect, whereas, in Lowell's opinion, a good press secretary should give little service and great respect.

Phil Murphy, who replaced him, was an early supporter of mine in Massachusetts, and as executive financial editor for the Boston *Herald Traveler*, he had written what I thought was a most competent article reviewing my background in economics and qualifications in that field. On a campaign swing through Boston in early April, Phil Murphy had said he would like to join the campaign. When the vacancy occurred, we called on him to join us and he did in late April.

For some reason at this time, the press began to worry about the effectiveness of my organization. Once one reporter began to worry, it seemed the whole press corps did. They reminded me of blackbirds on a telephone line. When one flies off, they all fly off; when one returns, they all return. The word went around that I was going to replace Blair Clark as campaign manager. I never could find out who started it, but there was no truth in it. Blair Clark had been most loyal and self-sacrificing in the whole effort.

The third event was my withdrawal of support from the joint Kennedy-McCarthy delegation in the District of Columbia primary. There were three reasons for withdrawal. One was the makeup of the delegation itself, which my supporters felt lacked balanced representation. The second was the manner in which the joint delegation was organized and operated, which was quite different from what we had been led to expect when we were asked to support it. The third was the fact the Kennedy campaign was using the joint effort to suggest that I had accepted his offer of help in primaries he had not entered, and that I was prepared to reduce my efforts in those primaries in which he and I both would be running. Even in the early stages there was no indication that the Kennedy supporters were preparing to help me, except as it might serve their own campaign. The withdrawal of my support from the District delegation made it very clear that my effort was a separate one and that there would be no compromise along the way.

Campaigning in Wisconsin was as pleasant and enjoyable as it had been in New Hampshire, although the response of the people was somewhat different. The character of the state was different, too, and, of course, the weather had changed as spring advanced. The snow was gone, although the northern lakes were still frozen over, and the geese in their northern migration walked about on gray April ice in a state of indecision and surprise. The brown of winter grass and corn stalks and of fields of stubble was the dominant color of the state, in contrast, for the most part, with the black of the plowed strips.

Here, as in New Hampshire, Robert Lowell traveled with me for several days. This was new country to him. In Wisconsin he was exposed to tamarack swamps and to the marks and influence of the great glaciers. At one place, after I had pointed out that the land over which we were traveling had once been under the great glacier and had made several references to terminal and lateral moraines, the poet commented that I was becoming a glacial bore. I dropped the subject and listened instead to his comments on wayside taverns selling beer and his observation that windmills had suffered a great deal in Wisconsin. (He meant, of course, that they suffered not from the attacks of Quixote, but from those of rural electrification. Many of the towers remain standing after the wheels and fans had either been taken down or blown down.)

There was more music in the campaign in Wisconsin. At almost every stop, we were met by a high school band or other musical group. One day at Superior, we heard a new song sung by students, nuns, and clerics: "Make the Scene With Gene." At Rhinelander, there was an Irish setter blanketed with a sign that read "All the way with Gene."

Not so pleasant were the reports of attempts to discredit me and my record in the Negro community and within the labor movement. Negro papers were being provided with charges from some unidentified source that I was against civil rights. The first report in a Negro paper claimed that I had not voted for civil rights sixteen or seventeen times. These were votes taken during the filibuster on the civil rights bill while I was campaigning in New Hampshire. They were unrelated to civil rights, but we were not able to get the paper to carry the correction until the day before the primary election.

Within the labor movement I had the endorsement of the Meat Cutters Union and the backing of the Amalgamated Clothing Workers in Milwaukee. The United Auto Workers remained officially neutral. Otherwise, the great body of organized labor officially supported President Johnson and the primary responsibility for keeping it in line rested in Al Barkan, the national director of COPE (the AFLCIO Committee on Political Education). Since my labor record throughout the years had been much closer than Lyndon Johnson's to what organized labor was asking for, I was disturbed to learn of efforts to discredit it. Such action seemed to repudiate the statement (later much-repeated) that "Labor stands by its friends."

In the closing days of the Wisconsin campaign, our canvassers reported increasing support for me. Their latest report on March 30, three days before the primary election, showed that I might get something like 62% of the vote.

Experts were not so optimistic. As late as March 28, Richard Nixon, who was also campaigning in Wisconsin, predicted a victory for President Johnson. And on the 29th, Vice President Humphrey predicted that President Johnson would be the Democratic nominee that fall. "I haven't the slightest doubt," he said, "that the election in November will be fought out by Mr. Johnson on the one hand and Mr. Nixon on the other. I imagine people expect me to say that, but I am one of those Democrats who is not panicked at all."

Two days later, on Sunday, March 31, President Johnson addressed the nation on television. He reported that in the interest of de-escalating the conflict, American bombing of North Vietnam was being limited to the area immediately north of the demilitarized zone. At the end of the speech he departed from his text and announced he would not be a candidate.

I had not anticipated the President would withdraw, even though I expected to win over him in Wisconsin. I did think that if he were defeated in a number of primaries it was unlikely he would go on as a candidate to the convention.

I took no personal satisfaction in victory over President Johnson. Withdrawal was a personally sad and difficult moment for a man who gave many years in the service of his country. It seemed to me Lyndon Johnson might in fact feel liberated by his withdrawal. I had once heard him speak of "the tattered sky of Texas."

After the President's announcement, our canvassers reported that my earlier 62% had dropped by three or four points.

When the votes were counted, I received 56.2%, President Johnson 34.6%, and Senator Kennedy 6.3% in write-ins. Vice President Humphrey and Gov. Wallace each had 1/2 of 1% in write-ins.

The Wisconsin victory was not complete and final for we faced the immediate problem of a contest with Senator Kennedy in Indiana and other primaries, and the entrance of Humphrey, if not in the primaries at least into the contest for the nomination.

I began to feel like a relay runner who after each lap had to face a different runner – starting in New Hampshire and Wisconsin when I ran against President Johnson – first as a write-in and then in his own name, and now Indiana where I was to run against Senator Kennedy, after which, I anticipated, Vice President Humphrey would certainly be on the track.

No Man's Land

The campaign was never planned simply as a delegate-gathering effort. Our aim was to change the political process – to make it more responsive to the people's wishes. We therefore crisscrossed the country and interrupted regular campaign schedules in an effort to reach and to involve as many people as possible. I left the New Hampshire campaign, for example, to make a speech to the Press Club in Atlanta, Georgia, and at the University of Georgia at Athens in January 1968, and again in February, for a speech at Holy Cross College in Worcester, Massachusetts, and for Business Executives Move for Vietnam Peace meeting in Philadelphia.

I had just arrived in Wisconsin in March and heard Senator Kennedy's announcement that he was entering the race when I had to leave to fulfill speaking obligations made earlier in Indiana, Massachusetts, and Maine. As hectic as many of these trips were, the ride from Woburn, Massachusetts, to Brunswick, Maine, was one of the better remembered of the campaign, both by me and the accompanying press. It was a rainy night and I rode in a converted Checker cab that seemed to be without shock absorbers. As we jolted along, I was reminded of "Maine," a poem by Philip Booth:

> When old cars get retired, they go to Maine.
> Thick as cows in backlots off the blacktop,
> East of Bucksport, down the washboard
> from Penobscot to Castine,
> they graze behind frame barns: a Ford
> turned tractor, Hudsons chopped to half-ton
> trucks, and Chevy panels, jacked up,
> tireless, geared to saw a cord of wood.
>
> Old engines never die. Not in Maine,
> Where men grind valves the way their wives grind axes.
> Ring-jobs burned-out down the Turnpike
> still make revolutions, turned marine.

89

If Hardscrabble Hill makes her knock,
Maine rigs the water-jacket salt: a man
can fish forever on converted sixes,
and for his mooring, sink a V-8 block

When fishing's poor, a man traps what he can.
Even when a one-horse hearse from Bangor fades
away, the body still survives:
painted lobster, baited – off Route 1 –
with home preserves and Indian knives,
she'll net a parlor-full of Fords and haul in
transient Cadillacs like crabs. Maine trades
in staying power not shiftless drives.[17]

He made no mention of old Checker cabs.

It was midnight when the cab reached Brunswick, but the students were still waiting. Their enthusiasm made the ride worthwhile, and the next day the response of the students at the University of Maine was as enthusiastic. At the end of the speech at the University of Maine, the master of ceremonies called for the Maine fight song. He said it had not been sung with so much enthusiasm for the last four years.

I interrupted the Wisconsin campaign again on March 27 to make a speech in Chicago for a businessmen's group. On the flight a conversation ensued between Robert Lowell and the officials of the business group about what Robert Lowell did for a living. After some hesitation, Lowell finally agreed that he was a free-lance poet.

On primary election day in Wisconsin, April 2, I flew to Omaha, Nebraska, for a rally planned by my supporters there before going back East again to Connecticut for rallies the next day in Hartford and New Haven. Connecticut, a non-primary state, was particularly significant because the party was strictly controlled by the State Democratic Chairman, John Bailey, who was also Chairman of the Democratic National Committee. Bailey had announced in January of 1968, eight months before the convention, that "the Democratic National Convention is as good as over. It will be Lyndon Johnson again, and that's that."

But, as in other non-primary states, a strong effort was being made to let the people decide and to open up the process so that they could. Shortly after I announced my decision to enter primaries, groups in Connecticut began to organize under the

---

[17] On a later visit to Maine for a few days' summer vacation, the first thing I saw on the highway was a pickup truck with a load of new tail pipes and mufflers, replacements for burned-out parts of old cars in Maine.

leadership of Anne Wexler, vice-chairman of the Westport Democratic County Committee, the Reverend Joseph Duffey, director of the Center for Urban Studies at Hartford Seminary, and Chester Kerr, director of Yale University Press. Members of these groups, motivated largely by opposition to the war and a concern over neglect of domestic problems, were characterized by Chester Kerr as "middle-aged liberals left over from the New Deal, former Stevenson volunteers who had infiltrated the Democratic organization ... and Kennedy fans tired of waiting." There were, in addition, many young people anxious to work for change in and through the political process.

Connecticut had never had primary elections. The usual procedure was for the state party at its convention in June of the presidential election year to select a slate of national delegates and then bind them to a unit rule. The entire state delegation of 44 faithful party members, selected by John Bailey, would then vote at the national convention as Bailey directed.

The strategy for breaking this procedure was formulated early in the year. Normally the 960 delegates to the state convention were selected at Democratic town committee meetings. But Geoff Cowan, a Yale Law Student, discovered a provision in the 1955 election law that allowed for a local party primary wherever 5% of the registered party members petitioned for it.

Thus rival slates of delegates were chosen to oppose the organization slates and the necessary petition signatures gathered. And by the early March deadline, the opposition forces had gained the right to hold primaries in thirty cities and towns, including the major population centers of Hartford and New Haven. Meantime, in the towns where there were no primaries, they won more than a hundred delegate seats before the regular organization really realized that there was any movement afoot.

On April 10, the day of the primary in the thirty cities and towns, our forces brought in 145 more delegates to the state convention. Unexpected victories by our slates in New Haven and New Britain were particular blows to the Bailey forces. Of all the Democrats voting in the new Connecticut primaries, 44% expressed their preference against the organization's slates – a solid victory for a spontaneous people's movement.

I crossed the continent from Connecticut to California and found changes under way there too, particularly among students. When I had spoken five months earlier at the University of California in Berkeley, the mood had been one of protest and dissent. Now, on my return, large numbers of students were prepared to support and participate in the political process. They abandoned the devices of the protest, the peace rally and the resistance march, to attend rallies, to work in headquarters, to canvass, and to perform other tasks.

The tragic news of the assassination of Dr. Martin Luther King, Jr., reached us April 4 in San Francisco. We immediately cut short all plans in order to return to Washington. I went on from Washington to Atlanta with the congressional delegation to attend the funeral. The funeral of Dr. King was near-perfect testimonial to his service to the cause of his own people and to his declared ideal of equality for all citizens of the United States. It was both a religious and a political observance – the best combination of the two.

Sitting in the church where Dr. King had so often and so eloquently spoken, I recalled his speech in Washington when he led the "March on Washington for Jobs and Freedom" in 1963 before we passed the civil rights bill. It was the first time we had met, and I sat on the steps of the Lincoln Memorial. At that time we were considering a set of civil rights which was clearly guaranteed under the Constitution of the United States. It would seem that we should not have had to march for that purpose or even to pass any legislation because the right to vote and the right to equality under the law – all of the principles in the Civil Rights Act that we were fighting for in 1963 and 1964 – were as old as the history of the country and should have been recognized without dispute or legislative contest, and certainly without a march on Washington. Yet Martin Luther King saw the need for the march. He saw the need to inspire the people, the need to demonstrate that action had to be taken, and certainly his efforts contributed to the passage of that new set of laws.

I did not resume campaigning until April 10, in Nebraska. The next day I spoke on civil rights at Boston University, in Massachusetts.[18] I said that, as Martin Luther King had understood and as the Kerner Commission[19] had underscored, the legal victories achieved in civil rights had done little to alleviate the social and economic conditions at the root of the problem. The same remarks still apply.

We must begin immediately and on a massive scale to attack the causes of unrest and to bring within the reach of all Americans, including those whom we have kept in a kind of colonial status in our midst, those things that make up what we call the good life.

---

[18] See Appendix 7.

[19] The Kerner Commission is the popularized name for the National Advisory Commission on Civil Disorders, established in1967 by President Johnson, under the chairmanship of Governor Otto Kerner of Illinois.

In addition to the traditional and constitutionally guaranteed civil rights, we must move to establish a whole new set of civil rights, rights that derive from basic human rights but that, when they are taken up and assured by society, become civil rights and citizens' rights. These include the right to a decent job, one becoming to the dignity of a man and one that will return him satisfaction as an intelligent and creative human being as well as an income with which he can support his family in dignity and decency; the right to adequate health care without regard to income, race, or habitation; the right to a decent house, not in a ghetto but in a neighborhood within a community that is part of the United States of America.

To assure these rights, I proposed in Boston: first, that the federal government determine what a minimum acceptable personal income is and attempt to insure it for all Americans; second, that we have a federally subsidized health insurance program for all citizens; third, that we have a massive federally subsidized program of adult education as well as expansion of educational programs for the young; fourth, that we carry out the Kerner Commission proposal to build six million housing units for low-and moderate-income families within the next five years.

Senator Robert Kennedy also made a speech on civil rights. He gave his in Indianapolis on April 4, immediately after hearing of Dr. King's assassination, and I thought it was the best speech of his campaign.

The April trip to Massachusetts was demanding. On most trips into Massachusetts the demands on a candidate are traditionally without limit. The speech that night at Boston University was preceded by one reception and followed by four more. Being delivered into the hands of the faithful is sometimes worse than being delivered into the hands of the enemy.

No one has a corner on the burdens to be borne in a campaign. It becomes a test not only of the candidate but of his schedulers, his speech writers, campaign workers, and everyone else who is serious involved. Something of the mood is reflected in "*Sonnet for a Political Worker*" by Cecil Day-Lewis:

> *Is this what wears you out – having to weigh*
> *One mote against another, the time spent*
> *Fitting each thumbed and jig-sawed argument*
> *Into a pattern clear to you as day?*
> *Boredom, the dull repetitive delay,*
> *Opponents' tricky call, the discontent*
> *Of friends, seem to deny what history meant*
> *When first she showed her hand for you to play.*

Do you not see that history's high tension
Must so be broken down to each man's need
And his frail filaments, that it may feed
Not blast all patience, love and warm invention?
On lines beyond your single comprehension
The circuit and full day of power proceed.

I took a four-day rest over Easter and then returned to the campaign trail, stopping on April 16 in Charleston, West Virginia, enroute to Pittsburgh for the Pennsylvania preferential primary.

We had argued the wisdom of running in Pennsylvania. Some felt that because it was a strongly organized state and because that organization would be working solidly for President Johnson we would not do well. Furthermore, the Pennsylvania primary is not binding; that is, the popularity contest of the preferential vote for president means nothing as far as delegates are concerned. Even though one got 100% of the preferential vote for president, he might not get a single delegate to the Chicago convention. Delegates in Pennsylvania are elected individually, 4 from each congressional district, and they are not identified on the ballot in any way except by name. Voters have to know or be told which delegates are personally pledged to vote for any particular presidential candidate. This, of course, meant that the regular Democratic party, with its organization and patronage-influenced vote, would have strong advantages in electing its delegates in the Democratic party.

By mid-February, however, straw polls throughout the state were indicating that my support might be more substantial than had been suspected. My groups had been working very hard, particularly in Pittsburgh and Philadelphia and in other counties where there were college and university campuses. We estimated we might get better than 200,000 votes, and I decided to run.

Since it was virtually impossible to beat the party organization in Pittsburgh and Philadelphia, it was thought better to run many candidates and depend on percentages. My supporters "flooded the ballot," getting 12 to 16 delegate candidates who supported me to file for the 4 delegate seats in each district. Ballot position is determined in Pennsylvania by drawing lots, and we were counting on some of our candidates making it to the top of the ballot where position alone could achieve election. *All* of the McCarthy delegate candidates were pledged to support the four McCarthy candidates in their districts who drew the top places on the ballot. Hence our vote would not be split, even though many candidates filed. In the suburbs and smaller towns, where the regular party was not as well organized, we ran slates of delegates directly opposed to the organization slates and of equal numbers.

Because of commitments in other states, I had only two days for campaigning in Pennsylvania. We made the most of them, thanks to Norval Reece, a master scheduler we discovered there. Norval is a Quaker of great patience and forbearance and very long-suffering. He joined our staff after the Pennsylvania primary and served as official scheduler for the rest of the campaign. The best advice I can give to any presidential candidate who runs in as many states as I did is to sign on a Quaker scheduler.

On the first of the two days in Pennsylvania, to demonstrate, Norval arranged for me to greet workers at the first shift change at the Jones & Laughlin steel plant, to give several newspaper, radio, and television interviews, to take a midday walk through the crowds at the Golden Triangle, to attend two luncheons, to visit with Mayor Joseph Barr and other leaders at Democratic headquarters, to see a group of ministers at a church, and to wind up the day in Pittsburgh with a speech at an evening rally.

The second day was like the first. It included a meeting with Congressman William Green in Philadelphia. At a subsequent conference Green said that if in the forthcoming preferential primary I got 200,000 votes it would not mean much, but if I got 400,00 votes, it would be highly significant.

Five days later, on April 23, the votes were counted, and I received 428,259. That was 71.6% of the Democratic vote, and it was the first time in recent Pennsylvania history that non-organization delegates were elected. Our vote-flooding strategy in Philadelphia succeeded; in the city's five congressional districts my delegate candidates got twelve of the twenty top places on the ballot and 6 were elected. In Luzerne County, a coal area where we pitted our slate directly against the organization's, my delegates won two of the four spots; in Montgomery County, three out of four.

Despite this showing, fewer than 29% of the Pennsylvania delegation at the national convention saw fit to follow the views of their state's voters. In fact, one-fourth of the delegation – the delegates-at-large – had been chosen even before the primary took place.

The preferential primary results had still less effect on the leaders in Pennsylvania. At their State Democratic Committee meeting in Harrisburg on May 27, Mayor James Tate of Philadelphia and Mayor Joseph Barr of Pittsburgh attempted to steer the whole delegation into endorsing Vice President Hubert Humphrey. The speaker at the meeting was Senator Walter Mondale, of Minnesota, a cochairman of the Vice President's campaign, and Senator Edward Kennedy also attended. Eighty-three delegates voted for Humphrey, 21 for McCarthy, 1 for Harry Truman, and 21 were listed as uncommitted. Congressman William Green voted no and later announced his support for Robert Kennedy. The attempt to impose the unit rule for Humphrey was dropped only when a court case was threatened.

Although the campaign in Pennsylvania differed from that in Connecticut because of the differences in the laws of the two states, it was in substance the same. Our effort always was to secure true representation of the people through those chosen to go to the Democratic National Convention in August. How much we would be thwarted in that goal was just beginning to show.

Good and Bad Signs

The Indiana primary was the first primary in which Senator Robert Kennedy was entered.

In announcing his candidacy on March 16, Senator Kennedy said that he was not going to run specifically against me. However, in his prepared statement, he made special reference to administrative experience in the executive branch of the government and especially in the National Security Council. Since at that time President Johnson was still a candidate, it was not possible that he was making this point to compare qualifications with those of the chief executive who is also chairman of the National Security Council. The only possible interpretation was that he intended to use it against the man he was "not going to run against."

In the weeks following his announcement, and before the Indiana primary, we began to get indications as to how his supporters intended to conduct the campaign against me. The word we got was that they were going to use my twenty-year record in the Congress to discredit me in much the same way they used Senator Kenneth Keating's record in the New York Senate campaign in 1964. Politicians rather commonly rely on what has succeeded for them before – a failing shown in military history as well where weapons used to make heroes in one victor are retained when they are no longer effective. This voting-record technique, when used against Senator Keating, was taken to the Fair Campaign Practices Committee for judgment and became the subject of public controversy in which the failure of the committee to stand by its judgment has left it a somewhat discredited organization.[20]

---

[20] The Fair Campaign Practices Committee was organized in 1954 as a non-profit, non-partisan group to investigate and report on violations of political campaign ethics as outlined in a code which has been agreed to in every campaign year since then by both national committees and by the major candidates.

On first hearing of the plan to attack my record, I did not look upon it as a particularly serious matter. I felt that I had made a consistent record without contradiction and that any honest person would agree and be discouraged from trying to distort it, especially in a primary in which other issues were of such overriding importance. I was mistaken.

In late March, we received the first reports from our local organizations of a so-called fact sheet. It was being circulated by Citizens for Kennedy, with a New York address, under the chairmanship of Dr. Martin Shepard. The same Dr. Shepard had volunteered to help earlier in our campaign in New Hampshire when he believed that Senator Kennedy would not be a candidate. His special field, he said, was that of news releases. His offer was rejected.

The fact sheet appeared in various forms. One was a letter addressed to my Massachusetts supporters, listing a number of what were alleged to be illiberal, somewhat hypocritical votes, ranging from a poll-tax amendment to rent control. The fact sheet was soon spread across the country. Signals from as far away as Hawaii indicated that by early April many universities in primary and non-primary states, as well as local Democratic organizations, had received some form of the sheet. In addition, in an April 2 mailing Dr. Shepard enclosed a list of key secretaries who would "take care of emergent material" in the Kennedy headquarters in Washington.

A fortnight later, on April 19, a press release from the office of Citizens for Kennedy in 1968, 30 West 96th Street, New York City, stated that Dr. Shepard was acting independently of Senator Kennedy's office. After the assassination, I asked one of the Kennedy people who had been responsible for the voting-record operation and was told it was Pierre Salinger.

The material continued to appear throughout the campaign. A full-page ad appeared in the UCLA *Bruin* entitled "A Time to Pause," sponsored by something called the "Ad Hock Committee of Students for a Second Look." The charges were variations on the Shepard "research," reworked, amplified, and given a somewhat new cast. In ads and in other forms, the distorted material appeared in more college newspapers and was given national distribution by volunteer organizations in Indiana, Nebraska, South Dakota, and California.

On May 7, Senator Kennedy publicly disavowed the Shepard pamphlet. Yet on the next day, May 8, 1968, Jimmy Breslin reported in the New York *Post* that Senator Kennedy, in talking with two of my volunteers, whom he was trying to win over, asked without waiting for an answer: "Why did he vote against giving the minimum wage to farm workers?" and "Why did he vote for excluding a large proportion of people from the Minimum Wage Act?"

The Senator should have known the explanation for these votes. Since my first term in Congress in 1949, as a representative of Minnesota's Fourth Congressional District, I have been a consistent advocate for the expansion of minimum wage coverage. Yet because of some votes on amendments to the Minimum Wage Act in 1960 and in 1966 reported out of context I was accused of "contradiction between statement and actions." The facts concerning the Minimum Wage bill of 1960 were certainly available to Senator Kennedy because his own brother, Senator John Kennedy, guided it through the Senate. John Kennedy had worked long and hard to raise the minimum wage by stages and to extend coverage to an estimated additional four million workers. As Chairman of a Senate Labor and Public Welfare Subcommittee, he, together with Senator Wayne Morse and other members, led the debate and helped secure the bill's ultimate adoption. I, of course, voted for it.

Debate on the bill centered on the provision extending coverage to employees of laundry and dry-cleaning and retail and service enterprises with annual gross sales of $1 million or more and engaged in activities affecting interstate commerce. Opponents felt that the "activities affecting" clause was an unwarranted extension of the federal government into an area which should remain under the control of the states. To limit the effect of the "activities" clause, they introduced an amendment, sponsored by Senator Mike Monroney, "restricting the proposed extension of the retail and service coverage to employees of chains operating in two or more states." The real test came on a motion to table (reject) the Monroney amendment. There the battle was joined. A vote in favor of the motion to table the Monroney amendment was in effect a vote in favor of significant extension of minimum wage coverage; a vote against the motion to table was a vote against significant minimum wage extension. I voted – with Senator John Kennedy – to table the amendment.

As part of the move to defeat the Monroney amendment, an amendment was offered by Senator Clinton Anderson which excluded from coverage some of those whom the new bill sought to include. Senator Morse clarified the reasons for accepting this amendment in the floor debate. He said, "If we must compromise on coverage under this bill in order to defeat the Monroney amendment with its serious legal consequences in respect to the application of the interstate commerce clause, then let me say I am ready to compromise. In doing so, I compromise no principle...I am sorry if it is necessary to compromise on the coverage on workers in the hotel, restaurant and automobile businesses, in order to enhance our chances of defeating the Monroney amendment, but I shall do it rather than permit a greater injury to millions of workers."

Many Senators,[21] including Democratic Senators Muskie and Humphrey together with such Republicans as Senators Jacob Javits and Tom Kuchel, followed the advice of Senator Morse as did I, and accepted the Anderson amendment in order to get the necessary votes to table the Monroney amendment. Failure to have done so would have jeopardized the adoption of the Minimum Wage Act of 1960. Yet the accusation in Robert Kennedy's campaign advertisement, "A Time to Pause," excerpted only those fragments of the debate on the bill which would show "that the image Senator McCarthy attempts to project is shattered by the truth of his legislative record."

The report of my vote on the amendment by Senator Tom Kuchel to the 1966 minimum wage bill involved similar distortion. The basic bill extended coverage to farm workers, and I supported this bill. The Kuchel amendment provided for gradual increases of the farm wage on 1.6% of the farms over a period of five years, with the adoption of the national minimum wage rate thereafter. Because this was the first time that agricultural workers would be granted meaningful protection under a federal act, the committee suggested that the increases be limited to $1.30 in February 1969 so that the Senate might then evaluate the program and study its effect on agriculture. I felt this was advisable and voted accordingly. The citation of this vote as proof of my hostility to the plight of farm workers can only be labeled as a misrepresentation.

The worst inaccuracy of all was the charge that I was against civil rights because of a vote against the poll-tax amendment offered to the civil rights bill. I had voted in the past to abolish poll taxes whenever this issue was before the Congress. But this particular time, the Justice Department had a case before the Supreme Court to outlaw poll taxes under the Constitution – not on the basis of a statute but by interpreting the Constitution. Attorney General Nicholas Katzenbach came and asked me, and other liberal members of the Senate, to vote against the amendment being offered by Senator Edward Kennedy because the Justice Department felt if it passed it would prejudice the case, and they believed they would win the case and the poll tax would be declared unconstitutional. Attorney General Katzenbach

---

[21] The vote was 87 for, 8 against, and 5 not voting.

pointed out that I had a good civil rights record and could afford to take chances as I would never be challenged. (How wrong he was.) And so we voted to defeat the amendment; the Justice Department won its case before the Supreme Court, and poll taxes were outlawed under the Constitution in 1966.

The final use of the material appeared in a direct-mailing piece in California that also carried two pictures: one of Senator Robert Kennedy and one of me. The picture of me must have been taken twenty years ago. It made me look young and rather furtive; it was not flattering.

When Senator Kennedy and I debated on June 1 on ABC's "Issues and Answers" program – the only time that he and I appeared on the same platform – Senator Kennedy referred to an ad placed in some California papers by some of my supporters. Though the ad properly charged him with some responsibility for the Vietnam buildup and also for the invasion of Cuba, it also suggested that he was responsible for the invasion of the Dominican Republic. The advertisement appeared without being cleared with me and without my having been aware of it, and as soon as I knew of it I had ordered it withdrawn. I acknowledged this when the issue was raised on the program and then asked Senator Kennedy about the attacks of my record which were being distributed in California. He replied that he did not know to what I was referring.

A number of college papers challenged the attack on my record almost immediately, some apologizing for having used the material. In a letter to the editor of *Bruin*, Susan Wheeler, a graduate student in history, wrote:

> *It is alarming to see the lengths to which Kennedy supporters are going already, not so much to illuminate what their candidate stands for, as to discredit Senator McCarthy. The ad which appeared in the Daily Bruin on Wednesday has come out in a number of college newspapers and seems to have taken a great deal of time and effort to get at the "facts." Unfortunately, the authors of this ad have resorted to some fantastic misrepresentations, either by taking issues out of the context of the bills in which they were presented by not mentioning that McCarthy voted for stronger, more enforceable legislation than some of the vaguely worded passages that they cite...*
>
> *It may seem strange to Mike Shatzkin, who wrote an article to go with the paid advertisement, that many of us who have been attracted to McCarthy have doubts about a lot of things, including the demand by Shatzkin that we must support Bobby unquestioningly, without doubts.*

The pretense of both the ad and Shatzkin that they are somehow presenting the "truth," is especially insulting being presented within an academic community, but its cynicism has somewhat the same ring as that displayed by the Senator from New York, when he announced that he was going to win the presidency of the United States, while supporting Senator McCarthy...Many of us have been extremely concerned about the "credibility gap" which has grown between the government and the people. I suggest that from the way Kennedy has been running his campaign and from the way his own record looks both before and after he decided he was to be president, that if he is elected, we will be faced with a credibility gap that will make that of the present administration look like a little crack in the plaster.

The only major newspaper we knew of that considered this attack a legitimate matter of inquiry was the New York *Times.*[22]

In the early months of the campaign when I was asked if I could support Senator Kennedy for the presidency, I said that I could. As the campaign wore on, and as the continued use of the dishonest attacks on my record remained in evidence, I began to have reservations. My final judgment was expressed in a press interview on May 21 when I said that I could support Vice President Humphrey if he changed his position on Vietnam and possibly Senator Kennedy if there was a change in his campaign methods.

The experience with this attack was for me the most disappointing part of the entire campaign. The effect of the misrepresentations continued to show nearly a year after they were first published. When I was scheduled to appear at the University of Notre Dame in March 1969, I received a copy of the school paper in which a student went on at length still using the same misinformation.

Senator Eugene McCarthy's support of Russell Long in last week's contest between Long and Edward Kennedy for the post of the Senator Majority Whip might have been fatal for the forces of liberal progress if 1) the Senate respected McCarthy or his logic and 2) Kennedy had not gained the kind of respect that did in fact elect him. Fortunately for those concerned with meeting Nixon's reactionism with liberal proposals, neither of those conditions were present, Kennedy won easily without McCarthy's support.

---

[22] See Appendix 8.

Indeed, the only fatality was McCarthy's credibility as a statesman, or, for that matter, a man. McCarthy's support of the racist Senator from Louisiana was, he said, based on his belief that Kennedy's election would not bring true reform to the Senate. McCarthy would then, on the face of things, seem to imply that Long's reelection would. That is so obvious an absurdity that even McCarthy must have been aware that such is not the case. But, in any case, if McCarthy did not believe Kennedy to be a qualified liberal, he himself should have sought the post. Certainly one more gallant crusade would not hurt Sir Bitterroot.

The reason for McCarthy's betrayal to both the Senate and liberals and his highly overrated constituency through the country is, of course, easily discerned by anyone familiar with McCarthy's mind and past political record. As one of his worshipping aides put it recently, McCarthy simply looks upon the Kennedy family as a chronic national disease. McCarthy supported Lyndon Johnson in 1960 and worked hard behind the scenes to help his Texan friend to beat Kennedy. While Lyndon called Kennedy's father a Nazi, and John Connally talked of Kennedy's responsibility to the Pope and dependence on drugs, McCarthy cloaked his support for Johnson in a supposed effort to nominate Adlai Stevenson for the third time.

By 1967 McCarthy realized that Lyndon was vulnerable on the war, and suddenly the man who had spoken so eloquently for the Gulf of Tonkin resolution three years before called the Vietnam war a catastrophe. Seeing a chance to humiliate Johnson, and perhaps get the kind of favorable publicity that sells books and lecture appearances and – who knows – maybe even the Presidency, McCarthy ran for the Democratic nomination against Johnson.

Suddenly, McCarthy's pro-Johnson, anti-Kennedy approach shifted completely. Now Johnson was a rube, an ogre, killing helpless women and enjoying it. Kennedy, now dead and somehow respected for being something greater than McCarthy had perceived, was now McCarthy's ideal...

At the kickoff speech of the campaign at the December 2, 1967, Conference for Concerned Democrats in Chicago, McCarthy even managed to evoke tears from the audience as he talked about his late friend "Jack." The display was as wet was it was deceitful.

However, New Hampshire was won, and from that point on McCarthy suddenly became Clean Gene – the holy warrior who had stood alone, the man the people found. And so the myth began...

Now Gene was the great hope of the black man. It didn't matter to McCarthy (or his supporters) that he had voted against the anti-poll tax amendment. Nor did it bother them that, somehow, he just couldn't bring himself to talk abut the black tragedy in America. That lack of public concern and his failure to visit the black ghettos more than three times in the course of his entire campaign didn't bother a lot of people, especially the anti-Kennedy element, the crossover Republicans and the large racist community from which he pulled so many votes for the "great crusade." McCarthy and the troops evidently saw no contradiction involved in this peace candidate's disdain and unconcern about gun control. This of course had almost everything to do with the single victory in Oregon. McCarthy even made a point of reiterating his stand against gun control the morning of Robert Kennedy's death...

McCarthy "libs" overlooked a lot of things in the Senator's past. Like his constant support of the oil-depletion allowance. His more youthful supporters were evidently unbothered by his votes against 18-year-olds voting in the District of Columbia. Nor were the peace types upset at his votes against draft deferments for Peace Corps and VISTA volunteers or his vote against any attempts at replacing the present draft system with a voluntary service system. Nor were these forces for peace at all disturbed by Gene's alliance with Barry Goldwater in 1961 in the fight against JFK's Arms Control and Disarmament Agency.

The liberals also seemed to have overlooked McCarthy's vote to remove some one million workers from the protection of the minimum wage act, or his vote against giving agricultural workers the same minimum wage protection as other workers. The McCarthy liberals concerned with the elderly chose to overlook McCarthy's vote against attempts to reduce the deductible feature of Medicare and his votes against measures that would have reduced considerably the price of drugs for senior citizens.

But now the focus is on 1972 and not 1968. And it is clear that Gene's intellectual arrogance and vindictive pettiness are all that remain of the Great Crusader. Perhaps that is best, for now those of us who are truly concerned with saving this country can get to the work at hand.

It is to be hoped that those who still support McCarthy will disenthrall themselves. Those who cannot, however, some advice: If Russell Long refuses to be Gene's running mate in 1972, there's always Curtis LeMay.

During the Indiana campaign we began to consider ways of countering attacks on my record. Consideration of our defense was made doubly unpleasant by virtue of the fact that from the time of Senator Kennedy's entering, the columnists had begun to write about the Kennedy-McCarthy feud, which reportedly went back to 1960 if not 1956. I found that once a thing has been said three times by three different columnists, the other columnists believe it. There is almost no use in denying it or trying to set the record straight. The feud idea was nourished by some of the Kennedy supporters as a way of showing special loyalty to their principal.

It is, of course, true that I supported Hubert Humphrey in the Chicago convention of 1956, when Adlai Stevenson opened the vice-presidential nomination to the convention. Senator Humphrey was the Minnesota candidate and the candidate of the Midwest, and it was a campaign which came on very short notice and involved not only the Humphrey candidacy but also the candidacies of Senators Estes Kefauver and Albert Gore. It produced no basis for establishing that I in any way was involved in a feud with John Kennedy. My relations with him in the House of Representatives had always been very friendly. I was among the members of Congress who were invited to attend his wedding. We had talked on at least one occasion of making a European trip together. Again, in the 1960 presidential contest, nothing happened to stir any particular animosity between John Kennedy and me, although I did not support him until after the nomination when I did campaign in sixteen states and worked very hard to try to bring Stevenson supporters and other liberals who were thought to be lukewarm to support his candidacy.

Within a few weeks after the election, I was hospitalized in Georgetown University Hospital with pneumonia. Mrs. Kennedy was there at the same time for the birth of John, Jr. President-elect Kennedy visited me in the hospital and discussed rather generally the problems of setting up the Administration and of how difficult it was to find people one really knew and trusted for cabinet posts. He also spoke about his loss of the state of Ohio which was, he said, beyond his understanding.

After leaving the hospital I went to Florida to recuperate. The President-elect was in Palm Beach then. I was called and asked to speak to him on behalf of Orville Freeman as Secretary of Agriculture. I did call the President-elect and noted the Governor's interest, including my recommendation of him for the appointment.

My relationships with President Kennedy during his term were all positive and friendly. Early in the Administration, March 1961, I was called upon to speak for the Democrats at the Gridiron Dinner in Washington. The tradition of this dinner was to have two speeches: one by the president for his party and the other by a speaker chosen by the club to speak for the opposition party. At the time that President Eisenhower became president, this tradition had been somewhat weakened. He and the Gridiron Club agreed that the club would choose both the Republican and Democratic speakers and that the president at the close of the dinner would respond to the toast. President Kennedy chose to follow the precedent of President Eisenhower. I learned later from Robert Riggs, who was chairman of the dinner, that the President had proposed me as the Democratic spokesman. The Gridiron Club accepted his recommendation, and I accepted their invitation.

During the three years of President Kennedy's administration, I gave consistent and strong support to all of his major legislative proposals, especially civil rights, the Test Ban Treaty, and his tax program which was the clearest rationalization and advancement of economic policy in all the years that I have been in Congress.

I was called upon to perform two limited special missions – or at least to make a limited report to the Administration on two things. I went to Chile to participate in the international conference of the Christian Democrats in July 1961, and was asked for a judgment on the strength and substance of the Christian Democratic party in Chile and on the quality of its leadership. On a visit to Rome during the Vatican Council, I was asked to tell what I learned of Vatican attitudes toward what was then described as the Italian government's receptivity to the Left. Whereas previous Popes might have been political, I reported back that Pope John was open to the Left and open to the Right and open to everyone.

November 22, 1963, in the city of Washington was a day out of season. It was a day both of spring and of fall, both of beginnings and of endings, one of endings and of beginnings. Into the quiet of that day came the word of the death of John Kennedy.

In the days that followed immediately, grief increased in depth and in breadth, both here and throughout the nation and the world.

President Kennedy was not merely a Washington President or a political President. He was a President in every home, every town, and every city – a President to everyone, both the very young and the very old, in the United States and in other countries of the world.

As I wrote in my testimonial, "It is not for us to attempt to measure or assign the guilt for his assassination and death, for the burden of that act is too great to be borne by any one man. The act and its consequences must be related to all our actions, and the burden of guilt must be shared by all who through the years have excited and stirred the simple and the anxious, who have raised questions and turned them about until they became suspicions, who have nurtured doubt until it bore the fruit of accusation and false charges, who have spread themselves to make a shade for fear and to save it from the light of truth until it grew to be a despair-like fear of fear; by all who stood in silent acquiescence or who protested too softly; by all who envied him or any man who wished him ill."

I feel now as I did then that John Fitzgerald Kennedy demonstrated in action his realization that there must be a judgment of nations as well as of persons. He demonstrated his awareness of the two great facts of contemporary history – first, that the mass, or volume, of current history, of the things which demand some judgment and some commitment from our nation and from us, is greater than ever before; second, that the movement of history itself is now at a rate more rapid than ever before known – and that in the face of these two ultimate facts, we are called upon to exercise, as best we can, and to the fullest possible measure, the power of human reason in attempting to control and give direction to life and to history.

John F. Kennedy's entire efforts demonstrated a confidence in the future, a hope that the world of men could and would be improved, a belief in the universality of mankind and, in these far-reaching searches, a belief that there was no satisfaction except in the intensification and perfection of the life of every person.

My acquaintance with Senator Robert Kennedy before 1968 was very limited. I do not recall that I had more than a half-dozen conversations with him, either social or political. What I knew of him as a politician and a person was derived largely from his public image. I had no personal experience that would confirm or deny any of the popular judgments that had been passed upon him. The Indiana campaign afforded me my closest and most continuous exposure to Robert Kennedy in action, and this was, of course, at a distance.

Our prime concern in Indiana was getting organized. Although we were criticized for being in bad shape, we were not. Our organization was so good that it included a statewide ham radio operation to use in the event of a threatened telephone strike. The telephone strike, however, did not materialize, and so the ham radio system, like many of the other organization devices, never became operative.

My schedulers seemed preoccupied with having me appear in every courthouse square in the state of Indiana. Still, there were rather pleasant stops, as stops go, especially in places like Greenfield, where an appearance could be combined with a visit to the home of James Whitcomb Riley. And in Franklin where the town turned out, and in Crawfordsville when the Baroque Quartet (harpsichord, cello, violin, and flute) from nearby Wabash College played Vivaldi's *Four Seasons* at the meeting. This was the first time, I believe, that a candidate for the presidency had been accompanied by a harpsichord.

The student door-to-door effort in Indiana was blunted by the Kennedy canvassers who planted difficult questions ahead of the student's calls. We considered preparing the students to attack the record of Senator Kennedy but rejected the idea. In Indiana, as in California and other states to come, we sent them out to make the same kind of case they had made in New Hampshire.

The candidacy of Governor Roger Branigin, a Democrat, complicated things. He made us wonder if we really were in a campaign. Sometimes he ran as a favorite son; sometimes as a stand-in for Vice President Humphrey; and at other times he suggested that he be given serious consideration either as a candidate for the presidency or the vice presidency. On some occasions he argued that Indiana should simply send him to the convention to make decisions for the state. The mayor of one of the cities of southern Indiana sustained this notion with argument that it would be good to send the Governor because the Indiana delegation might then get better hotel accommodations. The mayor said that in 1964 they had gone to Atlantic City committed to President Johnson, and consequently had been placed in one of the worst hotels.

Governor Branigin made a point of calling us out-of-state campaigners "interlopers." I thought I made the best answer in an appearance in Vincennes, which at one time was the capital of the Northwest Territory. Most of my former congressional district – the part of Minnesota which lies east of the Mississippi and west of the St. Croix rivers – was located in the Northwest Territory. I claimed a kind of native-son status by virtue of that historic fact. It did not do me much good.

There seemed to be a rather generalized defensiveness in Indiana against outsiders. In northern Indiana, especially Gary, people seemed worried about the prospect of being taken over by Chicago. In the south, they were threatened by Kentucky, in the west, by Illinois, and in the east, by Ohio. It was as though in

Indiana they have to think Indiana for fear that if they do not it will be absorbed by the outside world.

The Indianapolis *Star*, as I've noted, was not particularly unfriendly to me – it ignored me – but it supported the candidacy of Governor Branigin, was strongly opposed to the candidacy of Senator Kennedy and, what I had to say was almost always squeezed out. There was some evidence that this blackout was reflected in the votes in Marion County, which includes Indianapolis. Governor Branigin received 33% of the votes there and about 30% in the rest of the state. In Marion County I received 19%, compared with 28.5% elsewhere.

Despite some of these handicaps, the campaign in Indiana was generally pleasant. Spring had clearly come. The apple trees were in bloom, and as we drove through the state one was reminded of the tradition of Johnny Appleseed. The students who turned out in Bloomington in the early part of the campaign were the first we had seen in summer clothes, and were beginning to show the tan of late spring and early summer.

Where farms had been consolidated and houses and other buildings torn down, the people seemed to respect the lilac bushes; they left the lilacs standing. A cynic in our tour, who purported to know about bushes, remarked that it might not be romanticism that kept man from plowing out the lilac bushes, because lilacs were very difficult to get rid of, that they are many-branched and many-rooted and almost defy easy destruction. In cultivated fields, more than in any other state, trees were left standing, even in the middle of a field. It seemed not be a matter of the kind of tree but rather a regard for the tree as such.

We noted also a number of rather strange and interesting signs – signs which were changed from week to week: HE THINKS HE IS VERY WITTY – HE IS HALF WRIGHT; WOMEN THINK A GREAT DEAL – ABOUT MEN; and the promotion for a radio station: WE HAVE BEEN ENTERTAINING YOUR WIFE WHILE YOU WERE AWAY.

I had long been observing and thinking about signs, and found time in Indiana to finish three poems. Their overall title was *Three Bad Signs*. The first sign that struck me was GREEN RIVER ORDINANCE ENFORCED HERE. PEDDLERS NOT ALLOWED. Such signs appear in many Midwestern states and are derived from an ordinance passed in Green River, Wyoming, in 1931. The issue was carried all the way to the Supreme Court and was sustained by the Court. Adopted in substance by many small towns, the ordinance allows local communities to exclude all traveling peddlers from selling within their confines. I had first

seen the sign as a boy in my hometown of Watkins, Minnesota. I
saw it again in the campaign.

The second bad sign, MIXED DRINKS, is not peculiar to
Indiana but is found in gateway and bowery areas of cities across
the country. WE SERVE ALL FAITHS, the third sign, is similarly
universal. One has only to look closely at the billboards of the
mortuaries and morticians to see it.

Three Bad Signs

The first Bad Sign is this:
"Green River Ordinance Enforced Here.
Peddlers Not Allowed."

This is a clean, safe town.
No one can just come around
With ribbons and threads
Or new books to be read.
This is an established place.
We have accepted patterns in lace,
And ban itinerant vendors of new forms and whirls,
All things that turn the heads of girls.
We are not narrow, but we live with care.
Gypsies, hawkers and minstrels are right for a fair.
But transient peddlers, nuisances, we say
From Green River must be kept away.
Traveling preachers, actors with a play,
Can pass through, but may not stay.
Phoenicians, Jews, men of Venice –
Know that this is the home of Kiwanis.

All you have been round the world to find
Beauty in small things: read our sign
And move on.

The Second Bad Sign is this:
"Mixed Drinks."

"Mixed Drinks"
What mystery blinks
As in the thin blood of the neon sign
The uncertain hearts of the customers
Are tested there in the window.
Mixed drinks between the art movie
And the Reasonable Rates Hotel.
Mixed drinks are class,
Each requires a different glass.
Mixed drink is manhattan red
Between the adult movie and the unmade bed

110

Mixed drink is daiquiri green
Between the gospel mission and the sheen
Of hair oil on the rose planted paper.
Mixed drink is forgiveness
Between the vicarious sin
And the half-empty bottle of gin.
Mixed drink is remembrance between unshaded
40-watt bulbs hung from the ceiling,
Between the light a man cannot live by,
And the better darkness.
Mixed drink is the sign of contradiction.

The third Bad Sign is this:
"We Serve All Faiths."

We serve all faiths:
We the morticians.
Tobias is out, he has had it.
We do not bury the dead.
Not, He died, was buried and after three days arose.
But He died, was revived, & after three days was buried alive.
This is our scripture.
Do not disturb the established practitioner.
Do not disturb the traditional mortician:
Giving fans to the church, for hot days,
Dropping a calendar at the nursing home,
A pamphlet in the hospital waiting room,
An ad in the testimonial brochure at the retirement banquet.
Promising the right music, the artificial grass.
We bury faith of all kinds.
Foreverness does not come easily.
The rates should be higher.

We did not win in Indiana but we did better than the pollsters had predicted. Two days before the primary, the NBC poll had given Robert Kennedy 37% and me 24%. The Harris poll had given Senator Kennedy 45% and me 19%. In the actual voting, it was 42.3% for Kennedy and 27% for me.

As I prepared to leave Indiana, there was no indication of disappointment or disaffection among my supporters here or in other states. The vote tally certainly had not dampened the spirits of the young people at Indianapolis headquarters in the Claypool Hotel. Two signs went up on the bulletin board. One announced a STAFF MEETING: TOPIC – CALIFORNIA. The other asked for applicants from "all who wished to work at the Chicago Democratic convention." They meant to go all the way.

The Oregon Trail

Nebraska happened on the way west. After Indiana and before Oregon, I had only four days scheduled for campaigning there.

Although I hoped that I would not do too badly in Nebraska, I had no real reason to expect that I would run very well. Oregon was the critical state and we had to concentrate our money, time, and effort there, giving Nebraska little more than a quick once-over and hoping for the best.

Members of the Nebraska Democratic organization were friendly and hospitable, a welcome change from the way we had been received by regular Democrats in other states. My support in Nebraska was centered in the University of Nebraska at Lincoln. The campaign was directed by Mark Acuff, who has written with perception and humor about both the state and national campaign in the book called *The New Look in Politics* (University of New Mexico Press, 1968). Acuff, with the help of David Evans, a former political science professor, and those who worked with them, did exceedingly well under trying circumstances.

Although Nebraska was initiating a new open primary,[23] it was nearly impossible to get the Republicans to cross-register. In Nebraska, as Acuff says, 'Republicanism runs deep ... There are

---

[23] Mark Acuff describes it thus: "Nebraska's wide-open new primary law, untested before 1968, was an offspring of the 1964 Goldwater campaign. In Nebraska, as elsewhere, Goldwater's more hydrophobic supporters raided the party structure, stuffing caucuses and blitzing conventions until they had wrested control. No deviation from orthodoxy was permitted. These Goldwater tactics appalled a sizable number of the state's mild Republicans. They were moved to support a wide-open primary, making control of the party machinery essentially irrelevant to Presidential politics. The new law was written in such a way that the Secretary of State was empowered to place on the ballot the names of all and sundry who appeared to him to be genuine Presidential candidates, as well as those who organized any kind of campaign effort in the state and asked to be added. Only a formal affidavit of non-candidacy could remove a man's name. Only Nelson Rockefeller filed such an affidavit."

still small towns and certain strata of society in larger towns where it is not socially acceptable to be anything but a Republican. It is unthinkable – an utterly foreign notion – for these people to register as Democrats, even for two weeks." The farmers were about 100% Republican, but there was evidence that I appealed to them even if they did not feel free to vote Democratic. This was borne out later by a poll of Iowa farmers in *Wallace's Farmer*. That poll in late June gave me the lead over Vice President Humphrey in all age and educational groupings – 72 to 28%. Among Republican men on farms, I led the Vice President 82 to 19%; among Republican women, 76 to 24%. But in the Omaha-Lincoln metropolitan areas, the economic and cultural status of the Democrats was very much like that in areas in Indiana which gave Senator Kennedy strong support and those in Wisconsin where President Johnson drew strength.

The Republicans were as hospitable as the Democrats in Nebraska. On the morning of May 9, heading southeast after a rally at North Bend, our lead car suddenly swung north on Route 30 onto a country road. The farm land and the pastures bordering the road were beginning to show faint signs of green. It looked like the Nebraska described by Willa Cather in *O Pioneers*:

> *There are few scenes more gratifying than a spring plowing in that country, where the furrows of a single field often lie a mile in length, and the brown earth, with such a strong, clean smell, and such a power of growth and fertility in it, yields itself eagerly to the plow; rolls away from the shear, not even dimming the brightness of the metal, with a soft, deep sign of happiness.*

> *Evening and the flat land,*
> *Rich and sombre and always silent;*
> *The miles of fresh-plowed soil,*
> *Heavy and black, full of strength and harshness;*
> *The growing wheat, the growing weeds,*
> *The toiling horses, the tired men;*
> *The long empty roads,*
> *Sullen fires of sunset, fading,*
> *The eternal, unresponsive sky.*

Farther along the country road the car turned into a farm, and it was announced that we were making a scheduled lunch stop. Our host, A. A. Sibbersen, came forward to greet us, and so did his father. The elder Mr. Sibbersen, who had retired from farming, had been a pioneer in land management and crop rotation. He was

114

fully informed on the geological history of the entire area. The son, who now ran the farm, carried on his father's respect and affection for the land, its conservation, and its productivity.

The younger Sibbersen was an enthusiastic Nixon Republican, but he confided to me that he had almost succumbed to the temptation to reregister for the Democratic primary. Since he could not vote for me in the upcoming race, he said he was doing the next best thing by providing us with a typical Nebraska lunch – roast beef and strawberries.

Another pleasant memory for Nebraska is of an invocation given by the Catholic priest Father George Heinzen, in Nebraska City. It was the most far-reaching and complimentary invocation of the whole campaign. He began:

> *O God of Wisdom and Understanding, if your servant, the Apostle St. Paul, were here this morning and would have been privileged to give this invocation, he would have repeated an encouraging portion of his epistle to the Corinthians: "All the runners in the stadium take part in the race, but only one wins the prize. So I do not run like a man who doesn't see the goal. I do not fight like a boxer who punches the air." There have been cases of boxers punching the air, of not seeing the goal.*

Father Heinzen then said that I had proved myself "a serious runner," and he prayed that "we may see the wisdom in the quality of character and mature experience which can provide needed leadership, so that the future will see Senator McCarthy and his family in the White House." They did not see me in the White House; in fact, they could not see me in Nebraska City, either. I lost Nebraska City.

Our Democratic opposition was a lot less friendly. The Kennedy supporters in Nebraska used the same kind of tactics they had used in Indiana, only on a larger scale. Their canvassers continued to misrepresent my record and plant unsubstantiated doubts in the minds of voters. We began to believe their plan of systematic distortion was having serious effect when our canvassers in Omaha reported that about 15% of the voters they had approached said they were disturbed about my attendance record in the Senate. The facts were that in 1966 my voting participation record in the Senate was higher than that of Senator Kennedy, although in 1967 he had a higher percentage than I did. We did what we could to publicize the comparison and also suggested a comparison of my attendance record with Senator John Kennedy's in the hope that this might stop the nonsense.

The Kennedy organization was now also trying to draw young people away from my campaign with offers of more pay, educational assistance, and the like. They were not very successful. I had no objection to their taking professional politicians, if they could get them, like Dick Goodwin, and people like Arthur Schlesinger, Jr. but young persons who had worked with me, I felt, should not have been approached.

I was careful in the campaign not to let any of my aides express any opinions with regard to Senator Kennedy. Yet Pierre Salinger issued a public statement after the Nebraska vote that I was not a "credible candidate." I assumed that he meant to say "creditable."

By this time I had come to doubt whether Senator Kennedy and I could work out any satisfactory arrangement as he suggested. In public statements he regularly talked of a willingness to work out accord and expressed hope that we would be able to work together, but at no time in the campaign did he expressly say that he would support me as a candidate for the presidency.

When Senator Kennedy had announced his entry into the primaries I felt it meant that neither he nor I could be nominated. I was not sure that I could win any of the primaries in which he was entered against me, but I was sure that I could come close enough so that he could not claim any overwhelming mandate. And I was certain, also, that the people who had joined with me before New Hampshire and who had carried on with me in Wisconsin would not easily be moved to support his late entry. My hope remained, as we went on through the primaries, that the ultimate effect would not be a loss of strength on the issue of the war, and that my basic purpose – of raising the issue of Vietnam and changing Democratic party policy – would not be seriously jeopardized.

The total Democratic vote in Nebraska was predictably small. Senator Kennedy received 84,102 to my 50,655. He got 51.7%. I got 31.2% – again much more than the pollster predicted. The National Broadcasting Company released the Quayle poll on May 14 giving me just 22% – another questionable release of an unreliable poll on election day. (NBC was not the only network at fault; CBS had been significantly inaccurate in its polls in New Hampshire and was to be again in California.)

There were two interesting reports about my mood on the day after the Nebraska primary. One was by Richard Harwood of the Washington *Post*. Mr. Harwood saw me as having a "doomed look" and said that I was regularly secluding myself in the front cabin of the plane. On the same day, E. W. Kenworthy, writing in the New York *Times*, described me as being in good humor and expressing optimism about the future. He had been and talked to me that day.

Nebraska had not been so bad. There was no reason to think that the defeat would have any harmful effect whatsoever on the outcome in Oregon and California. As I reminded our friends in Nebraska, in the history of the westward movement it had been a relatively easy task to get the wagons to the Missouri, but after the crossing of the Missouri the real test took place on the Oregon Trail. I said that we had the best wagons and horses and the best men, and we expected to win the West.

In Oregon we had a better organization than we had in any other state. It had been working for six months[24] – long before the Kennedy and Humphrey announcements – and included representatives of the state Democratic party, the labor movement, some independents, and a number of Republicans. It was also the best financed of our efforts because we had money well enough in advance to plan the spending effectively. Elsewhere we were not so much beset by a shortage of money as by not having it at the right time. In our budget talks I was often reminded of Dorothy Day, leader of the Catholic Worker movement, who said that "the poor are never economical."

I looked forward to getting to Oregon not only because of the support of our own excellent organization but also because Senator Wayne Morse and Senator Mark Hatfield had taken a firm stand against the war, even before 1968. Both had publicly and privately always expressed approval of my effort in their state, and Senator Morse had publicly urged Senator Kennedy not to challenge me in the Oregon primary.

Unfortunately, because of earlier obligations, I was not free to go into Oregon right after the Nebraska primary. I was on the ballot in South Dakota. At the request of my supporters who had been working very hard for me there, I committed myself to one day of campaigning in the state, making three stops at Rapid City, Aberdeen, and Sioux Falls. Once again I was criticized for leaving the main trail. After nearly four months of covering our campaign, the press, in general, still did not accept that it was directed as much to education and giving people a chance to respond as it

---

[24] Among those responsible for the early organization were: Joseph Allman, a political science professor at the University of Oregon, Eugene, who became one of the state chairmen of Oregonians for McCarthy; Howard Morgan of Portland, a member of the Federal Power Commission from 1961 and 1963, appointed by President Kennedy, and a former Oregon state Democratic chairman; and Blaine Whipple of Portland, a former executive secretary of the state Democratic committee who was elected Democratic National committeeman in May 1968.

was to garnering delegates and drawing large crowds. The day spent in South Dakota was directed principally to the former ends, as were the next two days visiting five cities in Florida.

I returned to Oregon for the final drive to the wire on May 20. The campaign was moving along much as we hoped it would. There were no bloc votes. As one Oregonian said, "It was almost impossible to find a husband and wife who would vote together." Students and other campaign workers had had time to blunt the attack of the Kennedy people on my record and turn the case against them.

In Oregon, as in Nebraska, the labor movement made a substantial effort to advance the candidacy of Vice President Hubert Humphrey.[25] The state leadership of the Oregon labor council backed him. Some leaders and certainly some rank-and-file members of organized labor preferred Senator Kennedy. But in Oregon I got more support from organized labor than I had in any of the earlier primaries.

Among the many pleasant memories of the Oregon campaign was a breakfast meeting in Springfield held in the school gymnasium on the morning of May 25. The people attending ranged from the elderly to the very young. The food was Oregon apples, cookies, coffee, and milk. There was more spirit than anything else. Indeed there was so much spirit that no speech was really called for because it was more of a testimonial to the cause than to me.

It was this kind of spirit and the spontaneous, independent responses that made the campaign in Oregon so rewarding. Stanley Maveety, a professor of English at the University of Oregon, described the spirit and action in a report he wrote:

A doctor in John Day, Oregon, a town of 1500, set up a headquarters and bought his own McCarthy billboard. In Baker a housewife established a McCarthy headquarters in a tent since no building was available. A lady history professor at Eastern Oregon College set up the McCarthy headquarters in LeGrande with the help of a former Republican county official and of the President of the Student Body, formerly the Chairman of the Eastern Young Republicans of Oregon. One worker looking back on the campaign said, "Most of these headquarters were self-starting as hell."

The Astoria group in the northwest corner of the state had an enthusiasm all its own. Tugboats displayed their sign, "Fishermen for McCarthy." The McCarthy Astorians conducted a door-to-

---

[25] Vice President Humphrey, despite the boost from labor, had received but 7.4% of the vote (on write-ins) in Nebraska. President Johnson had polled 5.6%.

door campaign in areas so thinly populated that the canvassers rode horseback. This group, though self-reliant, wanted some supplies from state headquarters. To demonstrate their need they manufactured their own campaign buttons out of bottle caps, painted and fitted with a crude pin. To one of the workers in Eugene it was "a pretty crude affair, but beautiful!"

He also told how money was raised:

With his own money a Portland lawyer bought a minute of radio time to explain why he was for McCarthy. A man who came into the Eugene headquarters said he traveled up and down the coast on business and would like some handouts. He got his handouts, contributed $100, and did not bother to leave his name. In the Portland area alone, at least a thousand people volunteered their services. Often the headquarters was embarrassed because there was not enough work to go around. On one occasion 3,000 fund-raising letters had to be sent out on very short notice. Fifty of the people who had telephoned in were asked to pick up the letters at five o'clock and get them back before noon the next day. Of the fifty who called, fifty agreed; and of the fifty who agreed, not one failed to do the job – before the deadline.

The non-partisan, non-political, non-class, non-racial, and no-age group, characteristic of the Oregon campaign, was clearly reflected in his description of those who participated:

In Oregon as well as nationally the McCarthy movement has attracted a variety of supporters, among them, curiously enough, Goldwater people who, according to one worker, like McCarthy "because he's sincere." And McCarthy's success in Oregon does show his ability to get Republican votes. In Portland, Republicans called in every day requesting instructions on changing registration. In fact, a woman who had been answering such calls suddenly remembered, "I'd better go do that myself." She was not alone: two other women working in the Portland headquarters were also disenchanted Republicans. In the election the Republican vote for McCarthy was heavy, both because of such changes in registration and by means of write-ins.

Housewives were active everywhere. In Corvallis, a home of Oregon State University, and in Ashland, home of a summer Shakespeare festival, the headquarters were established and managed by housewives. In Eugene a single bake sale netted $600. In Oakridge it was a housewife for McCarthy who gave the town its first political headquarters: the mayor dropped in for the opening, and it became a minor historical occasion. But the location of the Salem headquarters could have been a symbol of McCarthy's over-all campaign: on one side of the former butcher shop was the U.S. Marine Recruiting Office, on the other a very psychedelic poster shop.

The young were also active and everywhere. A man phoned in from Pendleton and promptly became the Umatilla County representative. This "man," it turned out, was a junior in a Pendleton high school. Indeed, the role of young people in the McCarthy campaign was and is one of its distinctive aspects – even if it is exaggerated in the public imagination. Obviously they have contributed what they could: energy, persistence, and a high degree of mobility. In the last phase of the campaign hundreds of students from Washington, Idaho, and Montana poured into the state to canvass. In Portland eight hundred people volunteered accommodations, frequently including meals. One man and wife came in and said they could take three or four workers, then changed their minds and said seven. When seven arrived, their own seven children slept on the living-room floor so that the workers could have beds. A Portland physician, Dr. James Van Pelt, volunteered with other doctors to give these out-of-state students whatever medical attention they needed. Since the group had the look of the Children's Crusade, the fact that Dr. Van Pelt was a pediatrician was duly noted.

One young veteran from the Wisconsin campaign drove out alone to the state headquarters and asked for work. He was given the job of making financial arrangements with local printers for campaign literature. According to those in charge, his handling of the $70,000-$80,000 budget was better than that of a professional since wherever necessary he worked late into the night. The same mobility and enthusiasm characterized Oregon students after the primary. Even though it was just before final exams, hundreds went south to work in the California campaign.

In Lane County forms were mimeographed for statewide distribution giving instructions to Republicans who wanted to change their registration. High school and college students diligently went through 50,000 copies crossing out a word which had mistakenly been inserted. Skip Bracken, a young Negro, was in charge of the campaign in Portland's Albina District. Early in the campaign, young canvassers found a housewife there preparing dinner, so they helped her clean the fish while they told her about Eugene McCarthy. The

University of Oregon headquarters had a sign, "Eugene McCarthy is a Groovy Trip," and when the Senator was greeted in the rain by the largest crowd ever to assemble at Eugene's Mahlon Sweet Airport, one supporter held a "Make the Gene Scene!" placard. She was a grey-haired lady – yes, in tennis shoes!

The response of the people of Oregon, not just to the campaign but to the issues that had been raised, was the positive force in the election. But my campaign was also aided by the mistakes of the Kennedy campaigners, who began to show some panic in the face of possible defeat. First, they charged that I was spending more money than they were – a charge not taken very seriously by many people. Second, they resorted to blitz telephone canvassing. And third, they increased their efforts to discredit me as a candidate despite the fact that the polls by that time were showing me as a stronger national candidate than Senator Kennedy. They charged that I was simply a stand-in or a stalking-horse for Vice President Humphrey and an obstacle at best for Senator Kennedy.

Ten days before the balloting the local polls were showing the race to be very close, although Senator Kennedy was given a slight margin. Senator Kennedy had told the San Francisco Press Club, "If I get beaten in a primary, I'm not a very viable candidate." I did not believe that this was necessarily true, but it was my opinion that the candidate defeated in the Oregon primary would have a difficult time explaining defeat.

I won 43.9% of the vote, Senator Kennedy, 37.0%, President Johnson, 12.1%, and Vice President Humphrey, less than 1% in write-ins.

Weeks after the campaign, I read a poem by William Stafford and some things became a lot clearer to me. It was called "An Oregon Message":

When we moved here, pulled
the trees in around us, curled
our backs to the wind, no one
had ever hit the moon – no one.
Now our trees are safer than the stars,
and only other people's neglect
is our previous and abiding shell,
pierced by meteors, radar, and the telephone.

From our snug place we shout
religiously for attention, in order to hide;

only silence or evasion will bring
dangerous notice, the hovering hawk
of the state, or the sudden quiet stare
and fatal estimate of an alerted neighbor.

This message we smuggle out in
its plain cover, to be opened
quietly: Friends everywhere –
we are alive! Those moon rockets
have missed millions of secret
places! Best wishes.

Burn this.

I was not previously familiar with the poem, but reading it clarified a remark a man had made to me in a town on the southern border of Oregon. I had said that I was going on to California the next day, and the Oregonian said to me: "Don't tell them we are here."

California: They

The California campaign is the most difficult to write about for two reasons:

One, and the principal one, is that it ended in the assassination of Robert Kennedy. This tragedy cast a pall over the California contest and, in retrospect, over the whole year.

It is difficult to write about California, too, because it was more impersonal and remote than the primaries in other states. It was, I suppose, similar to what a national primary would be like, with a candidate somewhat detached and remote, relying mainly upon local efforts, upon advertising, and upon communications media. A state as large as California cannot be covered with a series of small meetings, nor can the campaign be carried by handshaking.

The campaign in California spread over a period from January 1968 until the primary on June 4. In those five months I was in the state about nineteen days. "They," my California supporters, were more responsible for any accomplishments than either "I" or the rather generalized "we" that I have sometimes used in this book.

The California campaign had its beginning more than six months before I announced my candidacy. A resolution adopted at the annual convention of the California Democratic Council in March 1967 called for a special CDC convention in September to form a slate of delegates to run in the California Democratic presidential primary in June 1968, pledged to a peace platform and candidates who would support it. At the special convention, held on September 30, in Long Beach, a detailed plan for electing delegates was agreed upon.[26]

---

[26] The convention also elected the seventy-five initiating members of a statewide steering committee which met the next day and added a group of non-CDC people, including labor leaders, Negroes, Mexican Americans, leaders of the ADA, and Dissenting Democrats, and others. This was the convention to which Gerald Hill had invited me in early

The steering committee adopted a resolution urging me to be a candidate. At its November meeting they set out an organizational plan which was to serve well. General meetings were called in each congressional district for December and January. These attracted great numbers of new people.

Early in January I designated Gerald Hill and Martin Stone, a young Los Angeles industrialist, as cochairmen of the California campaign. In addition to Hill and Stone, most able and loyal help came from the California congressional delegation. Don Edwards, the Ninth District Congressman, who had been involved in the cause of the Concerned Democrats before I became a candidate, answered every call for help both in his own state and other parts of the country. In the Los Angeles area my campaign was assisted by Congressman George Brown, one of the members of the House of Representatives who spoke out early on the issues and in behalf of my candidacy. Mrs. Ann Alanson, national committeewoman, became the first and only member of the Democratic National Committee to support my candidacy.

The decision to allow local people to run things proved its worth. Campaign operations were generally self-supporting, and headquarters were opened in storefronts or private homes. In small towns, people organized committees, started campaigns independently, and then called the state or district headquarters for recognition, materials, and instructions. We encouraged this local initiative; it caught the spirit of the movement. By the end of the campaign there were more than one hundred and forty local headquarters, locally financed except for three or four in poverty areas.

An indication of the enthusiasm and ingenuity of the California campaigners was the collection of the signatures needed to put our slate of delegates on the primary ballot. The idea of petition parties was offered by Jo Seidita, a San Fernando Valley housewife and secretary of the California Democratic Council.

The usual method was to distribute petitions during the thirty-day period of signing. March 6 through April 6. Some candidates had hired professional signature-collecting firms. Mrs. Seidita's party plan, however, envisioned as many as five-hundred late-evening parties for the night before the petitions were due, with signing to begin at midnight. If it worked, our local chairmen

---

August and which in turn led to my meeting with him again in October in Los Angeles.

would be ready to present their petitions to county registrars at the opening of business the next morning.[27]

Affidavits had to be secured for each delegate so that the petitions could be officially filed. Because my signature was necessary, Gerald Hill flew to Philadelphia on February 27, putting the forms in front of me as I was preparing to speak to a rally.

Many parties were under way by midnight of the 5th, and by 2 A.M. of the 6th, there were more than five hundred in progress. Like nearly everything in California, parties were a trifle unusual. Each party had a notary public, who could verify signatures, and a deputy registrar to re-register Republican or Peace & Freedom party voters. The parties were of all sorts, from dances to debates, speechmakings to cocktail parties and midnight suppers. There were seventeen people at one gathering in Hanford, a farm town, and more than a thousand at The Factory, a Los Angeles discotheque.

The morning after, sometime before sunup, more than 30,000 valid signatures were presented at courthouses around the state. Thirteen thousand signatures were gathered in Los Angeles County alone. A major traffic jam was reported in front of the Los Angeles county headquarters on Fairfax Avenue at 3 A.M. as petitions arrived from one hundred parties around that county.

On my first trip to California, in January, I undertook to touch the principal centers of active support and also to raise money. We had estimated the cost of the campaign in California at about $1 million. In the four days in Los Angeles, San Diego, Fresno, and San Francisco, I spoke at two universities (UCLA and Stanford) and at fund-raising breakfasts, lunches, and dinners, held press conferences in each city, met with the editorial board of the San Francisco *Chronicle*, with representatives of organized labor, and with party leaders who were not directly identified with my campaign.

---

[27] The plan had several advantages: participation of enthusiastic volunteers in an early and important effort; an opportunity for fund raising; and top listing on the ballot under California law, considered significant by some experts.

California delegates to a national Democratic convention have traditionally been chosen by a small and select committee of the candidate's principal supporters. My supporters chose instead to call unofficial local conventions to nominate candidates for the 172 delegate and alternate positions on the California slate. The conventions were remarkable not only in themselves but in the mixture of the young and the old, the new and the experienced politicians that they attracted. The 172 delegates and 172 alternates were finally confirmed by the 250-member steering committee.

There were at all times two aspects to the primary: the contest for the control of convention delegates and the contest for the control of the regular party organization in California, since a primary victory meant control of the party in the state.

When I spoke to the California Democratic Central Committee at Fresno, I made my case to the Democrats of that state. And perhaps it was a startling proposal. But the heart of it was that my position was not that of the dissident but instead was clearly consistent with what we had *promised* to the people in 1964. Here is how I argued the case:

In 1964, the Democratic party had won the greatest election victory of any party in this century. A Democratic President was elected by an unprecedented plurality – 16 million votes. Two-to-one Democratic majorities were obtained in both houses of Congress, paving the way for the enactment of liberal legislation that had waited for as long as twenty years.

In the years since 1964, something happened to the Democratic party. Slowly there began an erosion of spirit. Many people voted Republican in 1966, not necessarily because they found the Republican party attractive but because they were losing faith in the Democrats.

In California, only four votes in the Assembly kept the state safe from rampant Reaganism. The prospects nationally were not cheerful for Democrats.

What was the reason for the decline in Democratic spirit? Much of the answer, I thought, was that leadership of the party had itself dissented – moved away from long-standing principles of the party and misread the overwhelming mandate it received in 1964.

If Barry Goldwater had been elected in 1964 and pursued the course of every-widening escalation in Vietnam, Democratic unity would never have been more solid. The confusion of the party derived from the fact that it was not a Goldwater government but a Democratic administration that was following a Republican foreign policy. The Democrats on the Senate Foreign Relations Committee were not the dissenters. The dissenters were in the Administration.

What are the great principles of Democratic foreign policy? They are, I believe, five:

That America must not shrink from war when liberty is at stake, but that America must not conduct war against the poor, the backward, and the primitive.

That primary reliance in foreign policy must be placed on political rather than military solutions; that American B-52s and defoliation chemicals are no substitute for negotiations between internal political forces within a foreign country.

That in building world order and peace, the United States must work in concert with its friends; that "going it alone" is really what isolationism is all about.

That the standing of America in the world is not primarily determined by the size of America's arsenal or its willingness to use arms, but by the ideals that America embodies and, as Thomas Jefferson wrote nearly two hundred years ago, by the "decent respect" we pay to the opinions of mankind.

And that in foreign, as in domestic, policy the leaders of government must be truthful with the Congress and the people; that when they ask for a major commitment they must state their purpose clearly and without ruse.

These principles of Democratic foreign policy had been formulated and carried out by four great Democratic Presidents in this century, I reminded the California Central Committee. These presidents, while defending freedom, while protecting the national security, understood the yearnings of the other nations and other peoples, and in so doing won respect and affection for America within the world community.

It was Woodrow Wilson who first saw the need for a League of Nations; Franklin Roosevelt who put an end to military intervention in Latin America and adopted the policy of the Good Neighbor; Harry Truman who established the Marshall Plan for Europe and the Point Four Program for the developing nations; and John F. Kennedy who signed the Test Ban Treaty, launched the Peace Corps and the Alliance for Progress.

America today is more isolated than it has been since the heyday of isolationism, not by our withdrawal from the world but by the withdrawal of most of the world from us.

This blunt talk about who was dissenting from whom was not politic and was not music to all ears. In any case, when I expressed these sentiments, I received a standing ovation – from less than half of the crowd.

Before Senator Kennedy entered the primaries, we anticipated that we could win in California against President Johnson. It appeared as though we would have a strongly united liberal organization in California. Robert Kennedy's candidacy changed the picture there perhaps more than it did in any other state.

When he announced his candidacy on Saturday, March 16, 1968, the California Democratic Council was holding its annual convention in Anaheim. The night before, the convention had passed a resolution of support for my candidacy – the first primary endorsement for President in the organization's sixteen-year history – with only half-dozen dissenting votes. The Reverend Martin Luther King, Jr., making what was to be his last speech to a political group, addressed their luncheon, saying:

I want to commend your organization for the significant work that you have done since your existence. I also want to commend you for endorsing one of the truly outstanding, capable, brilliant, dedicated Americans, Senator Eugene McCarthy.

This was generous praise, and such an endorsement at that hour was welcome.

After Senator Kennedy's announcement, California Assembly Speaker Jesse Unruh, who in early 1967 had urged him to become a candidate, told the press that he was "sure that something would be worked out" between the Kennedy and McCarthy forces. Gerald Hill responded that this was not so, and pledged that there would be "no personal attacks on Senator Kennedy, but we reserve the right to defend ourselves."

Talk of "accommodation" continued, but only one county chairman and one delegate changed allegiance to Senator Kennedy.

New McCarthy headquarters were opened. Campus activity increased after attacks on my record, similar to the ones in Indiana, appeared in the *Daily Bruin* at UCLA, the *Daily Californian* at Berkeley, and the *Stanford Daily*. Our faculty and student supporters were prepared to refute the advertisements point by point.

By the time I spoke at the Cow Palace in San Francisco on May 22 – less than two weeks before the primary election – the change in the character of the campaign as the consequence of the entrance of Senator Kennedy and the withdrawal of President Johnson was clear. The issues which I had been raising earlier had become confused, and other issues and matters which were quite unrelated to the problems of 1968 had been injected into the campaign. In the Cow Palace speech I tried to make clear what the real issues were.

Months earlier, I pointed out, I had made the decision that a challenge had to be laid down, not just a challenge to the president but a challenge to the people. The challenge was on the war, on the question of what priorities we should set for the nation, and on what they considered America to be in the year 1968, and what they wanted it to be in what remains of this century and beyond.

At the time I decided to run in New Hampshire, I told the people in the Cow Palace, Senator Kennedy said that he did not want to divide the party. I thought the time had come to divide the party if it was not already divided. I thought the issues were important enough to the country that one had to run some risks. We should have been running the risk of further division, for ours was the party which in 1948 had raised the issue of civil rights and said we were prepared to go down on this issue because it was so important to the nation. But in 1968, Democrats were saying, "Let us have no dissent; let us have no disunity."

This was a time for every citizen to take some chances, I said, businessmen and professional men who would run the risk of losing business or losing clients, teachers and professors who would expose themselves to attack and to criticism, students who would miss a class or two, slip a grade or two because of the commitment to the future; artists and actors, who had been treated rather badly at times for getting involved with politics and knew what it was to take chances on their careers. And if we were going to ask every citizen in this country to take some risks, why should the politician not also run a risk?

Then in the speech I tried to make clear the continuing differences between the other candidates and me. Candidates, I said, who are now talking about reconciliation and unity.

I was for unity but it depended upon what basis we would unify. Vice President Humphrey's conception seemed to be a kind of homogenization of America, in a way pretending there were no serious problems. We could all just be happy together. As I read it, the Kennedy approach was to put together an "organization," to assemble pieces of America without any organic whole. His campaign organization was setting up twenty-six different committees to deal with different kinds of Americans. I did not know there were that many. A special committee to deal with the Polish, a special committee to deal with the Italians, even one to deal with the Irish. A special committee to deal with Negroes, a special committee to deal with the Puerto Ricans, and one for retired former public officials. (That was drawing the line rather finely. A retired public official would be a former public official unless there were some who could retire without having been former.)

These special appeals may have worked in the past. It may even have been proper to say to each group: "There are injustices; you have rights that ought to be attended to. Come in with us and we will look after your problems along with the problems of other people." In this way a kind of composite America was put together in the past out of which some good did come. It was something like the politics of the Depression, and it had worked.

But I did not think it was the kind of politics that was in order for 1968.

We had to deal with straight problems which are the concern of *every* citizen in this country – simply because he is a citizen and not because he is a member of any organization or group of minority. In this speech I emphasized that I was quite prepared to speak about the injustices in our country – against Negroes and against others – and was doing so, but only in order to get all of the people to respond, to accept their responsibility, and not to distract people from the *common* problems which faced us. Having judged that the war in Vietnam was a mistake without precedent in our history, we were called upon not only to correct our mistake but to search out the causes and the conditions that led us into it. The time required us to make the hardest and the harshest judgments about our national assumptions, about the institutions that embody them, and about some of the leaders who had become the spokesmen for them.

Involvement in Vietnam was no accident, I said. It did not happen overnight. We did not wake up one morning and find ourselves with half a million men in that part of the world just by chance. It was not a landing in the dark. It was no departure from the diplomacy which we had been following. It was not a surprise, really, for it was written in the past, if we had only seen it coming. It came out of the consensus of the policies which have long been the principal guidelines for American conduct in this world.

I was not convinced that Robert Kennedy had renounced those misconceptions nor that Hubert Humphrey was prepared to say that the process – as well as what it produces – could be wrong. The Kennedy campaign was to suggest that he was the new wave, and yet I found it difficult to see why he would use an endorsement from Robert McNamara, the former Secretary of Defense, who was one of the principal engineers of the policies he was against.

I then laid down a clear challenge to Senator Kennedy and Vice President Humphrey. I said first with reference to Senator Kennedy: "I think that I can campaign against the Senator from New York and, in doing so, give the people of this nation a clear basis upon which to choose between us." I also took issue with the Vice President on substantially the same grounds of his involvement in the development of the war in Vietnam.

So I said flatly that I would make no concessions to any other candidate, offer no deals and accept no deals. Instead, I would carry on to the end what we had begun the previous November and carried through the cold of January and February. By the end of the year, I hoped we would prove to ourselves and to the watching world that the politics of reason and of conscience could also be the politics of success.

As we went along in the campaign, Senator Kennedy began to water down his stand on Vietnam, by slight alterations in his own position and by attacks, direct and indirect, on my position, especially concerning a coalition government in South Vietnam. There was a unity movement in the other camps. Vice President Humphrey said: "Robert Kennedy and I came to hold remarkably similar views on many, many questions – and believe it or not, on one that seems to be in the forefront of people's thinking today, on Vietnam."[28]

This did involve some oversimplification on the part of the Vice President, I think, but the fact is that the change in recent Kennedy statements was moving him much closer to the stated position of the Vice President, and farther from me.

On the strength of his name and the appeals to ethnic and minority groups, we anticipated that Senator Kennedy would probably get 90% of the vote of the Mexican-Americans and Negroes in the California primary. There was little we could do about this except try to get my record before them. But even assuming that the record had not been distorted and that we had been able to get my record on civil rights and migrant labor to them, there was no practical reason to believe they would be moved to support me because of their personal identification with the late President Kennedy and Senator Robert Kennedy. I did have among my active colleagues in California leaders from the Mexican-American community,[29] a number of Negro spokesmen who were critical of Senator Kennedy's record on civil rights as Attorney General and who had also raised a wiretapping issue. Drew Pearson and Jack Anderson wrote in their nationally syndicated column of May 25, 1968, that Robert Kennedy, while Attorney General, had "ordered a wire-tap" on the telephone of Martin Luther King, Jr., on July 16, 1963.

Senator Kennedy, campaigning in Oregon, would not talk about it, referring reporters to his headquarters for a statement. In Portland, Oregon, Pierre Salinger said, "Senator Kennedy never authorized any eavesdropping while Attorney General. He did authorize wiretaps in cases involving national security and on written request of the Federal Bureau of Investigation." When Salinger was asked if Mr. Kennedy had authorized a wiretap on

---

[28] Speaking to the Liberal party at the Roosevelt Hotel in New York City on August 17.

[29] Among them, Dr. Ernesto Galarza, Evelyn Velarde Benson, Frank Lopez, Eddie Perez, Gonzalo Molina, Rene Nunez, Alicia Ramirez.

Dr. King, Salinger said, "Senator Kennedy has not in the past and will not now discuss individual cases." We made no general effort to exploit either of these issues in the campaign, but there is no doubt in my mind how they would have been used had I been Attorney General at the time the bugging was initiated.

We had no set strategy for the campaign. I would appear on college campuses, cover the major population centers in the state, and try to speak on the thorny issues that interested Californians, but which, in fact, affected much of the United States: population growth, educational needs, race, urbanization, conservation, water, air pollution, and agriculture.

My California state organization concentrated on producing and providing materials, scheduling my trips, handling press relations, and fund raising. The campaign schedules were well organized but overbooked; they usually had to be reduced by one-third in order to meet other commitments.

The results in the primary proved that our estimate of voting by minority groups was correct, and it also sustained our statement that these were voters who in a general election would support the Democratic nominee.[30]

We were constantly under pressure to spend more time in Negro and Mexican-American communities. A false issue emerged out of this: that I would not go into minority areas. Actually, we were in Watts twice, and in Compton, West Oakland, and the Fillmore District, and to Mexican-American rallies in both Los Angeles and San Francisco. There were other meetings with various leaders of the minority groups in California.

In a campaign, the candidate sees everyone, goes everywhere, and in some ways sees nothing. He can never really know what it is like day-to-day for the people who are working for him. At this point, in order to convey better than I can the special spirit of fun and adventure that pervaded the homes and offices and odd bits of real estate that were part of the McCarthy "movement," another writer's recollections are valuable. Beulah Roth, a southern Californian, has well described it:

> *McCarthy Campaign Headquarters banners appeared on vacant stores all over the city, like mushrooms after a hot damp summer. The coward's way out was to work some place near my home, but I chose an area quite a distance away because they were short of help in that district. Until recently the Beverly and Fairfax quarter was almost 100% Jewish, now the ratio has changed to 80% Jewish and 20% Hippie. An*

---

[30] See Appendix 9.

unlikely brotherhood, but highly compatible. Pot roast mingles with pot. Kosher neon signs blink harmoniously with psychedelic lights. Old men with beards discuss weather and war with young men with beards. Flower children share the sidewalk with Jewish housewives. The Free Press shares the newspaper stand with the Daily Forward, and The Jefferson Airplane and the Mamas and the Papas sing duets with Richard Tucker and Jan Peerce. Oh, Fairfax Avenue is a wonderful place!

And so was Senator McCarthy's headquarters, because the wonderful people on that wonderful street helped in every way they knew to insure McCarthy's success in the primary. I could write a sonnet to their devotion to licking stamps and ringing doorbells. A lot of money was collected there too. Working men's money. Pensioners' money. Butchers' money. Synagogue money. Love-In money. Tightly budgeted household money. It was all given with such love and such devotion that I could hardly see to write out a receipt because of the tears in my eyes. Yes, they all wanted a receipt.

The atmosphere in the Westwood Village campaign headquarters was quite different. The zeal and education were the same but the case of characters changed. Volunteers here were college students, educators, and upper-middleclass housewives from Brentwood, Bel Air, and Beverly Hills. Then, of course, busloads of students from campuses in Northern California came down to help with the workload of stamping, addressing, telephone answering, and doorbell ringing. There always seemed to be a deadline or a printing crisis, a misspelled name, a change of date, and a lack of funds. The grownup volunteers were imaginative and resourceful, but a small eleven year old boy who came in one day surprised everyone with his ingenuity.

It was a Saturday morning early in May. I was struggling with the ribbon on the ancient Smith Corona I was using. Worn to a shred in the center, brand new on the edges, it refused to move to the right or the left. Suddenly a small hand reached over my shoulder, touched something in the innards of the machine. Miraculously, the ribbon went on its merry way as typewriter ribbons were meant to do. "Anything else I can do? I want to help," asked the hand. It belonged to a boy certainly no older than eleven, an age which finds putting tacks on chairs and rubber lizards on desks a nice way to spend a Saturday morning.

"Anyone need help?" I announced. There was no reply except a suggestion from a nearby fellow-volunteer, sotto voce,

that the boy was a mini-agent provocateur sent by the Nixon people to undermine our operations. But Ethel Longstreet, almost drowned in papers and lists on the balcony, needed help badly, even from an agent provocateur. She delegated him to some simple sorting, part of a major operation of determining from long lists of names WHO was to receive an invitation to the reception for Eugene McCarthy at the home of Mr. And Mrs. Paul Newman. Names had to chosen on the basis of importance, affluence, and political affiliation. They then had to be alphabetized faultlessly, and arranged according to zip code and city. Finally, the envelopes had to be addressed and the invitations mailed. The job needed a staff of ten experienced workers, and all Ethel had was one little boy. But just as he had worked the miracle on my typewriter, so he accomplished another for Ethel. In a few minutes he had devised a system which could facilitate the procedure for her. Then, quietly, in a corner, he went to work himself. For the first time in that headquarters' history the invitations went out correctly and on time...

And the film stars [the Newmans, Barbara Bain, Martin Landau, Barbra Striesand, Walter Matthau, Jill St. John, Myrna Loy, John Forsythe, Carl Reiner, and others] really helped us when we McCarthy supporters went into the nightclub business. "Eugene's" was called a discotheque to be chic, but actually it was an old-fashioned night club with new fashioned music. There were some psychedelic light effects, too, which were no good for the astigmatic customers, McCarthyites or not. The rash of celebrities at "Eugene's" was so constant that soon table reservations became as hard to get as third row center for the Bolshoi Ballet. Situated in the heart of Beverly Hills...it became a Mecca for visiting tourists. People who had no more sense of social significance than my dog, gladly paid the cover charge just to get a glimpse of Barbra Striesand. When we added up those $5 bills, we found that Eugene McCarthy did more business than Disneyland.

What I remember is bright young faces, homemade posters, peace beads, and amulets. There was also one pleasant, short meeting with Mrs. Joseph Kennedy in the Fairmont Hotel in San Francisco. When I introduced myself, she smiled and said, "Have fun in the campaign" – a remark which reflected her openness of spirit and the honesty she had shown in her earlier frank response to criticism about campaign spending: "It's our money and we're free to spend it any way we please."

In a state as large and as complex as California, I found that gauging progress was difficult. The polls and other indicators showed that I continued to gain after the entry of Senator Kennedy.

The Field poll, a respected California poll taken in mid-May, after the Indiana and Nebraska primaries, reported Senator Kennedy with 39% to 25% for me, and 25% for Vice President Humphrey.

The poll readers pointed out that this was a gain of approximately 8 percentage points for me from the mid-March Field poll, which had shown Kennedy with 47% to my 17% and 29% for President Johnson.

Thus, during this period, Senator Kennedy declined 8% while the "undecideds" were increasing.

National polls throughout this period tended to sustain these findings. In most cases those polls appeared to indicate that when paired against Republican candidates, Senator Kennedy would not run as well as I would. The Harris polls, taken between March and May, showed me gaining over Mr. Nixon – going from a 34% to 43% advantage for Nixon to a 40% to 37% advantage for me, with Senator Kennedy losing ground – going from a 44% to 39% advantage to a 30% to 40% advantage for Mr. Nixon. At this time, Governor Rockefeller and I were running about even in the polls. Senator Kennedy began with a 9% advantage when paired against Governor Rockefeller, but by May this was changed and Governor Rockefeller had a 5% advantage.

Whatever the poll watchers thought, late in the campaign Senator Kennedy and his advisers decided to accept a debate with me. I had long been trying to get the Senator to debate, without effect. Now, he had agreed to the conditions of a debate as offered by the American Broadcasting Company.

I had not approved the format of the debate, as the press reported and I did not appreciate the likelihood that ABC might produce the smallest audience. A smaller audience might minimize the risk for a candidate who did not do well but it did not meet my need to reach as many people as possible. The network had first proposed that the debate follow the format of the original John F. Kennedy-Richard Nixon debates of 1960. But they had made concessions along the way without being fully open with the aides who were speaking for me. Once Senator Kennedy agreed to debate, it was practically impossible, in view of the fact that we had been urging a debate, for us to hold off or insist on other than the ABC terms.

It was our judgment that coming so late the debate would probably have little effect on the outcome of the primary, but that by accepting it Senator Kennedy could offset what he might lose by continuing to refuse to debate – as he had in other primaries and even earlier in the state of California.

There were few surprises in the debate, excepting Kennedy's denial that he knew of several events of which I felt quite sure he did have knowledge. When I mentioned the distortions of my record, for example, Senator Kennedy replied that he did not know to what I was referring. I was disappointed in the panel since I thought they did not press hard enough, with the exception of Bill Lawrence whose questions were discerning and probing. He questioned Senator Kennedy about whether he as Attorney General had specifically authorized or condoned a wiretap on the telephone of Dr. Martin Luther King. Senator Kennedy then responded that the law forbade him from saying whether or not such a wiretap was approved. He did say, however, that he had never given permission for "bugging."[31]

I described our joint appearance as a contest with three referees and the contestants wearing sixteen-ounce gloves.

The general conclusion was that the Kennedy people thought he had done well, and the people who were for me thought I had slightly the better of the meeting, and I thought that it had turned out almost a draw.

At the time Senator Kennedy first entered the primaries, I had serious reservations about him as a potential President, not because of any personal knowledge I had about him but rather on the basis of what others had said or written. I believed, however,

---

[31] This remark was consistent with the position stated by Pierre Salinger when this issue was raised in the Oregon primary. It was never clear to me exactly why this distinction between permitting wiretapping and not permitting bugging was considered important or an adequate answer. As a matter of fact, one can make a better case for allowing bugging, or electronic eavesdropping, than for wiretapping, since in the case of the former one can at least take limited precaution to protect privacy, precautions which are impossible when a tap on the telephone is used.

This same matter was the subject of testimony in a Federal Court in Houston in June 1969, when in the case involving former heavyweight champion Cassius Clay, FBI agents acknowledged that for a number of years electronic devices were used to listen to conversations of Dr. King. The FBI continues to say that each bugging was authorized in writing by the Attorney General before installation. Former Attorney General Ramsey Clark denied authorizing any wiretaps or bugs against Martin Luther King. The issue remains unresolved and perhaps it should remain so. But as to the future, it is my opinion that clarification of the procedures and power and responsibility of the FBI's director is indicated and necessary.

whatever these deficiencies might be, they would be more than made up for by the commitment he had and by the kind of people who would be his advisers. It was on the basis of these considerations and in reply to inquires early in the campaign as to whether I could support him for the nomination against Lyndon Johnson or other candidates that I had answered that I could.

But as we neared the end of the primary trail in California I began to have more and more doubts about the integrity and reliability and judgment of some of his supporters, who, it seemed to me, were more interested in having power, or being in the presence of power, than they were in the issues and, in some cases, in Robert Kennedy himself. At the same time I came to accept the honesty and depth of his own commitment and concern.

It appears as though he had too many counselors and some of them, at least, were not very good. He was badly advised by those who urged him not to enter the primaries at the time I decided to enter. He was badly advised by those who persuaded him to become a candidate under the conditions in which he entered the primaries in March 1968. He was badly advised in his first attack on Lyndon Johnson, when in Los Angeles on March 24, he accused the President of "calling upon the darker impulses of the American spirit – not perhaps deliberately but through its action and the example it sets – an example where integrity, truth, honor and all the rest seem like words to fill out speeches rather than guiding beliefs." It was my opinion that he was badly advised in the methods of campaigning he used against me, especially the attack on my record.[32]

Senator Kennedy not only had too many advisers, I think, but he also was too concerned about them. In a campaign such as 1968, or for that matter I suppose in any presidential campaign, the decisions one must take fall into three general categories:

First, the important decision about key issues on which one needs little advice because they are the substance of the campaign.

The second category includes decisions that are relatively unimportant or that cannot be determined with reasonable

---

[32] A very interesting point was raised, first, I believe, by Bob Healy of the Boston *Globe*, after the Oregon primary and before the California primary. He said that if Senator Kennedy at that time had announced that he was not going to challenge in California but was swinging his support to me, he could have won the support of most of my delegates at Chicago as well as that of my campaign workers. But if he persisted in fighting the California primary, Healy reasoned, it would be much more difficult for my supporters and my delegates to move to him at the August convention.

accuracy by *anyone* – such as whether one should travel by plane or by car or go to one town instead of another. These are decisions almost all of which can be made without any extensive consultation with the candidate.

And the third category of decisions, the practical political ones, for the most part should be made by the candidate himself. Unless he is the best-qualified man to make such decisions, he should not be the candidate.

I never believed that victory in all primaries would assure my nomination. When Senator Kennedy announced that he would not enter the primaries I felt that if he maintained the standby position which he then held (namely, that he more or less agreed with me and other critics of Administration policy in Vietnam but that he did not wish to divide the party and was supporting President Johnson for renomination), he would come into the convention with great strength and would probably be nominated.

Senator Kennedy won the California primary. Again, the results showed that he was able to get the almost solid vote of the minorities. They showed again that I could get votes for the Democratic party in 1968 that other candidates could not get. The margin of victory of Senator Kennedy was 4.5%, and the actual count showed a difference of 140,152 votes: Senator Kennedy receiving 1,445,880 against my 1,305,728.

I was working with members of the campaign staff in my suite in the Beverly Hilton Hotel, drafting a congratulatory telegram to Senator Kennedy on his California primary victory, when David Schoumacher of CBS came in and said, "Senator Kennedy has been shot." He said he would get more information. In a few minutes he returned and said that Kennedy had been shot in the head.

I remember having been surprised that Senator Kennedy had gone down to make his victory statement so early with the returns still so close. And all I can remember saying, when my wife and daughters and I heard the news, is "Maybe we should do it a different way; maybe we should have the English system of having the Cabinet choose the President. There must be some other way."

I paid my tribute to Senator Robert Kennedy, observing that among those who knew him well and outside the field of the politics, he elicited a deep and continuing friendship. These friendships were marked by great warmth and loyalty which transcended differences in age and political differences.

His record as a most loyal, ardent, and self-sacrificing aide of his brother was well known to all Senators, and to the American people, as was his record following the death of President Kennedy, when he assumed in a very special way the burden of carrying forward what had been started. In the same spirit, he had moved on into new fields of need and of concern in this nation.

He was the most worthy advocate – dedicated, energetic – committing all of his strength to the end of achieving the objectives which he had concluded were for the good of this country.

As Mary McGrory, a journalist who saw him as a friend and as a politician, wrote: "He intensified life for those who knew him and for those who did not."

I think the best statement of Senator Kennedy's character and of his campaign was that written by Robert Lowell, who was Robert Kennedy's friend as well as mine:

R.F.K

Here is my workroom, in its listlessness
of Vacancy, some old Victorian house,
airtight and sheeted for old summers,
far from the hornet yatter of the bond –
is loneliness, a thin smoke thread of vital
air. What can I catch from you now?
Doom was woven in your nerves, your shirt,
woven in the great clan; they too were loyal,
and you too more than loyal to them, to death.
For them like a prince, you daily left your tower
to walk through dirt in your best cloth. Untouched,
alone in my Plutacharn bubble, I miss
you, you out of the Plutarch, made by hand –
forever approaching our maturity.

The Great Delegate Hunt

My principal effort after the primaries was to try to build sufficient strength so that the position which Senator Kennedy and I had taken on the issue of Vietnam – although we differed somewhat – could be maintained and carried at the Democratic convention.

It had from the beginning been my intention to test as thoroughly as I could the entire process of the Democratic party, not just as it operated in states that had primaries but also in those that had modified primaries and in those in which the selection of delegates was made through the regular party processes of precinct caucuses, county, district, and state conventions. I hoped to leave delegates from these states without the defense that I had been indifferent to them, and also with the choice of rejecting or accepting my candidacy at the convention as their best, if not their only, chance for victory.

I also hoped that it might be possible to move the Vice President, who I expected would be nominated, to a break with the Administration and to make a clear statement on the war in Vietnam and other issues that had been raised in the campaign.

My most immediate concern was the choice of delegates in the New York primary election on June 18. My first campaigning, following the assassination of Senator Kennedy, took place in New York City on June 13. The New York primary, coming so soon after the California primary and the murder of Senator Kennedy, did not receive the attention that it might have in other circumstances. The intricacies of the petition and primary system in New York also contributed to difficulty in reporting such a vast and varied effort.

The Coalition for a Democratic Alternative formed the nucleus of the campaign organization headed by Mrs. Sarah Kovner, a former Democratic state committeewoman; Mrs. Eleanor Clark French, former vice-chairman of the Democratic State Committee; and Harold Ickes, Jr., son of President Franklin

D. Roosevelt's Secretary of the Interior. More than two hundred storefront headquarters were opened in New York City and throughout the state. This organization and related campaign committees not only took over the task of selecting and electing delegates in the New York primary but contributed substantially to supplying money and campaign workers in other primary states.

Under the New York system, 750 signatures are required to place the name of a delegate on the ballot. Three delegates and three alternates are elected from each of the forty-one congressional districts. The ballot lists candidates under their own names, with no official indication of presidential preference. Of the total 190 delegates allocated to New York, 123 are chosen in the primary, 65 are selected by the Democratic State Committee, and 2 votes are automatically allotted to the national committeeman and committeewoman.

More than 150,00 signatures were filed statewide to nominate candidates for delegates in support of my candidacy, but the delegates stood for election in their congressional districts only, making it impossible to publicize a statewide slate. Moreover, delegates could not even be identified with their presidential candidate on the ballot. To overcome such difficulty, campaign strategy was tailored to each district. A standard tabloid was prepared, explaining my record and the objectives of the campaign, but the last page was changed in each district to identify the local candidates for delegate. This was widely used in door-to-door campaigning in April and May.

Out of 123 delegates chosen in the election of June 18, 62 were pledged to me, 30 to the late Senator Kennedy, 19 were uncommitted, and 12 supported Vice President Humphrey. The "amateurs" had really surprised the party leaders. As a result of the victory, my supporters demanded half of the 65 delegates-at-large to be named by the state committee. As negotiations proceeded, they felt it necessary to trim their demand. But 28 delegates, they said, would be the absolute minimum, in fairness to the people of the state who had clearly expressed their preference at the polls through a procedure so cumbersome that it made the victory all the more impressive. Meeting on June 28, the New York State Democratic Committee allotted my supporters only 15 1/2 votes, and only seven or eight of the delegates named were recognized as persons publicly committed to my candidacy. Those who had worked so hard for so many months to test the system left the meeting in anger.

Subsequently, some of the delegates named by the state committee resigned or were replaced to increase representation of

Negroes and Puerto Ricans. Several leaders of the earlier Kennedy campaign announced support for me and joined the effort to obtain commitments from other delegates.[33]

In Chicago, the New York delegation cast 96 1/2 votes for Humphrey and 87 for me, although it voted 148 to 42 for the minority report on the Vietnam plank, which was then identified as my general position on the war. This confirmed my belief that many of the Kennedy delegates, although opposed to the war, were politically committed to the Administration nominee.

The test in New York was one of the most important of all because delegates had to run identified with a candidate but not under his name. This procedure, which comes closest to carrying out the constitutional provisions for the electoral college, should be developed as a national pattern. It is preferable to a national primary or even to a system in which separate primaries might be held in each state or in a large number of states.

In the New York primary, Paul O'Dwyer, an uncompromising supporter of my campaign and of my position, had been expected to run third in a three-man Democratic race for the United States senatorial nomination. He did not. He ran first with 36.1% of the vote. The organization candidate, a strong Kennedy supporter, Nassau County Executive Eugene Nickerson, came in second with 33.7%. Congressman Joseph Y. Resnick, a Humphrey supporter, ran third with 30.1%.

In many ways, campaigning for delegates was more demanding than the campaign in the primaries. Trying to satisfy demands from across the country was hard not only on the candidate but also on the schedules, the transportation and baggage handlers, and press-release writers. Moreover, there was need to respond, in some degree at least, to the advice and directions of the Secret Servicemen who were with me from California until after Chicago.

In the campaign for delegates, I spoke at conventions and party meetings across the entire United States. On June 14, I talked in Idaho Falls, Idaho; on the 15th, in Phoenix, Arizona; the 16th, in Albuquerque, New Mexico; the 17th, in the District of Columbia; the 18th, in Cleveland, Ohio. It went on like this through Minnesota, North Dakota, Oklahoma, Iowa, Michigan, and Illinois until the Fourth of July when I gave a farm speech at Corning, Iowa. After that appearance, I rested for a few days at St. John's University, in Minnesota, with friends and former teachers.

---

[33] Among them were Herman Badillo, Borough President of the Bronx; Eugene Nickerson, Nassau County Executive; and Jack English, chairman, Nassau County Democratic Committee.

I resumed campaigning in the West in Tacoma, Washington; Denver and Fort Collins, Colorado; and Salt Lake City, Utah. After stopping in Pittsburgh, Pennsylvania, on July 16, I spent four days in southern and border states, including Virginia, North Carolina, Georgia, Kentucky, Tennessee, and Maryland. Neither my campaign committee nor I expected to win many votes at the convention as a result of the latter trip. We did, however, wish to carry the case to the southern and border states to encourage those who had worked for the cause (in each of these states we did have strong and intensive support), and to lay the groundwork for party reform at the convention.

My message to the non-primary states was to report on what had happened in the primary states, to restate what the Democrats had promised to the country in the campaign of 1964, and to urge Democrats to send representative delegations to the convention in Chicago. By this time I was speaking more about the Democratic party than about my own candidacy. When I was asked whether I was interested in starting a third party or a fourth party, I said no, I thought that as long as I had the first party I was not going to worry about the others. I was trying to establish across the country that my position (and also Senator Kennedy's) on both the war and on domestic problems was the traditional Democratic position on these issues and that we were in the mainstream and simply asking Democrats to come back home.

You have heard it many times, I said. I have said it – I suppose nearly every candidate does, even the Republicans are now saying it – that 1968 is the year of decision. And it is a year of decision, but that is not enough. First we have to ask what we are to decide about? What is it that is really at stake in 1968? And when this question results in a rather difficult and hard answer which lays down a challenge to one's party, nonetheless the question must be asked and the chance for decision must be given. Where criticism is required and disagreement with one's own party, then I think the criticism must be spoken and the disagreement must be made evident. To a measurable extent, we Democrats are called upon to answer for things that happened under our administration in the last four years, for some things which might have taken place if we had had the right kind of policies and the persistence to carry through. But this is not one of those easy years that many of us remember, in which all we had to do was talk about the Republicans and their failures or simply contrast our achievements with what might have happened if we had not been in office. We are called upon to do the most difficult thing, I believe, for any party: to pass a judgment upon its own record, and having done that – assuming we are prepared to change our policy – to commit ourselves to changing the record, to ask the public for support for another four years. This was my message.

In 1964, we Democrats talked of peace. Promises were made of peace abroad and of progress at home. And similar promises were being made again in almost the same language as was used back in 1964. Most of us at Atlantic City accepted and said throughout the campaign that if our candidate was elected what has been happening in Vietnam would not have happened, and that if the other candidate was elected what is happening would have happened. So in a way we are answerable at least for what we said. We may explain it and discount it and give some justifications, because the movement of history is never a simple one. But, basically, I do not think we can explain what happened solely in terms of some historical movement of forces which were beyond the control of our administration in power.

And later on in 1965 and 1966, when the escalation of the war reached serious proportions, our administration said to the country, "We can fight two wars: the war on poverty and also the war in Vietnam." But we know that this promise has not been kept, I said, and that the war on poverty has been neglected. It has not carried forward; it has not been fought as it should have been fought. And the problems which we acknowledged in 1964, and which we acknowledged in 1965, were still with us in 1968.

The problem of poverty and the problem of our cities, I said then, as I continue to say today, have grown worse. We are threatened every day with disorder as a public manifestation of something which is more serious than disorder; that is, the despair of the people who live in our cities. It is not enough to blame the war and to say that once it is over we can take care of all these things; or to hope – as some do – for a cool summer.

The response and the success of our efforts varied from state to state, depending on state laws or tradition and on the experience of the people. Many of my supporters were new to politics and had to learn the rules – or lack of them. It was often like playing against the home team and against the home umpires.

Colorado was a model for non-primary procedures. For several years prior to the campaign of 1968, various groups – clergymen, businessmen, health organizations – had been organizing around the issues of the war and our national priorities. The leaders of the McCarthy movement in Colorado were thus able to identify the concerned people and organize them into a movement to support an alternative policy and candidate.

In January 1968, the Coalition for an Alternate Candidate was formed. This group did not specifically endorse me but left itself open to support any candidate who would oppose President

Johnson on the war. With the announcement of Senator Kennedy's candidacy, the coalition divided into two groups, one supporting me and the other, him. In Colorado, unlike other states, relatively good relations were maintained between his supporters and mine. (After Senator Kennedy's death, his supporters in some states went over to Humphrey, but not in Colorado. The emphasis on the issue in Colorado was the big factor in preventing defections.)

The open-party caucuses in May were heavily attended. Delegates elected at the precinct level to the county conventions represented the approximate division of strength in the state: 35% for Humphrey, 30% for Kennedy, and 35% for me.

In June, the county conventions elected delegates to the state convention and also to the national convention.[34] In the First Congressional District (Denver), the coalition won all 6 delegates: 3 for Kennedy and 3 for me. It won again in the Second District (Denver suburbs): 4 for me, 2 for Kennedy. In the Third District (Colorado Springs-Pueblo), the result was divided 3 for the coalition and 3 for Humphrey. In the Fourth District (Western slope, northeast, Fort Collins and Greeley), all 6 went to Humphrey, even though we estimated our strength at 35 to 40% there.

All 12 of the at-large national delegates chosen at the state convention supported me. This resulted in a final count within the Colorado national delegation of 19 delegate votes for the coalition and 16 for Humphrey – roughly proportional to our true strength in Colorado.

In North Dakota, we had time only to challenge the state party choices in one out of the some forty of the state senatorial districts – in the city of Fargo. At the precinct level in that district, my supporters were elected to 210 out of the 230 seats at the senatorial district convention. At the district level, of the 80 delegates sent on to the state convention, 70 were my supporters. Then at the state convention we were awarded 7 of the 25 North Dakota delegates to the Democratic National Convention. Had we been able to contest in the rest of the state, we might have shown sufficient strength to make the case for a higher proportion of the delegates to Chicago. But on the basis of measurable strength, the North Dakota distribution came close to being fair.

The fight for delegates in Iowa was an example of having potential but not realizing it. In the Iowa precinct caucuses held on March 25, my supporters took between 70 and 80% of the delegates, to the county conventions. A modest, but not very

---

[34] Twenty-four national delegates were elected, 6 from each of Colorado's four congressional districts. The 12 remaining delegate votes were elected at-large at the state convention.

serious, effort at the precinct level was mounted in favor of the candidacy of Senator Kennedy, who had announced a week before.

At the county conventions, however, my people failed to pay sufficient attention to the nominating committee which prepared the slates of delegates to the district and state conventions. As a result, the Kennedy people dealt with the Humphrey people and thus captured most of the strength we had won at the precinct level.

The Democratic party in Iowa was built up strongly by Governor Harold Hughes, who had the support and the admiration of most of the Democrats in the state. Hughes was running for the Senate on an anti-war platform, and there was reluctance among our people to make any move that might split the party and hurt the Governor's chances. Governor Hughes leaned to Kennedy, although he had not announced his support for any candidate. At the state convention on May 25, 1968, 25 of the delegate votes went to Kennedy, 2 to me, and the remaining 19 to Humphrey. After the assassination of Senator Kennedy, Governor Hughes put his full strength behind the effort to coalesce the anti-war sentiment, and he was able to influence a considerable portion of his delegation. Because opposition to the war was the most important question with many of the Iowa delegates, we did much better in the Iowa delegation in the polling at Chicago than we did in such delegations as Indiana where most of the Kennedy people went to Humphrey. Governor Hughes, of course, made the speech putting my name in nomination at the convention.

Michigan, with its 96 votes to the national convention, exemplified the workings of the old politics at its worst. Precinct elections for delegates to the county or district meetings, which in turn picked most of the national convention delegates, had been held in August 1966, two years before the 1968 Democratic National Convention. There was a choice of candidates in only 10% of the 5,000 precincts. In about half of the precincts, there was no opposition, and in the rest no elections at all. Most important, precinct representatives picked two years in advance were not likely to reflect how people felt about Vietnam or any other issue in August 1968.

We centered our challenge in Michigan in two congressional districts. In one of these, the Sixth, supporters of the Vice President, who were in a minority, refused to sit in the district caucus with our people, the majority. A "rump" caucus of Humphrey supporters was held. The Humphrey supporters in Ingham County demanded a proportionate rule, allowing representation to the minority Humphrey faction, but in two other

147

counties, where Humphrey supporters were in the majority, they had voted a unit rule, thus creating a pro-Humphrey majority in the Sixth District through unequal application of the unit rule. We challenged this inequality in the Sixth District at the national convention and failed, and in the end, 72 1/2 of Michigan's 96 votes went to the Vice President.

I could tell we were in for rough treatment when I appeared in Michigan before the delegation, well in advance of the Chicago convention, and Neil Staebler, a former Congressman and Democratic National Committeeman, asked me with reference to the war if I had not forgotten the lesson of the thirties and the invasion of Czechoslovakia by the Germans. I told him I had not forgotten. A second delegate, a Michigan labor leader, asked me the more or less standard question: whether I was prepared to pledge my support to whomever the Democratic party would nominate in Chicago. I said, as I had on other occasions, that I was not prepared to say that I would. The Michigan Democratic party is an example of liberalism gone wrong.

New Mexico was one of the hardest fought and most satisfying of the non-primary struggles. At every level, old-line party forces tried to steam-roller the insurgents, but my supporters persisted and finally won 11 of New Mexico's 24 votes to the Chicago convention.

New Mexico Democrats opposed to the war and anxious for a change in national priorities had begun to organize late in 1967, well before I announced my candidacy. In the preceding few years, I had spoken several times in the state and had become better known there than in many other states. Shortly after I announced, a state organization, chaired by State Senator Sterling Black of Los Alamos, son of Supreme Court Justice Hugo Black, was set up. Gross-roots work continued throughout the spring so that in mid-June, by the time of the precinct caucuses, Black estimated that statewide our supporters probably outnumbered those of Vice President Humphrey by 3 to 2. My supporters were elected to 205 of Albuquerque's 295 seats at the county convention and, after a stormy session, to 76 of Santa Fe's 84 seats.

In Los Alamos, a town dependent on government contracts, many persons who privately indicated their support and even willingness to work for my candidacy confessed a reluctance to be counted publicly. Nevertheless, my forces outnumbered Humphrey people 2 to 1 in Los Alamos, and we won all 22 of that county's delegates to the state convention.

Sterling Black has described the struggle in New Mexico against the party machinery. It was, in large measure, typical of

148

what we faced in many of the convention states. The old-time party officials, Black wrote, finally awakened to find themselves being overwhelmed by our strength, and they responded in the old ways. Delegate lists were illegally left open for several days after precinct meetings in an effort to round up more Humphrey votes. The old-timers undertook a frantic search of county registration records in an effort to prepare for credentials committee challenges. County credentials committees were stacked with Humphrey supporters. Attempts were made, in some places successfully, to throw out strong precinct delegations supporting me, afterward "compromising" by putting into the Humphrey delegations a few of my delegates to create a façade of fairness.

Yet through persistence and many a bitter fight, our people arrived at the New Mexico State Convention on June 29, 1968, with 510 firm delegates out of 1,256. At the state convention, they rehearsed, in effect, for what was to come two months later in Chicago. The Albuquerque, Santa Fe, and Los Alamos delegations, our strongest, were given seats in balcony bleachers as far as possible from the rostrum. There were no microphones in that section (despite promises of them), making it virtually impossible for our people to obtain recognition from the chair. (A bullhorn was quickly obtained.) Again, despite earlier agreement that delegates could carry signs on the floor, the sergeant-at-arms confiscated all McCarthy signs and took them out of the hall. Only after further negotiation was it finally agreed that signs would be permitted. There was also some harassment of our communications people who carried walkie-talkies.

The crucial moment in the New Mexico State Convention came in the battle over a resolution for proportional representation providing that a poll of the delegates be taken and that the 24 delegates to Chicago be named by my representative and the representative of the Vice President in direct proportion to the results of the poll. Our forces won the resolution by only 7 votes and were able, with this slim majority, to maintain control through much subsequent parliamentary maneuvering designed to neutralize the results of the vote.

It was a great victory for open politics in New Mexico. In the ensuing poll of the convention, delegates were permitted, for the first time in New Mexico history, to vote on their choice for their party's nominee for president. The 11 out of 24 votes in Chicago won by our forces were a tribute to responsible political leaders and should have been an example to others.

I made no personal campaign effort in my home state of Minnesota. A personal confrontation with the Vice President at that point would have had little effect on the outcome, and it would have deepened divisions within the party. Moreover, I had able and dedicated persons at work for me there: a state Conference of Concerned Democrats under the leadership of Professor John Wright and State Representative Alpha Smaby, and a state McCarthy for President Committee headed by John Connolly, a St. Paul attorney. Their organizations concentrated on the Minneapolis-St. Paul metropolitan areas. As in other states, local committees formed independently and then affiliated in a loose manner with one or the other of the state efforts.

Great numbers of students and teachers, including Roman Catholic nuns, carried on the major work in my behalf in Minneapolis and St. Paul. In the suburbs, the wearing day-to-day chores at the precinct level were done mainly by housewives and professional women.

The organizational effort aimed at the March precinct caucuses were staffed by regular Democratic-Farmer-Labor party members.[35] The Johnson-Humphrey campaign organization was aware of the concern about the war and about Administration domestic policies. Vice President Humphrey himself made a determined personal effort to keep the party in line. He asked for and received an endorsement of the Administration's Vietnam policies from the state executive council of the AFL-CIO Federation. He called together the 400-member DFL State Central Committee and more than 600 precinct chairman in December and delivered a two-hour defense of Vietnam policies. He entertained the state executive committee at his home in Waverly and again defended the Vietnam war effort at a major labor rally summoned for him in St. Paul.

Despite this personal attention, party leaders conceded that my supporters might have enough local strength to carry one congressional district and to elect five delegates to the national convention. And so, three weeks before the precinct caucuses, the Johnson-Humphrey campaign headquarters launched an intensive telephone campaign to get their supporters to the caucuses.[36]

---

[35] There were public announcements of support, for example, from Forrest Harris, Minneapolis, first vice-chairman of the state DFL; Mrs. Marilyn Gorlin, first vice-chairwoman; and Mrs. Joane Vail, White Bear Lake, Fourth District DFL chairwoman.

[36] Under Minnesota state law and the party constitution, a qualified voter who certifies that he is in agreement with the principles of the party is eligible to attend the precinct caucuses and vote for the election of delegates to the county conventions. County conventions, in turn, elect delegates to the eight congressional-district conventions. These delegates also become delegates to the state convention.

When the caucuses began on the evening of March 5, party officials were overwhelmed by the attendance. In precincts where fewer than a dozen voters had traditionally met, eighty to one hundred people were certified. Delegates supporting my candidacy won not only in precincts and wards populated by professors and students, as had been predicted, but in every kind of neighborhood, blue-collar as well as white-collar, wealthy suburbs as well as poor areas. They carried the three metropolitan congressional districts (containing half the state's population) by margins of up to 5 to 1.[37] And all but two or three elected party or public officials from these districts, who supported the Administration policies, were defeated in their home precincts.

The county conventions held later in March and in early April revealed that my supporters were somewhere between 100 and 150 votes short of a majority among the 1,106 delegates elected to the district and state conventions, which would select the 20 at-large delegates to the national convention. The state convention delegates were elected on the basis of one delegate for each 1,000 votes cast in the county for the leading statewide DFL candidate or national Democratic candidate at the last general or presidential election, whichever was greater. However, a minimum of 6 votes was allocated without regard to population or the DFL vote, thus weighing rural votes more heavily than urban votes and smaller rural counties more heavily than larger rural counties. Under this apportionment system, 172 delegates were elected to the state convention in addition to those elected on the basis of one delegate per 1,000 DFL voters.[38] The 172 excess delegates constituted almost one-sixth of the total of delegates.

For the national convention, Minnesota was allotted 52 votes, including a full vote each for the national committeeman and committeewoman. The state party allocated the 40 votes among 60 delegates, 40 of whom were elected from the eight congressional districts and 20 at-large by the state convention. Using their narrow rural-weighted majority, the supporters of Vice President Humphrey elected all 20 of the at-large delegates, giving the Vice President 38 1/2 votes and me 13 1/2, although it

---

[37] They carried 16 of the 20 wards in the Third District (suburban), 16 of the 18 legislative districts in the Fourth District (St. Paul), and 9 1/2 of the 13 wards in the Fifth District (Minneapolis). They also carried the cities of the First and Sixth Congressional districts and of the Iron Range in the Eighth District.

[38] Each delegate allocated to Cook County, the smallest county, represented 162 voters, for example, while each delegate allocated to urban centers such as St. Paul, Minneapolis, and Duluth represented 1,000 voters, or a ratio greater than 6 to 1.

was quite clear that about one-half of the party's people supported my positions.

The last weeks before the convention were highlighted by several major campaign rallies. The rallies had two purposes: to raise money and to demonstrate popular support of my candidacy. They were successful as money raisers. There was no way of telling, of course, what effect they had on delegates and party leaders. They did certainly draw people, however.

The rally at Fenway Park in Boston on July 25 was the largest in any campaign in recent history. The stadium, which holds 45,000, was filled. In addition, an estimated 10,000 lined Brookline and Jersey streets outside the ball park.

The rally in Fenway Park was unique not only for its attendance record, but also for the fact that people paid to get in. It was the first time in the history of Massachusetts politics that people had paid to attend a political rally. The charges for tickets were roughly the same as for tickets to a Boston Red Sox baseball game.

Two nights later, the 27th, we had another rally in Detroit. The long newspaper strike there had blacked out much of the news of the progress of my campaign. We hoped that a rally at Tiger Stadium would help influence the Michigan delegation in their preconvention deliberations and encourage the rank-and-file Democrats to make the delegates responsive to the prevailing Michigan mood on the issues. For one of the few times during the campaign, the weather almost forced us to postpone an event. Rains drenched the Detroit area throughout Saturday, but finally cleared in the early evening hours just before the program was scheduled to get under way. Despite the rain, nearly 25,000 turned out for this rally.

I went to both Columbus and Cleveland, Ohio, on August 7, where another experiment was under way. A group of Democrats in Ohio, feeling that members of their party should have a chance to voice their preference, as they put it, "for today's candidates, not yesterday's and not those who might have been," formed a Committee for a State Primary. They undertook a privately sponsored presidential preference poll known as the August Primary, giving Democratic voters a choice among Vice President Humphrey, Senators McGovern and Edward Kennedy, and myself. There was also a blank line for write-ins.

I won the Ohio straw vote by more than 2 to 1 over Vice President Humphrey with 50.7% of the vote. Humphrey took 23%, and the rest was divided among Senators George McGovern and Edward Kennedy and former Governor George Wallace of Alabama.

The rally technique culminated with McCarthy Day rallies in thirty different cities on August 15. The rally at Madison Square Garden in New York, where I spoke, was a sellout.

In the states I covered in the days just before the convention – Michigan, Ohio, Texas, Missouri, Illinois, New Jersey, and Pennsylvania – it was apparent that the delegates who were being sent to Chicago did not even come close to representing the attitude of many Democrats. We tried our best through private meetings, at rallies, and by letters and telegrams to reach the delegates. Nobody expected a very clear or immediate response, but since we had committed ourselves to test as best we could – and this was the only means available – we did what we could.

With the state delegations as unrepresentative as they were, our basic plan for attack at the convention centered on abolishing the unit rule.[39] The strategy planning was led by Stephen Mitchell, former Democratic National Chairman. Mitchell and his workers knew that a fight on the unit rule would not make any difference to some of the delegations, but in some states it might make a small difference. And, more important, a matter of principle and precedent was at stake that would affect, if not this convention, certainly many to come.

A number of states had in 1968 eliminated the unit rule or restricted its use:

The Kentucky state convention adopted a resolution on July 27 abandoning the use of the unit rule.

The Virginia state convention on July 27 defeated a move to adopt the rule.

The Maryland state convention bound its delegation to the unit rule on April 29, but the State Democratic Executive Committee on August 1 rescinded the action.

The Missouri state convention voted to abide by the unit rule only if two-thirds of the delegation voted to do so.

The Oklahoma delegation voted to adopt the unit rule only if it seemed necessary at the time of national convention balloting. The Oklahoma state convention had given Humphrey 37 of its 41 votes.

Connecticut and Rhode Island, which had used the unit rule in previous years, gave it up for this convention.

---

[39] The unit rule is an arrangement under which a delegation to a convention casts all of its votes as the majority of the delegation decides. For example, if a state delegation to a national convention is operating under the unit rule and is split 12 to 11 over a resolution before the convention or on two candidates for nomination, the position advocated by the 12 would receive all 23 votes.

The North Dakota state convention on June 29 picked 18 delegates favorable to Humphrey and 7 favorable to me. This allotment broke up North Dakota's traditional use of the unit rule.

In my own state of Minnesota, my supporters filed a lawsuit in the United States District Court in St. Paul, calling for re-allocation of the 52 convention votes to which the Minnesota delegation was entitled. As a minimum, my supporters asked for a 31-Humphrey and 21-McCarthy division. However, on August 5, Federal Judge Philip Neville dismissed the lawsuit, declaring that the courts should not become involved in internal party political matters. Judge Neville also ruled that the one-man, one-vote principle, cited by my supporters in their lawsuit, was not valid in this case. A few days later, the Eighth Circuit Court of Appeals, sitting in St. Paul, upheld Judge Neville's ruling – both bad rulings in my judgment.

In the state of Washington, my supporters also filed suit to prevent the seating of the Washington delegation at the national convention. They argued that the process by which the 23 delegates and 4 alternates were picked violated the constitutional rights of my supporters, and cited in support the First, Ninth, and Fourteenth Amendments to the United States Constitution. It was further alleged in this suit that Humphrey supporters at the state convention permitted 2 contested delegations to vote on their own seating, and that the state convention officials and committees did not follow their own rules and procedures.

All of these local differences were raised again at the national convention and remain, in fact, before the Democratic National Committee. The one that received the most attention and was played out in part on national television revolved around the Georgia delegation. A group known as the Georgia Democratic Party Forum (GDPF) had been organized to challenge the delegation headed by Governor Lester Maddox. Under Georgia law, the state Democratic Executive Committee Chairman chooses delegates with the Governor's advice and consent. This means that in practice the delegation is picked by the Governor. With Governor Maddox as chairman, the 64-member delegation included only 3 Negro delegates and 3 Negro alternates. Governor Maddox had removed the names of former Governor Carl Sanders and Atlanta Mayor Ivan Allen from the list originally presented to him by the state chairman, James H. Gray.

The Georgia Democratic Party Forum challenged the Maddox delegation on grounds of party loyalty, racial discrimination, and alleged non-representation of differing ideological views. It was contended that the Maddox group had been chosen in a "discriminatory, arbitrary and unrepresentative" way. So the GDPF offered an alternative: a delegation of 21 Negroes and 20 whites, led by State Representative Julian Bond and the Reverend James L. Hooten from Savannah.

The Credentials Committee of the national convention approved the seating of both delegations, splitting Georgia's 41 votes equally between them. Most of the Maddox group walked out, rejecting the compromise. At the August 27 session of the convention, the Credentials Committee report was approved, however, and on later roll calls Georgia cast separate votes by the two delegations.

This Georgia precedent, if honored and sustained and extended by the national Democratic party, can be the force that leads to a truly representative party convention. Chicago demonstrated how badly a true representation of the people is needed at party conventions.

Chicago: The Politics of Chaos

Chicago, Illinois, was the wrong place for the Democratic convention of 1968. There was first of all the danger of protests by residents of Chicago itself, and the likelihood of a great influx of student demonstrators. There was the almost certain identification of the convention with the organization of Mayor Richard Daley.

Well in advance of the convention, I sent word to as many student leaders as I could reach in the country, asking them to discourage students and other young people from coming to the Chicago streets. Without this request, instead of the 10,000 students who did gather in Chicago, the number could have been closer to 100,000. Before the convention, I spoke to Mayor Daley by telephone, offering to be of any help that I could in dealing with problems that might develop at the convention. He neither suggested what I might do, nor did he ask for suggestions.

The early reports of the rigging of the convention did not disturb me much. I was not particularly concerned about some of the contested details, about space on the convention floor, placement of delegations, hotel accommodations, and communications. The issues we were raising and the manner of my nomination was not the kind that could be settled by a phone call to the right person at the right time. ·

My convention committee did try, without much success, to be treated fairly and equitably. This effort was based more on principle than on a practical concern over the consequences of discrimination against us.

We hoped to do three things at the convention:

-To make clear the need for reform of processes within the Democratic party, both along the way to a convention and at conventions themselves, and to prepare the way for reform.

-To obtain the strongest possible platform plank seeking a change in Vietnam policy.

-To make the best possible challenge for the nomination.

157

The matter of reform had been well developed in preconvention hearings and in protests which were registered before the convention began.

A most important procedural matter raised at the convention was that of the unit rule. There was something like unanimity on abolishing this undemocratic edict; there was no unanimity on when it should go. The Rules Committee of the convention had recommended the abolition of the unit rule for the 1968 convention itself. A minority of 15 of the 110 Rules Committee members, from ten states led by Texas, proposed instead that the unit rule be abolished for the 1972 convention. The minority included among its signers delegates from Texas, Louisiana, South Carolina, Arkansas, Michigan, Arizona, Nevada, Utah, New Mexico, and the Canal Zone.

Vice President Hubert Humphrey, it was believed, favored the abolition of the unit rule and the action of the majority of the committee, on August 26 apparently changed his position to support the minority challenge. In an August 21 letter to the chairman of the Rules Committee, Humphrey had urged abolition of the unit rule "at this convention." But a question was raised during the floor debate on August 26 about when Humphrey wanted it abolished. A national committee man from Texas, Frank C. Erwin, Jr., speaking for the Rules Committee's minority, quoted Humphrey as saying to him the previous day, "If you want to abolish the unit rule, well and good. But let's pass a resolution here at this convention that is effective in 1972." Edwin said that the Vice President had told him that he did not "want to try to abolish what I think is an undemocratic rule by undemocratic procedure." It was Edwin's interpretation that the Vice President wanted the ban on the unit rule to take effect in 1972.

Challenging the unit rule at the beginning of a convention was somewhat justified. It was not unusual in states which use the unit rule to include among their delegates some who were opposed to the majority position. Even though all the votes had to be directed to one candidate or case unanimously on an issue, the minority position was at least represented in debate and in discussion.

What was basic in the debate over the unit rule was the question of the point in the process, from primaries and precinct caucuses on through to the convention, at which the minority position should be cut off. Abolition of the unit rule at the convention would not have affected the outcome of the voting in the 1968 convention much since in most states the minority, or opposing groups, had been eliminated at the county or state levels. This was the case in the Minnesota delegation in which, despite the fact that the state convention showed my strength to be very close to that of Vice President Humphrey, all of the at-large delegates selected at the state convention were his supporters. The convention overrode the objection of the minority, and the unit rule was rejected for the 1968 convention.

A second major challenge was that over the seating of the Mississippi delegation. The Mississippi challenge at the 1968 convention was based upon racial exclusion in the selection of delegates and was sustained as a similar challenge had been sustained in the 1964 Democratic Convention at Atlantic City, thus setting a desirable precedent. Action on the Georgia challenge (described in the previous chapter) also established a significant precedent for reform.

The many challenges and the report of the Hughes Commission (the Ad Hoc Commission on the Democratic Selection of Presidential Nominees) indicated the inequities of the delegate selection process. In February 1969, Mrs. Anne Wexler, who had been a delegate from Connecticut to the convention, described the abuses: "When we assembled in Chicago, we knew … that over 600 delegate votes out of 2,600 – almost 25% – would be cast by delegates selected two and four years before the convention. This meant that these delegates had little or no relation to the representative principle and could not possibly reflect current popular will."[40]

A major consequence of the challenges was the recommendation to the convention that the party set up a special committee to lay down rules of procedure for the selection of

---

[40] "One hundred and fifty-nine were sleeted by state convention delegates who had been chosen by state committees elected two and four years before, or by state committees constituting themselves as a state convention for the purpose of selecting national delegates.

"One hundred and ten were members of the Democratic National Committee, elected four years before.

"Sixty-five were chosen by state committees elected two years before.

"One hundred and twenty-five were chosen by state convention delegates picked by county, district, or precinct caucuses two years before the national convention.

"Eighty-six were chosen by district committees elected two years before, or by individuals chosen by precinct caucus winners elected two years before.

"Forty-one were chosen directly by the state chairman with the advice and consent of the governor--with no direct access to the people...

"The important fact is that almost 25% of the delegates to the Democratic National Convention were elected by systems which denied timely and direct access to the citizen and had no relationship to the candidates or issues that eventually emerged."

delegates to the 1972 convention so that state delegations would be fairly chosen and be representative of the democrats in the respective states.

This reform program was finally adopted by a roll call of 1,350 to 1,206 on August 27. The official party call to the 1972 convention is to specify that:

One, all convention delegates be elected through "procedures open to public participation." (The selection process used by several states in choosing those to attend the 1968 convention came under fire on the grounds that rank-and-file party members were either excluded or discouraged from participating.)

Two, the delegates be selected "within the calendar year of the convention," or no earlier than January 1972.

Three, the unit rule be eliminated at all levels of the delegate selection process down to the county or precinct level.

The war in Vietnam was the principal point of conflict at Chicago. From the outset, everyone knew that the fight over the Vietnam plank in the Democratic party platform would be abrasive. And it was.

The platform plank originally presented by my spokesmen at hearings held in Washington, D.C., said that the only possibility of peace lay in a negotiated settlement between the four principal parties: the South Vietnamese government in Saigon, the North Vietnamese government, the United States, and the National Liberation Front, or Vietcong. Any realistic settlement had to be a compromise between the conflicting groups and forces in Vietnam. Since neither side was able to defeat the other, both had to be prepared to yield some of their expressed objectives. In practical terms, this meant that any settlement which was both fair and realistic in light of the military situation must provide for a government in which all could have a share of power and responsibility. Any settlement which did not provide for this could only be won on the battlefield. The composition of the future government of South Vietnam had been the principal stake and the spur of battle for both sides in the conflict.

Any statement of principle or intention which did not deal with the future government of South Vietnam in specific terms was an evasion of responsibility. Statements of general principle and policy, however well-intentioned, did not or would not constitute a commitment to concrete terms necessary in any realistic foundation for peace.

We said that we would halt the bombing of North Vietnam immediately and all other attacks by sea or artillery on the territory of North Vietnam. It was evident that such a step was an essential prelude to any negotiations. Certainly a great nation could make a generous gesture toward peace, especially when there was no evidence that a halt to the bombing would gravely endanger our forces in the South. Next, we proposed that we immediately reduce the level of conflict in the south by halting the "search-and-destroy" operations and other offensive tactics by air and land which were resulting in widespread destruction of the Vietnamese countryside. And that we would not further widen the war either by increasing our forces or extending the conflict geographically.

Finally, we said that whether or not there was agreement on a cease-fire or troop withdrawal to fixed locations, we would propose a two-stage process toward a final peace. Ultimately, the government of South Vietnam should be freely chosen by all the people of that country. However, an agreement to hold such elections could only be realistically accepted when all the parties were confident that (a) free elections would be held, and (b) those elected would be allowed to assume power. This called for a new governing structure in Saigon. Just as we would not trust the NLF to hold free elections, it could not be expected to rely on the good faith of the existing military government of South Vietnam.

We proposed, therefore, to establish by negotiation a new government in South Vietnam containing all major elements of the population, including substantial participation by the National Liberation Front. It would be the job of this government to prepare for elections, under international supervision, with guarantees of a free election process. If the leaders of South Vietnam refused to agree to such a broadly based coalition, we would then withdraw our support and our forces since progress toward peace would no longer be possible.

Following the formation of a new government, all groups, including the National Liberation Front and all the Buddhists, were to be permitted to organize parties, designate candidates, and campaign throughout the country. Prior to such elections, all American and North Vietnamese forces would have withdrawn from the country, and there was to be a general cease-fire under some form of international supervision.

The government so selected would be free to determine the future course and relationship of South Vietnam, including its relations with North Vietnam.

With such a program we could have attained our only legitimate objective in South Vietnam: the self-determination of the Vietnamese people.

On August 19, the supporters of Vice President Humphrey presented to the Democratic Platform Committee the outlines of a compromise plank. This was put before the Platform Committee by Senator Edmund Muskie, and it proposed essentially that the Vice President would accept but not demand a cessation of the bombing of North Vietnam and the formation of a coalition government in South Vietnam. This was an avoidance of the issues. The point was not what one would accept but what one was prepared to propose for acceptance.

The proposal offered by Senator Muskie did not carry clear, official endorsement by the Vice President. Senator Muskie said that the Vice President had not indicated approval or disapproval, but suggested that the substance of this substitute had been discussed with him.

There was little reason for doubt as to who was directing and controlling the opposing forces. In Chicago, the outside influences showed plainly.

On the same day, a speech by President Johnson before the Veterans of Foreign Wars in Detroit strongly reaffirmed Administration policy. Two days later, Secretary Rusk appeared before the Platform Committee defending Administration policy. The combination of the Rusk appearance and President Johnson's statement indicated that the Administration was not prepared to accept anything but an endorsement of its policy by the convention.

On the same day that Rusk testified, the supporters of Senator Robert Kennedy proposed a Vietnam plank.

As the time for the floor fight drew closer, the need grew for a compromise which would unite the opponents of the war in Vietnam. Unity was more important than refinement of the plank.

The Vietnam plank on which we finally agreed with the Kennedy people by way of concession was drawn principally from a speech on Vietnam given by Senator Edward Kennedy in Massachusetts before the Worcester Chamber of Commerce on August 21. It contained these principal proposals:

First, an unconditional end to all bombing in North Vietnam, while continuing to provide in the South all necessary air and other support for American troops.

Second, negotiation of a mutual withdrawal of all United States forces and all North Vietnamese troops from South Vietnam, this phased withdrawal to take place in a relatively short period of time.

Third, encouragement of our South Vietnamese allies to negotiate a political reconciliation with the National Liberation Front looking toward a government which would be broadly representative of these and all elements in South Vietnamese society. The specific shape of this reconciliation was to be a matter for decision by the South Vietnamese, spurred into action, it was hoped, by the certain knowledge that the prop of American military support would soon be gone. In addition, the South Vietnamese were to assume increasing responsibility for determining their own political destiny. Meanwhile, the United States was to extend economic and other assistance to help rebuild the society which had been ravaged by war.

Fourth, reduction of casualties among American and Vietnamese soldiers and Vietnamese civilians by lowering the level of violence and reducing offensive operations in the Vietnamese countryside, thus enabling an early withdrawal of a significant number of our troops. In this way we could eliminate all foreign forces from South Vietnam. Our troops would leave and those of North Vietnam would also depart. It would be up to the South Vietnamese to achieve a political and social reconciliation among their warring peoples. We would also seek to enlist the participation of international authority to guarantee troop withdrawals and the granting of asylum to political refugees. Thus we could reasonably anticipate that as we left the Vietnamese would be well on the way to a solution of their own problems, and a government in which all could have a share of power and responsibility.

Some commentators quickly concluded that my spokesmen had given away an essential point of my position; namely, that of the acceptance of a coalition or a new government in South Vietnam. This was correct, but in my judgment the only way in which the major points of the plank we accepted could be achieved would be either through a new government or in anticipating the establishment of a new government, whether that government be called a coalition or a fusion government or simply a representative government in South Vietnam.

As the work of argument and compromise went on, it became clearer that the issue the convention would act on was not one of the language and terms of competing peace proposals. What was coming up was to be a vote of confidence in the Johnson administration.

Direct White House involvement grew bolder. Debate was interrupted by Hale Boggs, Chairman of the Platform Committee, for a special message from General Creighton W. Abrams, the U.S. commander in Vietnam. Boggs, Democratic Congressman from Louisiana, announced to the convention that he had asked at a White House briefing what additional casualties would result if the United States stopped the bombing unconditionally. The answer, he said now, was General Abrams' assessment that within two weeks North Vietnam would be able to increase its military capacity in the South fivefold.

This was not specifically responsive to the question. But it would seem now to require explanations, in view of the subsequent Administration decision to stop the bombing.

Chairman Boggs also involved the Soviet invasion of Czechoslovakia and tensions in the middle East, neither of which had any immediate bearing upon the issue of Vietnam.

The Administration's use of the invasion of Czechoslovakia during the convention helps to clarify the reason for my restrained response at the time of the invasion on August 21. I did not plan to make any statement about the invasion, but responded to the urging of some of the people in my campaign. I was rather severely criticized by the press and by some of my associates for not having responded, they said, "with sufficient emotion" to that incident, with not having exploited it, or at least used it, as an issue to help my campaign.

My response had been restrained for a number of reasons: first, because I had consistently throughout the campaign tried to keep the attention of the people and the politicians on the real issues and had tried to eliminate those things which were personal, distractions, or extraneous. The invasion of Czechoslovakia by the Russians was certainly not an issue upon which delegates should have been divided at the Democratic convention.

And I was restrained because I believed that at the time of the Hungarian revolt in 1956 statements of encouragement on the part of public officials of the United States had given false hopes to the Hungarian revolutionaries.

Finally, the Administration responded to the invasion as though it was a great international crisis, and the President's call for a midnight meeting of the National Security Council indicated to me that what he had in mind was using the Communist scare and the atmosphere of crisis to try to influence the convention to support his position on the war in Vietnam. The injection of Czechoslovakia into the debate at the convention sustained this earlier judgment on my part.

The fight on the platform plank did not go to the floor, and the showdown came in a vote on August 28. The Administration-supported position carried by a vote of 1,567 3/4 to 1,048 1/4.

The third important action at the convention was the nomination.

Our estimate was that I had approximately 800 votes. These were votes I had won in primaries, votes that had come over to me from Senator Robert Kennedy's people after his assassination, and scattered votes from the non-primary states. Nearly all of these had been committed to me before the convention began.

I appeared before a number of delegations at the convention, in some cases out of courtesy because they were supporting me, in others – like Indiana and Nebraska – in the hope that I could win over the delegates who in those primaries had been committed to Robert Kennedy. I also spoke before delegations from such states as Ohio, West Virginia, and Illinois. The critical question which came up in each of these meetings was whether or not I would support the nominee of the party. I said that it would depend upon the platform and what the candidate stood for. The response to this answer in nearly every delegation was a negative shaking of heads.

Senator George McGovern was an active candidate at the convention and for a short time before the convention assembled. In my opinion, his candidacy weakened my position at the convention, especially since he was publicly committed to supporting the party nominee chosen by the convention. At the convention, Channing Phillips, supported principally by the Washington, D.C. delegation, also became a candidate and his name was put in nomination.

On Wednesday night, I received 601 votes and Vice President Humphrey received 1,760 on the first ballot. (Senator McGovern received 146 1/2; Channing Phillips, 67 1/2.) Most of the votes that went to Senator McGovern would have gone to me if McGovern had not been a candidate. A few of those that went to Phillips would probably have gone to the Vice President. Our original 800 estimate was about right.

There were several things in the course of the convention which I think deserve some comment and explanation. One was the move to support Senator Edward Kennedy of Massachusetts.

I saw no evidence of the direct involvement of Senator Kennedy himself in this effort. There is little question that Vice President Humphrey would have been most happy to have Senator Kennedy as his vice-presidential running mate, and the early statements, if not moves, by Mayor Daley and others were directed to this end.

Senator Edward Kennedy himself seemed to stand aside from the convention effort. The principal evidence of interest or concern was the presence of his brother-in-law Stephen Smith, who was somewhat active in the preparation of the Vietnam plank and in the planning for its presentation upon the floor of the convention.

165

At no time, either in the period following the assassination of Senator Robert Kennedy or during the convention, did I have any offer or indication of support in any formal way from what might be called a recognized spokesman of Senator Edward Kennedy nor of what was left of Senator Robert Kennedy's organization. (Some of Robert Kennedy's people, of course, had come over to me on an individual basis, both in the national effort and also in a number of the states.)

A conversation between Steve Smith and me has been reported. I did not initiate action to see Smith nor does it appear that he initiated action to see me. In my opinion, intermediaries suggested to Steve Smith that I wanted to see him in much the same way that they suggested to me that he wished to see me. In the course of the convention week I talked to Richard Goodwin occasionally. Goodwin, I knew, throughout the campaign – both before and after the death of Senator Robert Kennedy – had been in touch with those generally included in the Kennedy organization. He was a kind of double agent but was identified as such and played an honest role. During the convention I had spoken to him a number of times on the platform fight and also, as rumors of the move to draft Senator Edward Kennedy began to develop, asked him about the rumors. When I first asked him about this matter, he said that he had not talked with Senator Edward Kennedy, but that he was sure that the Senator was not a candidate, that he did not want the nomination at this point, and that he did not believe that Senator Edward Kennedy would allow himself to be drafted in opposition to me. He said, further, that he did not think that Senator Edward Kennedy would allow his name to go before the convention under any circumstances.

I said, in reflecting upon the convention situation as I saw it developing, that Senator Kennedy and I together might be able to win and that I could be for him as a nominee.

I was certain before the convention began that barring some unforeseen occurrence I could not be nominated. This was especially true when it became evident that many of the delegates who had been committed by primaries to Senator Robert Kennedy would not support me. The nomination by the Republicans of Richard Nixon, a weaker candidate than Governor Rockefeller would have been, also gave strength to the Humphrey candidacy. I was still concerned that we make the best possible showing on the nomination. I hoped that my showing and the threat of Senator Kennedy as a possible nominee would put greater pressure on Vice President Humphrey to adopt a more liberal plank on Vietnam.

On Tuesday, I raised the question of the Edward Kennedy campaign again with Dick Goodwin. Goodwin then arranged a meeting with Steve Smith, who that afternoon came to my room in the Conrad Hilton. After some discussion of the Vietnam plank, we discussed an Edward Kennedy candidacy. Smith did not ask me to support Senator Kennedy nor did he suggest that he was running a campaign for him. The conversation reached a point at which I did say I could not get a nomination and that since Edward Kennedy and I had approximately the same views, I was willing to ask my delegates to vote for him. I wanted to have my name placed in nomination, especially for the sake of the people who had campaigned for me for most of the year, and to have a run on the first ballot, but that if this was not possible or if it would weaken the cause, I would forego the nomination and a first-ballot test. I did say, that because of the campaign which had been run against me, I could not have done the same for Senator Robert Kennedy. I did not hear either directly or indirectly from Steve Smith or any other spokesman for Edward Kennedy again during the convention.

The response of the Kennedy group to my offer came, I suppose, when on Wednesday morning Pierre Salinger reported that Stephen Smith, previously uninvolved in the McGovern campaign, was now making phone calls in behalf of McGovern. Salinger also said that Senator Edward Kennedy had informed McGovern of his plans to issue a disclaimer of any interest in a candidacy.

At that time influential Democratic politicians were still not flatly committed to Vice President Humphrey. Mayor Daley, for example, was still publicly uncommitted, as were some other delegates, if not delegations. It would have been difficult, I think, for Senator Kennedy to have obtained the nomination that late in the convention, but a boom for him on Tuesday afternoon would certainly have strengthened those who were advancing the anti-Vietnam plank that night.

On August 28, the day of the balloting for the presidential candidate, Senator Kennedy issued a final statement from his Washington office in which he asked the convention to choose its nominee from the candidates already in contention. He gave, as he had in the months previous, "personal and family reasons" for his withdrawal.

With his withdrawal, the question of the nomination became simply that of running out time and of calling the roll.

As the time for placing my name in nomination approached, the television sets in the hotel showed more and more trouble on the floor of the convention and more and more trouble in the streets. As the violence spread, I put in a call for Governor Harold Hughes of Iowa, the man prepared to put my name in nomination. I asked him to withdraw my name. I hoped that this action, if publicized, would help to ease tensions in the convention and in the city. But when I reached him, the roll call was already in progress or was just about to be called. I asked Governor Hughes, who had by then nominated me, to use his own discretion about withdrawing the nomination in view of conditions on the floor. He believed it was too late to help matters much.

In his nomination speech he said that our campaigning had "caused a clean wind of hope to blow across this land" – a hope that our country could mend its internal wounds and change from a collision course in world affairs. Hughes added that my "steely intellectual approach" meant, in effect, "We must think our problems through before we can see them through."

He said: "We must have *bold* leadership, willing to undertake the basic changes in our political system that are so necessary to its survival.

"We must seek a leader who can arrest the polarization in our society – the alienation of the blacks from the whites, the haves from the have-nots, and the old from the young.

"We must choose a man with the wisdom and the courage to change the direction of our foreign policy before it commits us for eternity to a maze of foreign involvements without clear purpose or moral justification.

"But most of all, the man we nominate must embody the aspirations of all those who seek to lift mankind to its highest potential. He must have that rare, intangible quality that can lift up our hearts and cleanse the soul of this troubled country.

"Gene McCarthy is such a man...

"We Democrats cannot claim to have found him. The people found Gene McCarthy for us. They found him; they followed him; they have urged him on us. He is more accurately the people's candidate than any other man in recent history."

This was followed by other, and elaborately flattering, largely doomed praise. The young Representative from Georgia, Julian Bond, seconded my nomination, saying that if it were not for the McCarthy campaign, "we would be meeting under very different conditions" – not an open convention, not a testing of procedures, not "considering our national priorities – we would be rubber-stamping the policies of the past four years. And, above all, we would not have had a national judgment on the war in Vietnam – an overwhelming rejection of a war the American people never chose and never supported – a rejection of the way we have carried on that war, a rejection of the role of the military in our foreign policy, a rejection of empty slogans and misleading propaganda.

"The American people are demanding a fundamental change that, I think, is the great lesson of the campaign of 1968. They are demanding an end to the politics of unfulfilled promises and exaggeration, an end to the politics of manipulation and control...

"We have seen," Bond said, "all that is best in America demanding an end to the immoral war in Vietnam and a full commitment to all those who are excluded in our country, to all those who are injured or insulted, to all who go hungry and powerless in the midst of affluence and luxury."

John Kenneth Galbraith spoke briefly and effectively:

"Mr. Chairman," he began, "at this convention we have sufficiently used speech, both to convey meaning and, on occasion, to suppress meaning. So, I will be brief. Only one man dared to challenge McCarthy in the primaries. That was Bob Kennedy.

"No one approaches Eugene McCarthy in the affection of the voters. Only the leaders and managers of our party, only those who put party orthodoxy and personal vanity above ideas reject him.

"...in all of the states where the people select the delegates in the primaries, the delegates voted overwhelmingly for peace.

"And, likewise, where the people had selected the delegates, the delegates are for McCarthy...

"He has shown that resort to violence first destroys those who employ it. His campaign has shown that this may not yet be the age of John Milton, but he has shown that it is not the age of John Wayne or even of John Connally.

"The American people have responded to Gene McCarthy's counsel. My generation favors him. So, overwhelmingly, does the next generation, those who will be in your seats, our seats, four and eight years from now.

"For you, we, no more than other men, have been endowed with immortality either.

"I beg that you heed this simple fact. Democrats do not reject the will of the majority of the people. Politicians do not reject the will of the majority. Old men do not reject the young – not, at least, if they are wise. So let us be true to Democratic faith. Let us be wise. Above all, let us try to be young. And let us, accordingly, nominate and elect Gene McCarthy."

Another occurrence at the convention which I think deserves some comment was the interview I gave to the Knight newspapers on August 27, in which I said that I did not have the votes to win the nomination. This was reported as a great political mistake. I do not think it was. First of all, estimates of how the voting would go were rather clear. Newspaper stories that my aides spent the night of August 27 working frantically to offset the interview were sheer nonsense. Second, I said what I did because I hoped that the statement might take the edge off the expectations of the young people who had come to Chicago and prepare them for the defeat. I did not, when I gave the interview, foresee the kind of violence that marked the later stages of the convention.

I did not anticipate that after Vice President Humphrey had been nominated serious beatings would take place on the street outside the Hilton Hotel and in Grant Park, across Michigan Avenue, or that under the direction of Dr. William Davidson and my brother, Austin, who was also a surgeon, an emergency hospital would be set up on the fifteenth floor of the Hilton Hotel, and the victims of the violence, both in the street and in the park, would be given emergency treatment.

The day after the nomination, Thursday, was a day for winding up the convention and awaiting the choice of the vice-president candidate, for closing down our headquarters, and preparing for the departure of our campaign workers.

I spent most of Thursday speaking: first to those who had supported me – volunteers, staff, and delegates, and to the Minnesota delegation.

In the afternoon I crossed Michigan Avenue to speak to those who were assembled in Grant Park. I knew Grant Park from a description of it in the book *Morte d'Urban* by J. F. Powers.

> *Give me Chicago. The most beautiful sound I know is the sound of whistles on Michigan Avenue at dusk, especially in the fall. I like to sit in Grant Park and listen to the cops calling to each other like nightingales. You know the Chicago whistle? Wheeeeeuhhhhweeeuuhh. I'd say it's a musical instrument, related to the clarinet, piccolo, oboe, and also related to the old-tie train whistle. It'd scare the hell out of you – rightly played, that is – if you didn't see the Wrigley Building. I like to see Michigan Avenue shining wet at night. I like to come out of the Blackstone or the Drake at dusk, especially in the fall, with two or three good ones in me, and hear those whistles, the mush and the whine of rubber, the distant roar – it always seems to be centered over LaSalle Street, to the south, but it's like a haze you can never see and never touch.*

By far the largest number assembled in the park were students, from Chicago and from outside of that city, who had come as witness to their concern. There was also a number of representatives of the Youth International Party. I sensed great disappointment and some frustration but no anger in the park that afternoon. The Secret Service did not object to the visit, although a day earlier they had raised serious objections, saying that the Chicago police would take over any such move on my part. They advised me against the risk.

I encouraged the group in the park not to give up hope. I listed positive achievements from my campaign and theirs. I urged them to become active in congressional campaigns, especially in the campaigns of Senators who were running for re-election and supported my position on the war, and finally told them that I thought that when I had opened the box to what America was I had found that the people of this nation were not wanting.

The choice of Senator Muskie as the vice presidential nominee was no surprise, if for no other reason than that I knew the Secret Servicemen were being transferred to the hotel area in which he was staying.

Early in August I had been approached by one or two of Vice President Humphrey's supporters, inquiring about my interest in the vice presidency, and I told them that I had no interest, and my recommendation was that I not be asked so that I would not have to say no and the Vice President would be under no compulsion to explain that I had turned down an offer. I had several meetings with the Vice President during the course of the campaign, and the names that figured most prominently were those of Governor Richard Hughes of New Jersey and Senator Muskie of Maine.

A representative of the Vice President called me on Thursday, asking me to appear on the platform with him that evening when he was to give his acceptance speech. I declined. To accept would have been fine for a show of party unity but, clearly inconsistent with the position I had taken both before and during the convention. It would certainly have been a disillusioning betrayal of trust to many of my supporters and would have eliminated the last slight possibility that by withholding support I might move the nominee of the party after the convention to indicate his position on the war and to assert his independence of the Administration.

On Thursday night all seemed quiet. My senior staff members continued to carry out their supervisory responsibilities on those floors where the young people were quartered in the Hilton Hotel. I went to bed about midnight and, without being called, woke up some time before five o'clock on Friday morning. I noticed small, warming fires still burning in the park across the street, and thought it might be well to go over and talk with those still keeping vigil. I called the Secret Service to alert them to my plans, and said I would meet them at the command station on my floor within a few minutes. When I reached the command desk, one of my young workers, George Yumich, was sitting there with his head bandaged and bleeding. He told me there was trouble on the fifteenth floor. I went to that floor and found the lobby in panic, and number of young people, especially girls, in tears.

The story, as I was able to piece it together from witnesses, was essentially this. It had been quiet on the floor. Some of the students were sleeping in the corridors, some were in their rooms, some were playing bridge. Then the elevator opened and some fifteen or twenty Chicago policemen, accompanied by hotel agents, burst into the floor lobby and proceeded to open doors and herd people into the space adjacent to the elevators. This was done without warrant or legal process. Those who had been gathered by the police were taken by elevator to the main lobby of the hotel. There they were again subject to police brutality of the kind described in the New York *Post* (August 30, 1968), which reported that at one point a policeman broke from the cordon surrounding the sitting youngsters and began clubbing one of them. This was done, in so far as anyone could tell, at random and without provocation. Mary Margaret Gillen, wife of a campaign aide to Vice President Humphrey, said she protested to another patrolman. "Is that against the law, Mrs. Bubble-Eyes?" the policeman replied, according to Mrs. Gillen. Finally, another officer pulled the policeman away from the youth, saying, "What are you doing?"

As soon as I learned on the fifteenth floor that there was more trouble on the main floor of the hotel, I went to that lobby. The young people were still under orders, huddled on the floor and surrounded by a ring of helmeted police; some of them bloodied by the beatings they had received from the police, and some of the girls were near hysteria.

I asked for the officer in charge. There was no answer. When no one assumed responsibility for the police action, I directed the young people to leave the lobby in groups of three or four and to return to their rooms. Upon returning to the fifteenth floor, we found that nearly all the rooms had been locked by hotel security men, and it took thirty to forty-five minutes to obtain keys from the hotel to open the doors so that the young people could go back into their quarters.

This is the story of one of the rooms on the invaded fifteenth floor on Friday morning, as reported by Dermot A. Ryan, who had come to Chicago from Ireland to help in my campaign. Ryan was no radical youth, but an Irish businessman approximately forty years old. He filed the following affidavit:

On the morning of Friday, August 30, at approximately 6 A.M., I was in a suite on the 15th floor of the Conrad Hilton Hotel. I had been there for approximately one and one-half hours. There were approximately sixteen people in the room. During this time nothing had taken place beyond quiet conversation about the Democratic Convention. No one had thrown anything whatsoever from the windows, nor had anyone leaned out of the windows. There were not more than three or four people looking out the windows.

Suddenly, a number of policemen strode violently into the room. In raucous, belligerent voices they demanded that the people in the room close the windows and leave the windows. The people protested quietly and were not aggressive. They explained that nothing had been thrown from the windows. The people closed the windows and moved to the other side of the room. The police then ordered them out of the room. They obeyed, and were herded with many unnecessary pushes and unnecessary shouts to the lobby of the 15th floor.

While in this room, I showed my key to room 1229 and my press pass, but was told "everybody out." In the lobby the people asked to be permitted to go to the 23rd floor. They were told "nobody goes anywhere but to the ground floor." About one-half of the people entered the elevator, including myself. As I entered the elevator, I received a violent push in the back from a policeman which sent me staggering.

I wish to say, under oath, clearly and explicitly that none of the people either shouted, used bad language, called names or said that they would not obey police instructions. I was personally harassed, both in the room and in the passage. As I stood in the elevator, I saw a policeman in the lobby, who had not been struck or acted towards in any way aggressively, raise a stick high in the air and bring it down with every ounce of strength he possessed on the head of a young person. This took place not more than twelve feet from me. I clearly heard a resounding crack as the stick struck the person's head.

I can testify with utter certainty that until this time there had been nothing but peaceful explanation and obedience to the police orders. While in the room in which I and the other people had been sitting, it had been indicated by the police, after they arrived, that a particular police captain was in charge. I took his name and number and can identify him.

In addition to this incident, I was a personal eye-witness:

(1) To the police in front of the Conrad Hilton Hotel at approximately 10:15 P.M., Thursday, August 29, firing not less than five tear gas bombs at a time when I could see no sign of aggressiveness on the part of people who were protesting. At this time I was standing quite near the front of the protestors while interviewing two of them on behalf of the Sunday Press, an Irish newspaper.

(2) On Wednesday, August 28, at approximately 8 P.M., I was standing looking through the second floor level windows of the Blackstone Hotel at Michigan Avenue. I saw a policeman bring his stick down with all his strength upon a person who was attempting to leave the scene of the protest.

Finally, I wish to state that prior to the police arrival at the suite on the 15th floor, I had been interviewing the people in that suite on behalf of the Sunday Press. They had specifically informed that they had been working for McCarthy in various cities throughout the United States for from upwards of three months. They were not demonstrators and they had not come to Chicago to demonstrate.

After getting the young people from the main-floor lobby back into their rooms, I went again to the lobby on the fifteenth floor to see bloody carpets, a bloodstained bridge table, and my supporters sitting around on sofas and the floor shaking their heads in disbelief. On boy strummed a guitar hesitantly as they began to sing, "We Shall Overcome," and then, I am embarrassed to recall, "We Love Gene McCarthy."...they had lost some blood, and a few more ideals, but not, happily, their sense of humor. One girl said that when the police broke in, she was simply playing bridge and that a 21-point hand had been destroyed by the raid.

All inquiries concerning the fifteenth floor failed to turn up any reason for the massive police raid at five o'clock in the morning; in fact, they failed to turn up even minor irregularities. If there had been any, the proper way to proceed would have been through the use of the hotel detectives, aided, if necessary, by one or two policemen. What did occur was the massive invasion of privacy – action without precedent in the history of American politics. Even attempts to put calls through to me had been blocked by the hotel switchboard.

Most of the people who were on the fifteenth floor had campaigned with me in at least one or more states across the country and had been tested and proven. We had never had an incident in any city or in any hotel or motel from New Hampshire through California. And on the night of the 29th, we had, as was our custom, a number of adults alert for any possible trouble.

I had planned to leave Chicago about ten o'clock on Friday morning, but on receiving warnings that the police planned more arrests, if not more raids, on my campaign workers as soon as I or my senior staff members were gone, I delayed my departure until we were sure that all of our people had left the hotels, had left Chicago, or at least were beyond the reach of the Chicago police. As our chartered plane flew out of Midway Airport about six o'clock, the pilot said, "We are leaving Prague."

The Secret Servicemen who had been assigned to me following the assassination of Senator Kennedy in California were under orders to remain with me until our first stop after leaving Chicago. That, they said, could be any place in the world if we were prepared to fly on. We were not, of course, and after landing Washington and escorting me to my residence in Washington that night, their responsibility and their vigil were ended.

The spirit of the young people in Chicago was never so clear to me as when, after the campaign, I received a poem sent by Sue Brown of Syracuse University, not as a tribute to me, but as an expression of the simplicity, courage, and commitment of the people in the campaign of 1968.

In the park a soft rush of wings –
Pigeons play tag with balloons.
Fountains gently burst into crystal fireworks.
A bit of laughing smoke named Terrance
Drifts in a quiet lake of green and gold.
A bit of smiling wind named Melissa
Sits in the petals of the fountain.
The park is filled with bells and thoughts.
Their guitar strings tremble with wishes.
Their hands hold trust.
A man comes into the park,
Bringing wheatfields and candles
And gentle white horses.
And he takes the gift
Of their bells
And their trust,
And protects it
With a shield of promises....

II
The balloons are left behind,
And vanish into the sky.

The people in the park
Sling their guitars and their questions,
Over their shoulders,
And march
To fight the gray men
Who use brass bands
To cover the sound of guns.
The gray men wave signs,
And spin webs of barbed wire
Where questions are caught and strangled.
Night in a blue helmet
Crashes through the park,
Blindly slashing at trees.
The birds rise
In a rushing gray cloud of panic.
Terrance shouts some four-letter word.
A club swings,
Battering the word
Into the shape
Of an empty slogan.
Melissa cries.
A club swings,
Battering the tears
Into the shape
Of an empty cheer.
Innocence fades like drifting smoke.
The clubs swing
At blue jeans and beards,
Wanting to batter them
Into mindless gray.
Eyes full of strangled questions
Gaze through a forest of bayonets,
Waiting for the tanks.
A guitar sings;
A bell whispers.
The clubs swing,
And the silence is filled
With brass bands,
And speeches,
And guns.
Gray men with technicolor masks
Scream out pious excuses,
Swinging their parliamentary clubs,
Getting tangled in their own barbed wire,
And applauding their imagined victory...

III
The gentle man is not applauding
There are no brass bands
For his real victory,
For those who love him
Offer their bells
And with his children
He returns to the park,
To mend the trampled questions,
And touch the broken guitars
With songs of green of gold.

The Choice

What I did after Chicago was indicated in the program I set out for my delegates and supporters in Chicago on August 29. What we must do, I told them, was to go on, to continue to present to the people as best we could for judgment between then and November the issues we had been raising for nine months. We would continue to demand explanations from the candidates. More important than that, we would support those candidates, particularly for the United States Senate, who had stood with us and to identify the issues with candidates. "I hesitate to say that the fate of the republic may rest upon the United States Senate," I said. "It might cause great grief in the land and despondency." The fact is that this may have been true, particularly as far as foreign policy is concerned. We must get from every institution that we have developed – whether it be the Senate or the House of Representatives or the Supreme Court – the fullest possible measure of its strength and power. I disapprove of the seeming transfer of power to the executive branch of the government. It is not really power the branch has taken; it has simply taken all of the weapons – more than it can use – which is something different. "We do not have necessarily the strongest President but the best-armed one. The fact is that he was so well armed that there were no arms left for the troops. That did not make for good government," I said, "and we know it did not make for a good Democratic party."

"We can continue to raise the same issues for judgment," I urged, "and identify ourselves with the candidacies of men like Paul O'Dwyer and Harold Hughes. If we can elect candidates who are with us on the issues and send them to the Senate, we can again begin to establish what the drafters of the Constitution envisaged: a body of responsible men who have a share of obligation and also of power over the foreign policy of this country. We have not lost the fight on the issue. We have not lost

179

it in terms of the potential of the American system to respond in a time of need."

There was a great upsurge in Richard Nixon's popular rating after the Republican convention, but the narrowing of the gap between his and Vice President Humphrey's popularity rating that was widely anticipated immediately after the Democratic convention did not occur. On the contrary, Vice President Humphrey's popularity dropped.[41]

This decline should not have surprised many people in view of what had happened at the convention. It strengthened the desire on the part of some to get me to endorse Vice President Humphrey. But there were three factors keeping me from openly supporting him.

One was the way in which my delegates had been treated on the convention floor and also the way in which my campaign workers had been abused in the Hilton Hotel. I, of course, did not hold the Vice President wholly responsible for what Mayor Daley had done. I felt, however, that he could have had more influence on the way in which the convention was handled, both at the convention hall and in the city of Chicago, if he had not been so concerned with holding the support of Mayor Daley and the Illinois delegation and if he had been somewhat more willing to challenge the Johnson control over the convention. His concern not to offend Daley, was somewhat understandable, since almost every time Daley spoke of what he really wanted, he implied that he was not wholly committed to the candidacy of Vice President Humphrey.[42]

The second consideration was that some of the congressional candidates who shared my views and whom I had promised to support – most notably Paul O'Dwyer of New York – were denying support to the national Democratic ticket. I believed that I would have hurt O'Dwyer's cause and the cause of others had I immediately supported the Humphrey candidacy.

---

[41] In the July 29 Harris poll, the Vice President led Mr. Nixon 41 to 36%. A month later on August 27, Mr. Nixon had moved ahead of Mr. Humphrey 40 to 34%, and on September 23, although Mr. Nixon remained about the same, the Vice President had dropped to 31%. The Gallup poll, over the same period, showed a similar decline. On July 11, Humphrey led Nixon 40 to 35%. On August 21, just before the convention, the Vice President had declined to 29% against Mr. Nixon's 45%. And on September 29, the Vice President had dropped to 28%.

[42] After the election, on March 5, 1969. Daley said, upon hearing of a Humphrey remark suggesting that Daley's support had been less than wholehearted, "We should have had a stronger candidate."

180

The third was the issue of the war itself. The Vice President's position remained essentially the same as that which President Johnson had been maintaining when I challenged his candidacy in the New Hampshire primary. What happened at the convention had simply reinforced that position.

In order to give the Vice President as open a run as possible, my supporters and I did whatever we could to keep my name from appearing on the ballot in the twenty-five states where efforts were being made to have my name listed. The only ballots I seriously considered having my name on were the New York and the California. There was a possibility that I could carry California and New York, and that if the election were thrown into the House of Representatives – as some people believed it could be – these states might have constituted the balance of power in a House election and offset the anticipated Wallace effect.

After two weeks of meetings designed to terminate various activities connected with the campaign and convention, I took a ten-day vacation in Europe, after which I covered the World Series for *Life* magazine. I then returned to campaigning in behalf of candidates for the Senate and the House of Representatives in New York, California, Oregon, Alaska, Ohio, Wisconsin, Illinois, Massachusetts, and New Hampshire.

My appearances on campuses were met with much the same enthusiasm that had greeted them before Chicago. I was pleased to find many of the student campaign workers involved in the congressional races, as I had urged. Although some of them had joined my adult workers in supporting Vice President Humphrey and Senator Muskie, the hard core of my support declined to endorse the national ticket.

I remained hopeful that despite convention action the Vice President might take a more acceptable stand on the war in Vietnam. The convention, of course, was the point at which a change in policy should have been made. If Senator Edward Kennedy and some of the other presidential and congressional candidates had not been so quick to say that they would support the nominee of the party, no matter who he was, the likelihood of the adoption of a strong Vietnam plank would have been increased. And if they withheld their support they might have effected a change even after the convention.

In this interim period no concentrated efforts were made to get me to support the Democratic ticket. I received about the same amount of mail from those urging me to support the Vice President, those urging me not to support him and those who wanted some kind of guidance or direction. One group of approximately thirty American Negroes, including the Reverend

Martin Luther King, Sr., Bayard Rustin, Charles Evers, Mayor Carl Stokes of Cleveland, ran a full-page ad in the New York *Times* on October 24, calling upon me to support Vice President Humphrey. There were some efforts through organized labor, too, especially in my own state, and some direct approaches of the kind indicated in these excerpts from three letters sent by the same person between September 4 and October 14:

On September 4, 1968

You have achieved a great political triumph. Indeed you have pulled off a political miracle. You have emerged as a great national figure and indeed a world figure.

May I now plead with you to support Hubert? I think you owe this to the party. More importantly, I think you owe it to the country.

If Nixon becomes president, due to your failure to support Hubert, you will have much to answer for – to your conscience, to your family, to your state, your party and your country.

May I say that I also feel strongly that the support of Hubert is in your own personal interest? It will greatly build up your potential for the future.

On October 4, 1968

I also hear that you have taken a spot on TV on October 8. I earnestly hope that this portends your endorsement of Hubert. I think you have a wonderful line which you can take:

"I have been in Europe. I've been trying to get our country in better perspective after the two conventions. I have had the opportunity to think about the grave problems that confront us in this hour of tragedy and crisis.

"I have decided that I owe it to the country to endorse my former colleague in the Senate from Minnesota. This is not only because of my own respect for his record and his integrity, though I have differed with him seriously in recent times, but, more importantly, it is because of my feeling that it would be a disaster if our country turned to Nixon and Agnew for leadership."

Then light into Nixon and Agnew.

And finally on October 14, 1968

182

I do not think you can know how many of your friends agree with the attached editorial in the New York Times. (October 11, 1968, "Political Dropouts") I hope you will not be confused by the adulation and cheers which you received at a dinner such as that for O'Dwyer the other night. You are going to lose very powerful friends who want to number themselves as your supporters – if you do not come out in strong and vigorous opposition to Nixon and Wallace.

These three letters in sequence rather curiously covered the three classical biblical temptations – the offer of material gain, the offer of political power, and the promise of respect and honor. I do not mean to leave the impression that I overcame these great temptations with any show of spirit because I cannot recall having seen two of the letters until after the election was over.

As the time of the election approached, it appeared that no concession would be forthcoming from the Vice President and that the only choice left me was between the position which he was then taking and that of Mr. Nixon.

At a meeting of the New Democratic Coalition in Minneapolis on October 5, it was reported that I had laid down four conditions for my support of Vice President Humphrey. These were: a halt to the bombing of North Vietnam; support for a South Vietnam election in which the National Liberation Front would participate; a reform of the draft, allowing noncombatant status to persons opposed to military service on moral as well as religious grounds; and electoral reform of the Democratic party. This statement was made without authorization on my part and did not accurately present the conditions which I had in mind. Subsequently, at a dinner for Paul O'Dwyer on October 8, I stated clearly what my position was. We proved something, I said, along the campaign trail in the primaries. We proved something about what the Democrats wanted presented to the nation by their party in November. And what we proved in those states for the most part was not accepted in our convention in Chicago. So in the weeks since, we have had to prove again that what was indicated in the primaries before the convention is what the people of this country should have, and want to have, presented to them. There are three vital areas for decision and participation.

First, the issues of the war in Vietnam itself. We are not really satisfied by the grand intentions of free elections at some time in the future or qualified statements about stopping the bombing. We have to be willing to accept a new government in South Vietnam because that is what the war has been about.

The second area is the sharing of more of the burden of moral responsibility and in some cases the guilt that rests upon the young people of this country who are called upon to fight the war. We must give to those who are called and who do respond at least a genuine hope that they are participating in an action that will be brought to an end. And we must also do something about the draft itself. It is not enough to say that we are going to pick people on the basis of a lottery. That does not answer any questions. Nor is it enough to say that some time in the future we will have a professional army; that raises more questions than it answers.

The third area I described was improvement in the political processes of this country: "So that we shall not have another Chicago, so that we will not have to fight over one man-one vote and whether we have a representative convention again, let us take care of those problems along the way. Only thus can we have a convention in which the Democratic party sets an example and does not run behind the nation but ahead in its trust in peoples' judgment."

In the course of the campaign, the Vice President had come reasonably close to supporting the changes in the administration of the draft which I was recommending and had even reached the point of saying that he would replace General Hershey as Director of the Selective Service System. Although he had hedged at the convention, he did, when it was over, take a very firm stand in favor of reform of party procedures. It was on the basic question of the war and how to bring it to an end that we continued to disagree.

I set the day following my scheduled Madison Square Garden speech of October 28 as the time I would announce my position on the national ticket. By that time the Vice President might at least have moved to an open endorsement of a bombing halt as preliminary to discussions. I did not believe I should announce before the New York rally, which was planned principally in support of the Senate race of Paul O'Dwyer, who was still not supporting the national ticket. Any endorsement by me of the national ticket before then would certainly have hurt his rally if not his candidacy.

On October 29, I gave as positive and affirmative an endorsement to the Humphrey candidacy as I could in conscience give:

*I have been urged by many persons to support the
Democratic candidate for the presidency. I have been urged by*

many not to support him. I have also been asked by many to suggest to them how they should vote.

Most Americans today, I think, are quite capable of making their own decision about the presidency. Many, if not most, of my supporters have, I believe, already made this decision. To those, however, who may be waiting for my decision, I wish to announce that on November 5 I intend to vote for Vice President Hubert Humphrey and recommend that those who have waited for this statement of my position do the same.

The position of the Democratic candidate on the principal issues that have been raised in my campaign – namely, the ending of the war in Vietnam, the demilitarization of United States government policy, and the reform of the draft laws so as to make them responsive to individual conscience, together with the reform of the political process within the Democratic party – falls far short of what I think it should be. The choice, however, is between Vice President Hubert Humphrey and Richard Nixon. My support of Hubert Humphrey is based on two considerations:

The first, that on the basis of what he has stood for in the past and what he has said about domestic problems in this campaign, Hubert Humphrey has shown a better understanding of our domestic needs and stronger will to act than has been shown by Richard Nixon.

The second, that with Hubert Humphrey as President, the possibility of scaling down the arms race and reducing military tensions in the world would be much greater than it *would be with Richard Nixon as President of the United States.*

I wish to make it as clear as I can to the young people and to the others who supported me this year after I asked them to test the established political processes of the Democratic party that I will not make that request of them again unless those processes have clearly been changed. I wish to assure them that I intend to work to that end, and, at the same time, to continue to discuss the substantive issues of American politics.

In order to make it clear that this endorsement is in no way intended to reinstate me in the good graces of the Democratic party leaders, nor in any way to suggest my having forgotten or condoned the things that happened both before Chicago and at Chicago, I announce at this time that I will not be a candidate of my party for re-election to the Senate from the state of Minnesota in 1970. Nor will I seek the presidential nomination of the Democratic party in 1972.

185

The Vice President expressed satisfaction over my endorsement, and the endorsement was generally well received by my supporters, although some of them protested it. Paul O'Dwyer continued his independent course. Five persons who had worked hard in my campaign – Sam Brown, Paul Gorman, Martin Peretz, Robert Pirie, and Harold Ickes – signed a dissenting statement that was representative of the views of those who disagreed with my action. It read: "We will not vote for Hubert Humphrey…We make that choice in principle, not pique – to sustain the purpose, the continuity and the moral force of the movement Eugene McCarthy stood for in America."

In the early evening of October 31, President Johnson appeared on national television to announce that he had "ordered that all air, naval, and artillery bombardment of North Vietnam cease as of 8 A.M., Washington time, Friday morning." Thus was the bombing halt finally achieved on November 1, just four days before the national election. It had been preceded by extensive activity by our negotiators in Paris and conferences at the White House between the President and the top field commander in Vietnam, General Abrams. The President spoke that night, too, of "hopeful events" that had occurred in South Vietnam and of "progress" in the Paris talks.

President Johnson's announcement of a bombing halt was endorsed immediately by Vice President Humphrey. With the announcement of the bombing halt, Paul O'Dwyer gave his support to the candidacy of Vice President Humphrey. If the announcement had come sooner or if Vice President Humphrey had spoken up for such a halt, I could have endorsed his candidacy earlier.

In the closing days of the campaign, I spoke for the national ticket in California, Alaska, and Oregon, and especially for senatorial candidates Cranston, Gruening, and Morse. And so at last we went on to the election itself.

Poets and Politicians

Clemenceau, in speaking about the Dreyfus case in France, said that a country cannot be ruled by its philosophers, poets, artists, or scholars, but it is perilous for it to turn on them, to reject their judgment, to ignore their warnings. If it did not turn against the scholars and artists, the Democratic party for the first time in the twentieth century did in 1967 and 1968 reject their warning.

My campaign was, of course, not the first in recent times in which poetry was used. John Kennedy, in the campaign of 1960, regularly quoted from the works of Robert Frost and T. S. Eliot. His favorite Eliot quotation was from *The Rock*: "And the wind shall say: 'These were decent people. Their only monument the asphalt road and a thousand lost golf balls,'" which he followed with his own statement, "We can do better than that." And from the Robert Frost poem "Stopping by Woods on a Snowy Evening":

> *But I have promises to keep,*
> *And miles to go before I sleep.*
> *And miles to go before I sleep.*

He also quoted occasionally from the writings of the nineteenth-century English poet Arthur Clough.

Senator Robert Kennedy used poetry quite freely in his speeches. Speaking in Indianapolis, following the assassination of Martin Luther King, Jr., he quoted what were said to be his favorite lines from his favorite poet Aeschylus:

> *Even in our sleep, pain which cannot forget falls drop by*
> *drop upon the heart until in our own despair, against our own*
> *will, comes wisdom through the awful grace of God.*

The poet most openly identified with my campaign was Robert Lowell, who spent a few days in nearly every one of the states in which primaries were held and who was also with me in

187

Chicago. I had known Lowell personally for many years and known him as a poet for much longer. Poets are generally good company, and especially so when most of one's day is given, as it was in the campaign, to the practicalities of politics. His role was not that of a political adviser, nor did he propose quotations from literature for inclusion in my speeches; he was there more as an observer and more importantly as a presence.

These lines from his poem "Walking Early Sunday Morning" reflected something of the anxiety and concern and distress that, I thought, was growing in America in 1967 and 1968. I quoted them early in the campaign:

> *O to break loose. All life's grandeur*
> *is something with a girl in summer...*
> *elated as the President*
> *girdled by his establishment*
> *this Sunday morning, free to chaff*
> *his own thoughts with his bear-cuffed staff,*
> *swimming nude, unbuttoned, sick*
> *of his ghost-written rhetoric!*
>
> *No weekends for the gods now. Wars*
> *flicker, earth licks its open sores,*
> *fresh breakage, fresh promotions, chance*
> *assassinations, no advance.*
> *Only man thinning out his kind*
> *sounds through the Sabbath noon, the blind*
> *swipe of the pruner and his knife*
> *busy about the tree of life...*
>
> *Pity the planet, all joy gone*
> *from this sweet volcanic cone;*
> *peace to our children when they fall*
> *in small war on the heels of small*
> *war – until the end of time*
> *to police the earth, a ghost orbiting forever lost*
> *in our monotonous sublime.*

Many other established poets in the United States, and not a few unestablished ones, sent me letters of encouragement and often included either volumes of their poems or particular poems which they thought had bearing on the problems of 1968. Reed Whittemore, who was consultant in poetry at the Library of Congress in 1964 and 1965, talked to me often and sent poems, made suggestions, and offered to help in writing speeches. The same was true of Denise Levertov, Lewis Turco, Joseph Leonard Grucci, Joseph Langland, and Ogden Nash, among others. Before his appointment as consultant in poetry at the Library of Congress, William Jay Smith, made a special point of telling those who appointed him that he was supporting my candidacy.

Other writers and artists helped too. Arthur Miller, for example, campaigned very actively in my behalf, and at Chicago, before I was visited by Stephen Smith, recommended that I support Senator Edward Kennedy of Massachusetts because by doing so we might be able to carry the convention. He wrote what might have been the text of the speech in support of Senator Kennedy had that developed. These excerpts are from the text, which he sent to me in the Hilton Hotel in Chicago:

I have tried over the past year to put before the American people what I believe is the most decisive issue in the life of the country – the war in Vietnam. There can be no conflicting opinions about many of the consequences of this war but about one fact there can be no doubt any longer. In contest after contest I, and the late Senator Robert Kennedy, have demonstrated conclusively that the Democratic voter is overwhelmingly in favor of a new approach to peace. I have spelled out my differences with Administration policy, as Robert Kennedy did for himself, as Senator McGovern has done, and as Senator Edward Kennedy has done.

The question of whether to go on as we have, to continue the present sterile rhetoric, the hopeless hope that without changing policy the facts of life may miraculously change – this question the Vice President has also answered. He insists on the validity of what has failed and what continues to fail. I regard this fixed attitude as a tragedy for all of us.

But the issue of peace is far larger than any man or the candidacy of any man. Just as the office of the Presidency is larger than any man or of any man's personal ambition.

My candidacy has been from the beginning an expression of what I believed in the beginning and believe now to be a yearning, a desire, a demand in the American people for peace. My campaign has called forth tens of thousands of people to enter the political life of this country – again for that single purpose, the achievement of peace.

I believe that the great domestic crisis which we face cannot be solved until we first achieve peace. All our hopes and all our plans for the reconstruction of our nation fall to earth under the merciless gaze of this terrible war. Without peace there can begin nothing; all our promises – the very

promise of America itself – is being eaten alive by this daily
waste of our men and our resources.
The issue stands. No rhetoric can banish it.

I, therefore, ask all who have this issue at the center of
their concern, all who have heard me and joined me, to join
with me now in offering our strength to any of the candidates
who as President of the United States will support those
approaches and policies which I have advanced.

The issue of war is the issue of life, and ought not to be the
property of any one man. Our country must be given the
choice of life, the choice of a policy which is not the policy of
the majority report, the policy of the last four years. Richard
Nixon will not afford that choice to the country; he too is
bound by the past and its failure. America deserves better of
us than this endless kowtowing to what has failed.

There are men among us who are free to find the new road.
We must do this; we must have a candidate and President for
whom the past is a warning rather than a chain binding him to
error.

Ben Shahn, the artist who died in March of 1969, designed a
special poster for the campaign which was the best graphic
representation of the spirit of our whole effort and one which in a
most unusual way seemed to express the aspirations and the
purposes of the young people who were involved in my campaign.
It ran through many printings and reproductions during the
campaign and appears on the jacket, endpapers, and binding of
this book. It continues to be the most popular and appropriate
symbol of the politics of 1968.

A number of folk singers and other artists served in the
campaign, not just as entertainers but as persons committed to the
cause. The most active were Peter, Paul and Mary, Theodore
Bikel, the Smothers Brothers, Simon and Garfunkel, Phil Ochs,
Leon Bibb, and Tom Lehrer. Among the many actresses and
actors both from the stage and motion pictures, the earliest to help
were Paul Newman and his wife, Joanne Woodward, Tony
Randall, Phyllis Newman, Dustin Hoffman, and Myrna Loy.
These were especially helpful in the New York effort and in
California. Many others campaigned and raised funds.

One poet I quoted regularly was George Seferis, the Greek
diplomat who was a winner of the Nobel Prize for Literature. In
March of 1969, Seferis spoke out against the military regime that
had taken power in his country two years before, accusing it of
muzzling freedom and "enforcing a state of torpor in which all
intellectual values...are being submerged in a swamp." The Greek

190

government accused Seferis of being a Communist agent, intellectually barren, and less worthy of the Nobel Prize than other more patriotic Greeks.

Several lines from poems of his were especially pertinent to my campaign: "The time has come to say the few words we have to say for tomorrow our souls set sail."..."As one grows older so increase the number of judges who are prepared to condemn him." Lines from another Seferis poem tell of three mules; one of which slips while carrying the Queen. The Queen falls and breaks her neck and dies. Soon after, the spirit of the Queen appears to the mule handler and says, "Do not punish the mule for I was full of the will of God and that was too much of a burden for any beast to carry." Two of my favorite Dylan Thomas quotations I used somewhat out of context and with variations. His lines, "Do not go gentle into that good night," made me think, I said, of what the United States Senate could become. When someone asked me if I was not concerned about my political future, this line of his crossed my mind: "My immortality must matter less to me than the death of other men." In my variation I said my political future bothered me less than the death of men in Vietnam.

There were a number of poems which I did not quote but which, to my mind, had particular pertinence to the war and to the campaign. One of these was by William Butler Yeats, entitled "An Irish Airman Foresees His Death":

> *I know that I shall meet my fate*
> *Somewhere among the clouds above;*
> *Those that I fight I do not hate,*
> *Those that I guard I do not love;*
> *My country is Kiltartan Cross,*
> *My countrymen Kiltartan's poor,*
> *No likely end could bring them loss*
> *Or leave them happier than before.*
> *Nor law, nor duty bade me fight,*
> *Nor public men, nor cheering crowds,*
> *A lonely impulse of delight*
> *Drove to this tumult in the clouds;*
> *I balanced all, brought all to mind,*
> *The years to come seemed waste of breath,*
> *A waste of breath the years behind*
> *In balance with this life, this death.*

More interesting and perhaps more significant than the contributions of the established poets and artists was the poetic and artistic response that welled up from students and adults throughout the country. It was evident in advertisements and, particularly, in the signs and posters that appeared at almost every stop and in the poems given or sent to me during the campaign. Some were selected as favorite or pertinent poems, but many were written by the senders themselves. I include these examples:

Convention
By Gladys Johnson (Lincoln, Massachusetts)

Think of a time-space filled with aimless wingless ants
Hunters of Man lurking in narrow spaces
Newsreels
Comment, report aimless motion
Of predetermined chaos
(Render the unit rule useless)
Leaders pursue their prey
Prone to their unscrupulous compromise
Easy win is their goal.
Birthday celebration? Not for this tyranny of Mind.
Summation of youthful hope
Ripen to a still birth. Act III
We have gained from you the poem written for them,
Of what you lost
To the executor's pen brandish.
(And the postscript: You see how one can get inspired,
even by the "unit rule.")

The Candidates
By Caroline Kandler (New York City)

So much like the synthetic Lincoln at the fair,
The programmed running men
Repeat their HonorablePeaceandLawandOrder tape
Through their machinery.
Their followers who live in Disneyland
Attend, cheering to believe.

Others, small move players, stand by,
Measuring the line
Of their own fears.
They claim that even the tin soldier
When melted down
Revealed a human heart.

We'll wait
Until their tapes fall out.

A few poems were sent to me from other countries and many came from very young children. This one was written by a nine-year-old:

The Pyramids
By Annette Williams (Winchester, Massachusetts)

The pyramids that reach so high
Have a fulfillment to make before they die.
The colors so bright that never fade,
The giant stones that were painstakingly laid
How the ancients used no cement,
Yet the stones stayed where they were meant.
Six hundred miles those stones were taken,
Fifty tons of rock were laden on human men.
They dragged the tons of stone to make the Pharoh's long-used den.

All this they must show
Before the tons of rock crumble and go.

As a general rule, I believe the artist should remain somewhat detached and independent of politics, but when the issues are as crucial as they were in 1968, no citizen, no matter what his vocation or profession may be, can remain completely aloof. It was a year in which artists had to be, as Albert Camus has said, both artists and men even to the point of being prepared to neglect their special work or calling in order to involve their person, their time, and their art in the country's problems. "If we intervene as men," wrote Camus, "that experience will have an effect upon our language. And if we are not artists in our language first of all, what sort of artists are we?"

In 1968, the artists served their land and language well.

America Is Hard to See

This last chapter of the book is the most difficult to write because it deals with the significance of the events of 1968 as well as my part in them. As last chapters usually do, this one calls for a projection into the future. It is harder to explain why things happen than to describe their happening.[43] It is even harder to establish any claim to having been a principal or significant force in influencing events.

I would like first to accept what Tom Wicker said about "The Movement," as he called it, in the New York *Times Magazine* of August 25, 1968 – the Sunday before the convention:

> *And what The Movement might not fully appreciate is that in a sense they have already won. With McCarthy, they set in motion a chain of events which caused the withdrawal from the race of an incumbent President, brought a warring nation to the negotiating table, probably guaranteed peace planks in the platforms of both major parties and may well have turned around the fundamental institutional tendencies of the nation's involvement in Vietnam. The primaries were McCarthy's ballpark (or sandlot), as it were.*

It is true, as he wrote, that an incumbent President did withdraw from the contest for the nomination of his own party. Whether he withdrew because of my challenge or because of Senator Robert Kennedy's (as Senator Kennedy was reported to have speculated) or for other reasons can be explained only by President Johnson himself. It is my opinion that he would not have withdrawn as soon as he did if Senator Kennedy had not become a candidate, but it is quite likely that the President would

---

[43] Probably the best summary of the goals, spirit, and the achievements of the campaign was that written by E. W. Kenworthy of the *New York Times* at the close of the Chicago convention. See Appendix 10.

have withdrawn if I had defeated him as I expected to do in subsequent primaries.

The withdrawal of the President following an open challenge certainly proved wrong the political judgment of those commentators who said that an incumbent President could not be challenged successfully, and their more personal judgment that President Johnson particularly could not be dislodged.

It is possible that President Johnson might have gone to the negotiating table whether he had been challenged or not. My campaign at least built some pressure on him to stop the bombing and begin negotiating, and probably advanced the date at which negotiations did begin. And, consequently, if one accepts that there is a set of stages through which negotiations must run before any settlement can be achieved, my campaign may have advanced the date at which the settlement of the war finally took place.

The campaign was quite properly labeled "new politics." It was not just the politics of the outs trying to get in, or of the independents wresting control from the machine. It was new politics in every aspect: the new kind of people who were involved; the new ways that were opened for raising a challenge; and new in the substance of the challenge itself.

One cannot overrate the contribution of the new people. There has not been a campaign in the history of this country in which persons below the voting age were as extensively and directly and effectively involved as they were in the campaign of 1968. There were more of them involved than ever, they were given more responsibility, and they were truly, because of their mobility, a national force. In consequence of the campaign, there are thousands of young people who will never again be indifferent to politics.

There were risks involved in using young people as we did. Few of them had had any political experience, and yet they were quite ready to challenge the position of older, practiced people. Although our procedures for screening those who were admitted to official and active roles in the campaign were careful and thorough, there was always the fear that agitators might attach themselves, not only to the detriment of the campaign but also to the reputation of the whole student movement. There was also a continuing fear of accidents to the busses and cars in which the young people traveled. From the beginning in New Hampshire in January through the primaries and summer, there was not a serious incident until the attack on our student group by the Chicago police at the August Democratic convention.

196

Many adults, who had previously been indifferent or not actively involved, joined the students in what came to be known as "participatory politics − a rather awkward term that encompasses acceptance of civic responsibility and, following that, political action. Included among them and deserving special attention were members of the academic community, a large number of nuns, a great many educated young women − professional women as well as wives and mothers, especially in the suburban areas. There were also business and professional men who traditionally have shied away from politics, especially liberal politics, who committed themselves openly in my campaign.

Except for the nomination of Senator Goldwater by the Republicans in 1964, the contests within the major political parties in recent presidential years have centered more on personalities than on issues. Because the position on issues taken by Senator Goldwater was not shared by many Republicans, they were left in 1964 without a candidate who came close to what they felt they had a right to expect from their party. The electorate was really challenged to make a serious choice because of the extreme position taken by Senator Goldwater, and so victory went to President Johnson, a victory almost by default, misinterpreted as a mandate.

By 1968, however, the division within the Democratic party was not one of personality, but at root a difference on an issue and on an approach to government and politics. The party, acting through a majority of the delegates at the Democratic convention, refused to adjust the official party position to what a strong minority at the convention was advocating. Instead, the Democratic party went to the electorate with a foreign policy which was practically indistinguishable from that of the Republicans. Consequently, a large section of American voters was denied a chance in the general election to make the kind of choice which the voters had clearly demonstrated in Democratic primaries across the land they wanted to make. When, in fact, there was a deep difference of opinion in the general public's mind about the war, the two parties acted as if there was no contest. The technique of the Humphrey and Nixon campaigns was like freezing in professional basketball. When a game is tight, or in the case of a tie − the team in possession will hold onto the ball in the closing moments, hoping to shoot at the last second and score when there is not enough time left for the opposition to take the ball and make any offensive move.

Those who were frozen out of the electoral process in 1968 want reform − particularly in the Democratic party. Though party leaders in the past have taken account of what a strong minority wanted, they have done so often through undemocratic procedures. Now, I believe, the demand is for a perfection of procedures so that the position of a strong minority is sure to be reflected in the party platform and the position of its candidates and not left to chance. When the party deals with an issue like the war in Vietnam it will not be enough to say that a majority of the party at a convention has prevailed. The moral and emotional weight of such an issue raises it to a level of importance beyond what can be measured by a simple percentage of delegate votes. Without procedural reform, I doubt very much whether anyone could persuade the young people or the relatively independent practitioners of politics to test the processes within the Democratic party again in 1972.

The establishing of the Commission on Party Reform and Delegate Selection indicates that progress of this kind may take place within the Democratic party, although the preliminary announcement in April 1969 of extensive hearings was not particularly encouraging. Enough was already known about the undemocratic procedures within the party to establish a basis for reform without the delay or distraction of hearings across the country.

If party procedures are not reformed, both in the Democratic party and the Republican party, I anticipate that a third party or a fourth party will develop on the liberal side with the same strength and thrust that the George Wallace party had on the conservative side of 1968. There was growing evidence in 1968 that those who had been content to be considered independents, hoping to influence parties and candidates by this means, are more and more coming to the view that it is not effective to exercise such a second-class or residual citizenship in presidential years, passing judgment only after the two parties have developed platforms and chosen presidential candidates. They are beginning to see that it is necessary to be active in decisions both as to platform and as to candidates. The Wallace decision not to go the primary route in 1968 was a politically sound decision on his part.[44]

---

[44] Mark Acuff, the writer, who directed our campaign in Nebraska, said of the McCarthy movement: "I am certain that it is far more important than any of the issues raised in the campaign to date--more important than early settlement of the war, more important than relief for the ghettos, and far more important than the solution of the balance of payments problem. For in a way, the problem of the ghettos and the poor is linked closely with McCarthy's middle-class movement, though perhaps only a few Blacks see it that way. And the exasperation and helplessness so painful to the youth of the prosperous middle class,

The concept of one man-one vote, which has now been clearly defined by the Supreme Court in setting up legislative districts, must be established not only in the practices of the political parties, but in many other areas of American life: on college campuses for both faculty and students who want to have something more to say about their life on campus and their education; at stockholders' meetings at which participant stockholders accept that they have an intellectual and moral responsibility for the operation of the corporation; in movements like the National Farmers Organization in agriculture.

More important than politics and power was the substance of the challenge of 1968 and the response of the people of the country. Some time during the period of the primaries before California, a judgment was passed by the people of this country against the war. In a subtle way this judgment affected the politics after the primaries and also affected the action at the convention. When they were still giving it intellectual and moral support, the people of the country generally were more concerned about the war and about casualty reports. Following their judgment against the war, however, I sensed that they felt a release from responsibility – as though the war was no longer theirs but belonged to the administration in power.

This attitude still persists. Ever since President Johnson withdrew from the presidential race, the war became an official or administration or politicians' war rather than a "popular," or people's, war. The change in attitude might have taken place without a primary challenge, but I doubt it. The primaries gave the people a chance to pass a judgment on the war, and in Democratic primary after primary they indicated their opposition. In part because of that opposition, President Nixon became free to act –

___

though we call the problem 'alienation,' is not, at base, much different from the disfranchisement of the black man and the urban poor.

"Assorted Swedes and Frenchmen have been warning us for years that our inherently most difficult problem will be the adaptation of democracy to a technological culture with a population of hundreds of millions. Today, however, it is not only the Black and the poor and the young who feel powerless to affect the machinations of the system. In the last half of the 20th century, the smog-bound, tax-hounded, and radar-trapped suburbanite also feels cast adrift in a sea of technocracy where no one cares and, worse, no one listens.

"To my way of thinking, the failure of the system to provide a mechanism for the people to involve themselves in the ordering of government and society is more to blame for riots, arson and crime waves than any immediate economic and social deprivation. And George Wallace is every bit as much the benefactor of this upwelling of frustration as is McCarthy."

with little practical danger – to bring the war in Vietnam to an end and also free to adopt much more open policies toward Russia and mainland China. This would also have been true, I believe of Hubert Humphrey if he had been elected.

The campaign also helped to strengthen the challenge to the militarization of American life and American foreign policy – the challenge that was being raised especially by the Foreign Relations Committee of the Senate before my campaign, which was pursued by it during the campaign, and which is still being pushed with courage and vigor.

The Foreign Relations Committee began early in 1965 to assert itself in three major areas: first, by looking into the operation of the Central Intelligence Agency; second, by inquiring into the power and influence of the Department of Defense on foreign policy; and third, by beginning an examination of the whole foreign policy making process.

In keeping with these three purposes, the committee moved in 1965 to secure representation of the Senate Foreign Relations Committee on the Senate subcommittee which exercised control over the Central Intelligence Agency. Although the final move to secure that representation was defeated in the Senate in 1966, three members of the Foreign Relations Committee were accepted on this CIA advisory committee by the informal agreement, but were not give the right to vote.

In 1965, the Foreign Relations Committee made an inquiry into American intervention into the Dominican revolt. This inquiry gave particular attention to the process by which the United States decided to intervene. The hearings were held in executive session; no formal report was issued and the hearings had never been made public by the committee. On September 15, 1965, however, Senator Fulbright, the committee chairman, in a speech on the floor of the Senate, presented his conclusions based on his review of the extremely complex situation and testimony. "United States policy in the Dominican crisis," Senator Fulbright said, "was characterized initially by over-timidity and subsequently by over-reaction." and, "Through the whole affair, it has also been characterized by a lack of candor."

In 1966, the committee took up the Tonkin Gulf Resolution, which it had approved in 1964,[45] and challenged its use by the Administration to establish the legitimacy of the war in Vietnam

---

[45] The Tonkin Gulf Resolution was presented as a response to a specific instance of unprovoked armed attack on American warships engaged in what was described as "routine patrol" in international waters. It did not seek to commit the United States to maintain the independence and integrity of the nations of the area.

and also to silence critics. By virtue of the various interpretations that had been placed on the Tonkin Gulf Resolution, it had taken on a meaning and a significance which had not been attributed to it when the resolution was passed.

The following year at a presidential press conference on August 18, 1967, when the question of presidential authority to carry on the war in Vietnam was raised, the President talked again about the Tonkin Gulf Resolution. This time he did say with great frankness: "We stated then, and we repeat now, we did not think the resolution was necessary to do what we did and what we are doing." And in that same response, the President gave a very candid explanation of what the function of the resolution had been: "Back in May and June, 1964, before the Tonkin Gulf, we considered what we should do in order to keep the Congress informed, to keep them in place, and to keep them in agreement with what our action should be there in case of contingencies." This was the real point of the Tonkin Gulf Resolution.

Subsequent inquiries into the Tonkin Gulf incident itself raised serious question as to the truth of what had been reported at the time of the incident.

In March 1966, the Foreign Relations Committee held a series of educational hearings on the subject of mainland China. For the first time since 1949, when the Communists had taken control of China, American policy toward China was discussed in a restrained, responsible manner.

In the summer of the following year, 1967, the committee held hearings for the purpose of determining the constitutional role of the Congress in making foreign policy. Senator Fulbright expressed concern over a "a marked constitutional imbalance between the Executive and the Congress" in foreign policy matters. He noted that over the previous six years, the United States had undertaken four major military actions "on the basis of executive decisions made either secretly or under such alleged conditions of urgency as to preclude meaningful consultation with the Congress." In only one of those cases, the Cuban missile crisis of 1962, was there real urgency; in the others, the Bay of Pigs, the intervention in Vietnam, and the intervention in the Dominican Republic, it would have been better had action been delayed to permit careful consultation with the Congress.

My interpretation of the debate that took place among the drafters of the Constitution is that the only separation of powers intended in foreign policy was between the execution of policies and policy determination. There is no separation of power in our Constitution as to determination of policy. The whole thrust of the Constitution Convention was to share power and to share

201

responsibility, not to separate them. The Administration's testimony, presented by Undersecretary of State Nicholas Katzenbach on August 17, 1967, was therefore most significant. Said Katzenbach:

> *The President, of necessity, has a preeminent responsibility in this field.*
> *But to say this is not to denigrate the role of Congress. Whatever the powers of the President to act alone on his own authority – and I doubt that any President has ever acted to the full limits of that authority – there can be no question that he acts most effectively when he acts with the support and authority of the Congress.*
> *And so it is that every President seeks in various ways – formal and informal – the support of Congress for the policies which the United States pursues in its foreign relations.*
> *In part, the Constitution compels such support. It gives the President the responsibilities for leadership. It also gives the Congress specific powers which can on the one hand frustrate and distort and on the other hand support and implement.*
> *Obviously, then, there are great advantages to the Nation in the conduct of its foreign policy when circumstances permit the President and the Congress to act together...*

Katzenbach's statement was essentially a prescription for a kind of four-year dictatorship in foreign policy, even though it might be a benevolent dictatorship. It was reported that I was so shocked and enraged by the Katzenbach testimony that I "jumped up" and left the hearing room, saying that there was only one thing to do – take it to the country.

I did not jump up and leave the hearing room, but I did say, either before or on leaving the hearing, that I thought it was the wildest testimony on this issue that I had ever heard. The report that I decided to run at that moment is not accurate.

The Foreign Relations Committee continued to hold hearings during the primary campaigns in early 1968, and their inquiry and their findings consistently supported the challenge that I was making both as to the substance of foreign policy and as to the process by which it is determined and administered.

It was with the purpose in mind of making the Foreign Relations Committee even more effective that I resigned my membership on that committee at the time the 91st Congress was organized in January 1969. The Reorganization Act of 1946 provided for a Foreign Relations committee of thirteen members. In the years since that act was passed, the number of members on that committee had been gradually increased, over the objection of the chairman, until it finally had nineteen members. With the exception of the Appropriations Committee, which is very different in structure from the authorizing committees of the Senate, the Foreign Relations Committee was the largest of all committees in the Senate.

The committee was too large, as its chairman said, to be truly effective. When the Steering Committee of the Democrats in the Senate met in January 1969, Chairman Fulbright appeared before the committee and asked that the Foreign Relations Committee be reduced or held at fifteen, as provided in a new Legislative Reorganization Act which the Senate had approved in the 90th Congress. I was hopeful that his request would be honored because only fourteen members of the committee of the 90th Congress had returned in the 91st Congress.[46]

I was a member of the Democratic Steering Committee. When the committee responded to Senator Fulbright's request, there were a number who said they were obligated to restore Senator Gale McGee of Wyoming to the Foreign Relations Committee as he had been taken from the committee two years before when the Democratic majority in the Senate was reduced. If he had been added to the committee, because of the ratio of Democrats to Republicans in the Senate, the Republicans could have asserted the right to two new members on the committee instead of one, and the size of the committee would have been increased again to eighteen or nineteen.

In order to achieve the reduction that I thought was essential to the effective operation of the committee I gave up my place on the committee so that the members of the Steering Committee could honor their commitment to Senator McGee. Although Senator McGee has in some cases opposed the majority of the committee, he has been either a sole dissenter or one of a very small minority on the committee. Reports that I had taken this action to retaliate against Senator Fulbright for his failure to support me in 1968 were utterly false. The action was taken after consultation with him, and he has a number of times expressed his appreciation to me for helping to make the committee a more effective instrument of the Senate.

The committee with 15 members is operating very effectively in challenging the militarization and the personalization of the

---

[46] Two Republican members, Senator Frank Carlson of Kansas and Senator Bourke Hickenlooper of Iowa had not run for re-election, leaving two vacancies on the Republican side, and three Democratic members had been defeated: Senator Wayne Morse of Oregon, Senator Frank Lausche of Ohio, and Senator Joseph Clark of Pennsylvania.

foreign policy of this country. Even while awaiting legislative recommendations from the new Administration, the committee has moved into important areas of national policy. Three subcommittees, especially, have made valuable contributions. The Subcommittee on International Organization and Disarmament Affairs, under the chairmanship of Senator Albert Gore, has held hearings on the anti-ballistic missile and chemical and biological warfare. Senator Stuart Symington's Subcommittee on United States Security Agreements and Commitments Abroad has undertaken extensive study of United States commitments and agreements around the world. Senator Frank Church's Subcommittee on Western Hemisphere Affairs is studying the Alliance for Progress program, with particular attention to the influence of the military on Latin-American policy, and the full committee is undertaking another review of Vietnam policy.

The effectiveness of the committee has in part been responsible for the fact that the Nixon presidency was more impersonal than either the Johnson or the Kennedy presidency. Its cabinet members have certainly been given more freedom to speak and to act within the framework of Administration policies than the Johnson cabinet. In its relationship to the Congress the Nixon administration has shown a clearer understanding and respect for the separation and sharing of powers defined in the Constitution. And Congress, especially in the field of foreign and military policy, has shown greater independence than it did under the two previous administrations.

Our challenge of 1968 was characterized by Secretary of Agriculture Orville Freeman during the campaign as "only a footnote in history." Paraphrasing Churchill, I replied, "But what a footnote." It could well become part of the main text.

The American people were tested in 1968, and they were not found wanting. A general constituency of conscience was shown to exist in America. And there was a return of the spirit that moved this country in 1776 and 1789 – a sprit of "public happiness" described by John Adams as a delight in public office, in participating in public activities and in the government. John Adams said that the men of colonial America went to town meetings and participated in assemblies because they delighted in the dialogue, because they delighted in discussion – not because they had any special interest which they wished to advance, but because they were concerned with advancing the public good.

The campaign demonstrated clearly that the political system of America is really much more open than people believe it to be. If a group has an issue and a reasonably good candidate, neither the lack of funds nor the lack of organization nor the power of party opposition need deter it from making a challenge. Finances are less important than they have been in the past if proper use of public media is made.

Despite all that happened in 1968, the year revealed that there is within the people of this country a great reservoir of good will as well as ability and energy. We have always done best for our country and for the world when we were prepared to make mistakes, if we had to make them, on the side of excess of trust rather than on the side of mistrust or suspicion; when we were willing to make mistakes because of an excess of liberality or generosity, rather than an excess of self-seeking and self-concern; when we were prepared to make mistakes because of an excess of hope rather than an excess of fear. These have been the marks of America in its best times and the marks of America at its best in politics: reason and trust and generosity and hope. These were the marks that distinguished our new politics of 1968.

"America is hard to see," as Robert Frost has written, but if one looks hard and long one will see much that is good.

Statement by Sen. Eugene McCarthy, November 30, 1967

I intend to enter the Democratic primaries in Wisconsin, Oregon, California, and Nebraska. The decision with reference to Massachusetts and New Hampshire will be made within two weeks. In so far as Massachusetts is concerned, it will depend principally upon the outcome of the meeting of the Democratic State Committee this weekend.

Since I first said that I thought the issue of Vietnam and other related issues should be raised in the primaries, I have talked to Democratic party leaders in twenty-six states, to candidates – especially Senate candidates – who will be up for re-election next year, and to many other persons.

My decision to challenge the President's position has been strengthened by recent announcements from the Administration of plans for continued escalation and intensification of the war in Vietnam and, on the other hand, by the absence of any positive indications or suggestions for a compromise or negotiated political settlement. I am concerned that the Administration seems to have set no limits on the price that it will pay for military victory.

Let me summarize the cost of the war up to this point:

-the physical destruction of much of a small, weak nation by the military operations of the most powerful nation on this earth;

-100,000 to 150,000 civilian casualties in South Vietnam alone, according to the estimates of the Senate subcommittee on refugees;

-the uprooting and fracturing of the social structure of South Vietnam, where one-fourth to one-third of the population are now refugees;

-the United States, 15,058 combat dead and 94,469 wounded through November 25, 1967;

-a monthly expenditure by the United States of between $2 and $3 billion on the war;

I am also concerned over the bearing of the war on other areas of United States responsibility:

-the failure to appropriate adequate funds for the poverty program, for housing, for education and other national needs, and the prospect of additional cuts as a condition for congressional approval of a tax bill;

-the drastic reduction of our foreign aid program in other parts of the world;

-the dangerous rise of inflation and, as an indirect but serious consequence, the devaluation of the British pound which is more important east of Suez than is the British navy.

There is growing evidence of a deepening moral crisis in America: discontent, frustration, and a disposition to extralegal – if not illegal – manifestations of protest.

I am hopeful that a challenge may alleviate the sense of political helplessness and restore to many people a belief in the processes of American politics and of American government. On college campuses especially, but also among other thoughtful adult Americans, it may counter the growing sense of alienation from politics which is currently reflected in a tendency to withdraw in either frustration or cynicism, to talk of non-participation and to make threats of support for a third party or fourth party or other irregular political movements.

I do not see in my move any great threat to the unity and the strength of the Democratic party.

The issue of the war in Vietnam is not a separate issue but is one which must be dealt with in the configuration of problems in which it occurs. It is within this context that I intend to take the case to the people of the United States.

I am not for peace at any price but for an honorable, rational, and political solution to this war; a solution which I believe will enhance our world position, encourage the respect of our allies and potential adversaries, which will permit us to give the necessary attention to our other commitments abroad – both military and non-military – and leave us with both resources and moral energy to deal effectively with the pressing domestic problems of the United States itself. In this total effort, I believe we can restore to this nation a clearer sense of purpose and of dedication to the achievement of that purpose.

APPENDIX 2

Nominating Speech by Sen. Eugene McCarthy for Adlai Stevenson, Democratic National Convention, Los Angeles, California, July 13, 1960

Mr. Chairman, Democratic delegates at this great convention:

We now approach the hour of all-important decision. You are the chosen people out of 172,000,000 Americans, the chosen of the Democratic party, come here to Los Angeles not only to choose a man to lead this Democratic party in the campaign of this fall and this November, but to choose a man who we hope will lead this country and all of our friends and all of those peoples who look to us for help, who look to us for understanding, who look to us for leadership.

We are here participating in the great test of democratic society. As you know, our way of life is being challenged today. There are those, the enemies of democracy, who say that free men and free women cannot exercise that measure of intellectual responsibility, cannot demonstrate that measure of moral responsibility, which is called for to make the kind of decisions that we free people are called upon to make in this year of 1960, and there are those, I remind you, who are the friends of democracy, who have expressed some doubt and some reservation as to whether or not this ideology, this way of life, these institutions of ours, can survive.

Let me ask you at this time to put aside all of your prejudices, to put aside any kind of unwarranted regional loyalties, to put aside for the time being preferences which are based purely upon questions of personality. Put aside, if you can, early decisions – decisions which were made before all of the candidates were in the race, decisions which were made when the issues were not clear, as they are today.

I say to those of you – candidates and spokesmen for candidates – who say you are confident of the strength that you have at this convention, who say that you are confident and believe in democracy – let this go to a second ballot.

I say let this go to a second ballot, when every delegate who is here will be as free as he can be free to make a decision.

Let us strike off the fetters of instructed delegations. Let Governors say to their people: This is the moment of decision and we want you to make it as free Americans, responsible to your own conscience and to the people of the state that sent you here, and to the people of this country.

This I say is the real test of democracy. Do you have confidence in the people at this convention to make a fair and responsible choice, or do you not have that confidence?

What has happened in this world and what has happened in this United States has been described to you here by great speakers. Each new headline every day that we've been here has been a shock to us; each new headline has been a shock.

These times, men say, are out of joint. They say these are the worst of times without being the best of times – this may be true. But I say to you these external signs, these practical problems which face us are nothing compared to the problems of the mind and of the spirit which face the United States and the free world today.

If the mind is clouded and if the will is confused and uncertain, there can be no sound decision and no sound action.

There's demagoguery abroad in the land at all times, and demagoguery, I say to you, takes many forms. There's that which says "here is wealth, and here is material comfort." We suffer a little from that in the United States.

There's demagoguery which promises people power, which is used for improper purposes and ends. And we have seen in this century and in this generation what happens when power is abused.

I say to you there's a subtle kind of demagoguery which erodes the spirit. And this is the demagoguery which has affected this United States in the last eight years.

What are we told? What have we been told? We've been told that we can be strong without sacrifice. This is what we've been told. We've been told that we can be good without any kind of discipline if we just say we're humble and sincere – this is the nature of goodness. We've been told that we can be wise without reflection. We can be wise without study, we've been told. I say this is the erosion of the spirit which has taken place in this United States in the last eight years. And I say to you that the time has come to raise again the cry of the ancient prophet. What did he say? He said the prophets prophesy falsely and the high priests, he said, ruled by their word, and my people love to have it so. But what will be the end?

I say to you the political prophets have prophesized falsely in these eight years. And the high priests of Government have ruled by that false prophecy. And the people seemed to have loved it so.

But there was one man – there was one man who did not prophesy falsely, let me remind you. There was one man who said: Let's talk sense to the American people.

What did the scoffers say? The scoffers said: Nonsense. They said: Catastrophic nonsense. But we know it was the essential and the basic and the fundamental truth that he spoke to us.

There was a man who talked sense to the American people. There was one man who said: This is a time for self-examination. This is a time for us to take stock, he said. This is a time to decide where we are and where we're going.

This, he said, is a time for virtue. But what virtues did he say we needed? Oh yes, he said we need the heroic virtues – we always do. We need fortitude; we need courage; we need justice. Everyone cheers when you speak out for those virtues.

But what did he say in addition to that? He said we need the unheroic virtues in America. We need the virtue, he said, of patience. There were those who said we've had too much of patience.

We need, he said, the virtue of tolerance. We need the virtue of forbearance. We need the virtues of patience and understanding.

This was what the prophet said. This is what he said to the American people. I ask you, did he prophesy falsely? Did he prophesy falsely?

He said this is a time for greatness. This is a time for greatness for America. He did not say he possessed it. He did not even say he was destined for it. He did say that the heritage of America is one of greatness.

And he described that heritage to us. And he said the promise of America is a promise of greatness. And he said this promise we must fulfill.

This was his call to greatness. This was the call to greatness that was issued in 1952.

He does not seek it for himself today.

This man knows – this man knows, as all of us do from history, that power often comes to those who seek it. But history does not prove that power is always well used by those who seek it.

On the contrary, the whole history of democratic politics is to this end, that power is best exercised by those who are sought out by the people, by those to whom power is given by a free people.

And so I say to you Democrats here assembled: Do not turn away from this man. Do not reject this man. He has fought gallantly. He has fought courageously. He has fought honorably. In 1952 in the great battle. In 1956 he fought bravely. And between those years and since, he has stood off the guerrilla attacks of his enemies and the sniping attacks of those who should have been his friends. Do not reject this man who, his enemies said, spoke above the heads of the people, but they said it only because they didn't want the people to listen. He spoke to the people. He moved their minds and stirred their hearts, and this was what was objected to. Do not leave this prophet without honor in his own party. Do not reject this man.

I submit to you a man who is not the favorite son of any one state. I submit to you the man who is the favorite son of fifty states.

And not only of fifty states but the favorite son of every country in the world in which he is known – the favorite son in every country in which he is unknown but in which some spark, even though unexpressed, of desire for liberty and freedom still lives.

This favorite son I submit to you: Adlai E. Stevenson of Illinois.

APPENDIX 3

Nominating Speech by Senator Eugene J. McCarthy for Hubert H. Humphrey, Democratic National Convention, Atlantic city, New Jersey, August 26, 1964

Mr. Speaker, Mr. President, Distinguished Delegates and Visitors to this great Democratic convention, I assure you that the name which I shall give to you as I finish my speech will be the same as that which the President of the United States has just given you.

At no time in the recent history of any political party has a party presented to its convention and beyond that to the people of this country two men who are so alike in energy, in ability, in experience, in dedication, and in compassion as the two men whom this Democratic party will present to the people of this nation for approval in November of 1964: one of them from the State of Texas, the Lone Star State, and one from the State of Minnesota, the North Star State.

Neither of these men has been proved in one shining hour, but each has been tested in the slow trials of time. They have known hardship and poverty and have seen the edge of despair. They know both the weaknesses and the strength of America. Both of them are qualified to provide leadership for the United States of America.

They have been leaders in the great Democratic party – our party – this, the party of war and party of peace. We acknowledge this to be true; for when the safety of this nation and the honor of our country call for military action, we have been prepared to take such action and we are prepared to take it today. We are also the party of peace. When we have been called upon as the party in power to make commitments to the future, to act in hope, and to act in trust that a better world may be established we have not hesitated and we have not delayed in expressing that trust and in working to establish and strengthen the basis for peace.

We are the party of poverty when poverty calls for action, and it calls for action today in the midst of plenty. We are also the party of plenty and the party of progress. We are the party of promises, but we are also the party of fulfillment.

We, the Democratic party, are the party of history. We accept the traditions of America. We accept the history of the East – of the old and the new. We accept the history of the South – of the old and of the new and of the changing South. We accept the North and we accept the West. We accept all of this America as our America, and beyond that are willing to accept responsibility in every part of the world in which we have some power to influence people for good or to help them achieve the good and the full life.

What have the Republicans set against us in 1964: their spokesman and leader – a prophet of despair, their presidential candidate – the greatest "no-sayer" in the recent history of this country; a man who has chosen to vote "no" in the three great tests to which the Congress of this United States has been placed in the last four years. He has stood outside the conference room of discussion and outside the conference room of decision, shouting objections from the corridor of "no commitment," refusing to come in and to take the responsibility for decision.

On the Test Ban Treaty in which we acknowledged, with trust in Providence, that the powers which men have developed can be brought under some kind of moral control, he said, "No." He stood aside.

In the test of civil rights, in which we were called upon to affirm our belief in the universality of human dignity and of human rights, again the man who leads and speaks for the Republican party excused himself. He stepped out of the scene. He refused responsibility.

And finally in the great effort to eliminate poverty and to make the economy of this country produce so as to meet the needs of our people and to make it possible for us to meet the obligations which we carry around the world – again his was the voice of fear and his was the vote of no confidence. At a time when we were giving positive answers to every criticism which the Marxists have directed at our economy, proving that we can produce without depression, proving that we can prosper without exploitation, proving that we can progress without the class struggle and meet all of the needs of our people and meet our obligation in justice around the world, this man who now speaks for the Republican party, who now leads the Republican party, chose again to stay in a world of his own: a world in which the calendar has no years, in which the clock has no hands, and in which glasses have no lenses. In that strange world – in that strange world in which he lives – the pale horse of death and of destruction and the white horse of conquest and of victory are indistinguishable.

I call upon you here tonight, Democrats all, to affirm America. This is a time for all of us to enter into the fabric of our own time and to accept the challenge of the history of the 20th century, to declare and manifest our belief that the power of reason can give some direction to the movement of history itself.

I call upon you here tonight to dedicate yourselves to the efforts of our party, to dedicate yourselves again in support of Lyndon Johnson as President, and to accept my colleague, the friend of the President and my friend, Hubert Humphrey as Vice President.

Appendix 4

Speech of Sen. Eugene McCarthy, US Senate, Oct. 16, 1967

On Thursday, October 12, the Secretary of State, Mr. Dean Rusk, opened his press conference with a statement which has been marked by editors and commentators as significant. They are not altogether in agreement as to what constitutes the significance, but generally it has been labeled as bold and clarifying. I do not see it as being any more bold than previous statements made by the Secretary nor any clearer, since the style and language are those of the Secretary, unless the clarification is in the more simplified and restricted statement of our purpose and objectives in Vietnam. The Secretary did not speak of bringing the good life or the Great Society to Southeast Asia as a purpose of the war or of honoring the pledges of four Presidents, nor did he suggest that we cannot improve life in our own cities unless we make improvements in Vietnam. He said that we are in Vietnam in our own national interest and to honor our commitment. "Our commitment is clear and our national interest is real," he said.

I do not intend to reopen the question as to whether or not our commitment is clear, since this point has been subject to serious debate and challenge for nearly a year and a half.

The Tonkin Gulf Resolution in 1964 gave the President no power which he did not already have, nor was it in any way an open-ended license for expansion and intensification of the war free from congressional restraint or criticism. Our commitment under the SEATO Treaty, signed in 1954, was a limited one, imposing a limited obligation upon us, an obligation which was contingent at least in part on the concurrent response of the other major nations in the Treaty organization. There is little to be gained from arguing these quasi-legal points. Any worthwhile debate must deal with the realities of Southeast Asia. The debate on Vietnam is not a matter of variations on a theme. Although the Secretary evidently wants to have it considered within those limits, it is a debate upon the theme itself and beyond that on the nature of the music which the State Department is playing.

Let me consider first the positive statements made by the Secretary. He said there is "no significant body of American opinion which would have us withdraw from Vietnam" and "no serious opinion among us which wishes to transform this struggle into a general war." I do not know whether this is an accurate statement or not, but in any case it is irrelevant since the debate on our policy in Vietnam falls between these two extremes.

Early in his remarks the Secretary speaks of the fate which Asian communism has planned for Southeast Asia. Asian communism, for that matter world communism, undoubtedly has a fate planned for Southeast Asia and for all the world, but the fact that it has such plans does not necessarily mean that they are possible of realization, or that we have to respond to every action as thought the total plan were in operation and likely to be realized.

On the record, the Secretary has not shown himself to be the most accurate judge of Chinese intentions or potential or of the other forces running within the world. I quote from his May 18, 1951, speech before the China Institute in New York: he describes the "greedy hands" of Russian stretching out to dismember China; China, he said, was being "sacrificed to the ambitions of the communist conspiracy. China has been driven by foreign masters into an adventure of foreign aggression..." (Korea); "The Peiping regime may be a colonial Russian government – a Slavic Manchukuo on a larger scale. It is not the government of China. It does not pass the first test. It is not Chinese." He said of the Nationalist Chinese government: "We believe it more authentically represents the views of the great body of the people of China, particularly their historical demand for independence from foreign control."

The debate on Vietnam is not, as the Secretary states, essentially over procedures for carrying out policies on which the nation is united. This is a debate on matters of great substance over which the nation is indeed deeply divided and concerned. The Secretary may speak as solemnly as he can – and he can speak solemnly – but the members of Congress and the people of the country must continue to ask and seek answers to the question, "What is America's proper role in the world and what is the bearing of the policy in Vietnam on the fulfillment of that role?" We cannot permit the Secretary to dismiss, even solemnly, the United Nations and the recommendations of members of the Senate, including the Majority Leader, Senator Mansfield, with the easy remark that "there are some problems about going through an exercise of futility...to satisfy some critics among our own people."

Members of the Senate have a clear constitutional responsibility, which becomes personal because of their position, to be concerned over foreign policy; a responsibility which in the case of the Secretary of State exists only by delegation or proxy. As a matter of fact, much of what has been done or what is being done in Vietnam may be a costly exercise in futility: that the bombing of North Vietnam, for example, if we are to accept the recent testimony of the Secretary of Defense regarding the failure of the bombing to reduce significantly the supply of arms and men to the South may be such an exercise; that the much publicized program of pacification, more recently labeled "revolutionary development," which is essentially an attempt to graft on to Asian society Western values and institutions and practices, may also be an exercise in futility.

The one rather clear conclusion from his remarks is that, in his mind, the United States must establish and maintain an anti-Communist bastion in South Vietnam and that this is essential as a part of the overall strategy of containing China through encirclement, and that all of this bears quite directly on our national interest, if not our survival. This is a continuing application of the strategic theory of John Foster Dulles and reflects in action the ancient fear of the "yellow peril," presented to us now in a new image by the Secretary in his words that "within the next decade or two there will be a billion Chinese on the mainland, armed with nuclear weapons, with no certainty about what their attitude toward the rest of Asia will be." If this is the specter that is haunting Asia, it is difficult to see how we will rid Asia of it even though we achieve an unpredictable and total victory in South Vietnam.

The Secretary seems to accept the Chinese Communists' belief that their doctrine of world revolution is applicable to the entire underdeveloped world. It must be encouraging to the Chinese propagandists to see this basic tenet of their political philosophy accepted and endorsed by the American Secretary of State.

What is the measure of the Chinese threat?

What is its record?

Although there is every reason to believe that the leaders in Peking are firmly convinced that their revolution will serve as a model for the developing world and for the eventual defeat of the industrial "cities" by the countryside of the "people," in reality the Chinese experience has, with no significant exception, almost no relevance outside China. In no other country or part of the world do precisely the same conditions exist under which the Chinese Communists achieved power. Mao was able to gain control of China because he gained leadership of the Chinese nationalist movement, consolidating and leading it against a foreign invader in World War II. Only in Vietnam has this feat been duplicated. Ho Chi Minh is the only Communist leader in the underdeveloped world who was able to gain control of his country's nationalist movement at the time of resistance to a foreign invasion.

Throughout the underdeveloped world, Chinese attempts to promote their style of revolution have met with failure, largely because of internal forces of which nationalism is the most important.

The failure of the Communist attempt to gain control of Indonesia in late 1965 was a disaster of major proportions. China's attack on India in 1962 and her support of Pakistan on the Kashmir issue have dealt a severe blow to whatever hopes Indian Communists might have had for capitalizing on India's internal problems and divisions.

In Japan the Communist party has followed the Peking line at great cost, alienating the trade unions and the powerful Japanese Socialist Party. Even North Korea has proclaimed its "neutrality" in the Sino-Soviet struggle.

China's lack of success in Africa has also been noteworthy. The government of Malawi had to get rid of some cabinet ministers for allegedly conspiring with the Chinese; Kenya expelled the New China News Agency correspondent "in the interest of national security"; Burundi, once regarded as safely in the Chinese camp, expelled Peking's diplomatic mission. In Latin America, the Chinese have had even less success. Even Fidel Castro, whose rise to power had been hailed in Peking as a demonstration of the validity of the Chinese analysis of the Latin-American revolutionary situation, has denounced China.

China continues to talk a world-power game, but, even with nuclear weapons, the evidence of internal economic difficulties, particularly the food-population problem and the political struggle, which may be only a dress rehearsal for what will come after Mao passes from the scene, suggests that China's principal concern and effort will remain domestic and internal.

China's foreign policy objectives are of concern to us, but there is significant disagreement about her ability to pursue these objectives successfully. She seeks recognition as a great power whose voice is heard in the world's councils. China, understandably, seeks to overcome the bitter legacy of a hundred years of humiliation by the West. Recognition as a great power is essentially a nationalist rather than an ideological objective. All Chinese, Communist and non-Communist, agree on its importance.

China also seeks recovery of the "lost territories": Hong Kong, Macao, parts of Soviet Asia, Taiwan and the off-shore islands, and land along the Sino-Indian frontier. This is also an essentially nationalist objective, shared by all Chinese. In Chinese eyes, territories were taken forcibly from China by the unequal treaties imposed on her during the nineteenth century, or, in the case of Taiwan, were denied to her by the military power of the United States Seventh Fleet.

China seeks to re-establish what she considers her traditional sphere of influence in Southeast Asia and to eradicate United States military power from the Asian mainland. Chinese political domination in that area has not been clear or consistent, at least not since the tenth century when Vietnam achieved "independence" from China. At times the relationship appears to have meant little more than tacit agreement not to aid China's enemies.

China's desire to eliminate United States power and influence from the Asian mainland, while it conforms to Communist ideological opposition to democratic philosophy, is basically nationalistic, and there is little reason to believe that a non-Communist Chinese government would welcome a United States presence on the Asian mainland any more than the present government in Peking does.

Our policy in the Far East is based largely on unsubstantiated assumptions.

First, we assume that revolutions throughout the less-developed world are a Chinese-inspired wave of the future, and that Vietnam is a test case for guerrilla war and for wars of national liberation. There is no good reason for accepting this characterization of the war in Vietnam. The techniques of the Chinese revolution have not yet proved fully successful in China; they are a long way from inspiring revolution in other parts of the world.

Second, we assert that the Southeast Asia situation is analogous to previous situations and experiences in Asia and in Europe. Military containment worked in Europe and in Korea, according to the theory; thus it is the method to be applied in Southeast Asia or in any other test area. But the conditions under which containment was effective in Europe and in Korea do not exist in Southeast Asia, which is marked by deep ethnic and social divisions, by instability – political and social, by deep antagonism to Western colonialism, and by a desire for change rather than for a return to the past.

Many of our problems today are the result of our unwillingness or inability in the past to participate what might be the shape of the world twenty years in the future. Few Americans expected in 1945 that twenty years later we would still have 225,000 troops in Europe. We have 55,000 troops in South Korea fourteen years after the end of the fighting, yet, at the height of the Korean conflict, we never had as many troops committed as we have today in Vietnam. We must ask whether we are prepared to maintain from 100,000 to 200,000 troops in South Vietnam as well for fifteen or twenty years after the fighting stops. If we are not prepared to do so, the process must be reversed before temporary commitment assumes the character of a permanent establishment and an irritation in the changed context of another generation. We must begin now the adjustments of attitude which will be necessary if we are to reduce or liquidate our commitments in Asia.

The long-range question is whether the United States and China are on a collision course. The likelihood of confrontation, of ultimate showdown, is not immediate, not inevitable.

With regret I must conclude that the Secretary has added nothing constructive to the debate of American involvement in Southeast Asia by way of new facts, new policies, strategy or understanding; but rather because of the posture, almost of defiance, the careless or intentional abuse of the language can serve only to raise the emotional level of the debate, obscure the issues upon which judgment should be made, and cause further frustration and division within the country as well as between the Congress and the Executive Branch of the government.

APPENDIX 5

Address of Senator Eugene J. McCarthy
Conference of Concerned Democrats, Conrad Hilton Hotel, Chicago, Illinois, December 2, 1967

In 1952, in this city of Chicago, the Democratic party nominated as its candidate for the presidency Adlai Stevenson.

His promise to his party and to the people of the country then was that he would talk sense to them. And he did in the clearest tones. He did not speak above the people, as his enemies charged, but he raised the hard and difficult questions and proposed the difficult answers. His voice became the voice of America. He lifted the spirit of this land. The country, in his language, was purified and given direction.

Before most other men, he recognized the problem of our cities and called for action.

Before other men, he measured the threat of nuclear war and called for a test ban treaty.

Before other men, he anticipated the problem of conscience which he saw must come with maintaining a peacetime army and a limited draft, and urged the political leaders of this country to put their wisdom to the task.

In all of these things he was heard by many but not followed, until under the presidency of John F. Kennedy his ideas were revived in new language and in a new spirit. To the clear sound of the horn was added the beat of a steady and certain drum.

John Kennedy set free the spirit of America. The honest optimism was released. Quiet courage and civility became the mark of American government, and new programs of promise and of dedication were presented: the Peace Corps, the Alliance for Progress, the promise of equal rights for all Americans and not just the promise, but the beginning of the achievement of that promise.

All the world looked to the United States with new hope, for here was youth and confidence and an openness to the future. Here was a country not being held by the dead hand of the past, not frightened by the violent hand of the future which was grasping at the world.

This was the spirit of 1963.

What is the spirit of 1967? What is the mood of America and of the world toward America today?

It is a joyless spirit – a mood of frustration, of anxiety, of uncertainty.

In place of the enthusiasm of the Peace Corps among the young people of America, we have protests and demonstrations.

In place of the enthusiasm of the Alliance for Progress, we have distrust and disappointment.

Instead of the language of promise and of hope, we have in politics today a new vocabulary in which the critical word is war: war on poverty, war on ignorance, war on crime, war on pollution. None of these problems can be solved by war but only by persistent, dedicated, and thoughtful attention.

But we do have one war which is properly called a war – the war in Vietnam, which is central to all of the problems of America.

A war of questionable legality and questionable constitutionality.

A war which is diplomatically indefensible; the first war in this century in which the United States, which at its founding made an appeal to the decent opinion of mankind in the Declaration of Independence, finds itself without the support of the decent opinion of mankind.

A war which cannot be defended in the context of the judgment of history. It is being presented in the context of an historical judgment of an era which is past. Munich appears to be the starting point of history for the Secretary of State and for those who attempt to support his policies. What is necessary is a realization that the United States is a part of the movement of history itself; that it cannot stand apart, attempting to control the world by imposing covenants and treaties and by violent military intervention; that our role is not to police the planet but to use military strength with restraint and within . limits, while at the same time we make available to the world the great power of our economy, of our knowledge, and of our good will.

A war which is not defensible even in military terms; which runs contrary to the advice of our greatest generals – Eisenhower, Ridgway, Bradley, and MacArthur – all of whom admonished us against becoming involved in a land war in Asia. Events have proved them right, as estimate after estimate as to the time of success and the military commitment necessary to success has had to be revised – always upward: more troops, more extensive bombing, a widening and intensification of the war. Extension and intensification have been the rule, and projection after projection of success have been proved wrong.

With the escalation of our military commitment has come a parallel of overleaping of objectives: from protecting South Vietnam, to nation building in South Vietnam, to protecting all of Southeast Asia, and ultimately to suggesting that the safety and security of the United States itself is at stake.

Finally, it is a war which is morally wrong. The most recent statement of objectives cannot be accepted as an honest judgment as to why we are in Vietnam. It has become increasingly difficult to justify the methods we are using and the instruments of war which we are using as we have moved from limited targets and somewhat restricted weapons to greater variety and more destructive instruments of war, and also have extended the area of operations almost to the heart of North Vietnam.

Even assuming that both objectives and methods can be defended, the war cannot stand the test of proportion and of prudent judgment. It is no longer possible to prove that the good that may come with what is called victory, or projected as victory, is proportionate to the loss of life and property and to other disorders that follow from this war.

Let me summarize the cost of the war up to this point:

-the physical destruction of much of a small, weak nation by the military operations of the most powerful nation on earth;

-100,000 to 150,000 civilian casualties in South Vietnam alone, according to the estimates of the Senate subcommittee on refugees;

-the uprooting and fracturing of the social structure of South Vietnam, where one-fourth to one-third of the population are now refugees;

-the United States, 15,058 combat dead and 94,469 wounded through November 25, 1967;

-a monthly expenditure by the United States of between \$2 and \$3 billion on the war.

Beyond all of these considerations, two further judgments must be passed; a judgment of individual conscience, and another in the broader context of the movement of history itself.

The problem of individual conscience is, I think, set most clearly before us in the words of Charles Péguy in writing about the Dreyfus case:

> ...*a single injustice, a single crime, a single illegality, if it is officially recorded, confirmed, a single wrong to humanity, a single wrong to justice and to right, particularly if it is universally, legally, nationally, commodiously accepted ... a single crime shatters and is sufficient to shatter the whole social contract ... a single legal crime, a single dishonorable act will bring about the loss of one's honor, the dishonor of a whole people.*

And the broader historical judgment as suggested by Arnold Toynbee in his comments on Rome's war with Carthage:

Nemesis is a potent goddess ... War posthumously avenges the dead on the survivors, and the vanquished on the victors. The nemesis of war is intrinsic. It did not need the invention of the atomic weapon to make this apparent. It was illustrated more than two thousand years before our time, by Hannibal's legacy to Rome.

Hannibal gained a posthumous victory over Rome. Although he failed to defeat the great nation militarily because of the magnitude of her military manpower and solidity of the structure of the Roman Commonwealth, he did succeed in inflicting grievous wounds on the Commonwealth's body social and economic. They were so grievous that they festered into the revolution that was precipitated by Tiberius Gracchus and that did not cease till it was arrested by Augustus a hundred years later...this revolution," Toynbee said, "was the nemesis of Rome's superficially triumphant career of military conquest," and ended, of course, the Republic and substituted for it the spirit of the dictators and of the Caesars.

Those of us who are gathered here tonight are not advocating peace at any price. We are willing to pay a high price for peace – for an honorable, rational, and political solution to this war; a solution which will enhance our world position, which will permit us to give the necessary attention to our other commitments abroad, both military and non-military, and leave us with both human and physical resources and with moral energy to deal effectively with the pressing domestic problems of the United States itself.

I see little evidence that the Administration has set any limits on the price which it will pay for a military victory which becomes less and less sure and more hollow and empty in promise.

The scriptural promise of the good life is one in which the old men see visions and the young men dream dreams. In the context of this war and all of its implications, the young men of America do not dream dreams, but many live in the nightmare of moral anxiety, of concern and great apprehension; and the old men, instead of visions which they can offer to the young, are projecting, in the language of the Secretary of State, a specter of one billion Chinese threatening the peace and safety of the world – a frightening and intimidating future.

The message from the Administration today is a message of apprehension, a message of fear, yes – even a message of fear of fear.

This is not the real spirit of America. I do not believe that it is. This is a time to test the mood and spirit:

To offer in place of doubt – trust.

In place of expediency – right judgment.

In place of ghettos, let us have neighborhoods and communities.

In place of incredibility – integrity.

In place of murmuring, let us have clear speech; let us again hear America singing.

In place of disunity, let us have dedication of purpose.

In place of near despair, let us have hope.

This is the promise of greatness which was stated for us by Adlai Stevenson and which was brought to form and positive action in the words and actions of John Kennedy.

Let us pick up again these lost strands and weave them again into the fabric of America.

Let us sort out the music from the sounds and again respond to the trumpet and the steady drum.

Speech by Sen. Eugene McCarthy, Pfister Hotel, Milwaukee, Wisconsin, March 23, 1968

You in Wisconsin will understand that I was almost certain to win when in New Hampshire they asked me whether I felt a groundswell in February, and I said it felt more like a frost heave. We have gone on from that to frost heaves here in Wisconsin and also some sense of groundswell. If things continue as they are going, I think we will have to try to advance the date of the national elections. People are restless; they want to vote right now.

I do not want to take upon myself as much credit as Henry Reuss has given to me. You know I have been accused of being friendly to the poets. I have found them rather useful; I have a friend here tonight, Robert Lowell. Even the poets are restless now; they are not content to go along with Shelley and be the unacknowledged legislators of the world. They want to be acknowledged just a little bit. I have one very good line – it is really a variation from one of Robert Lowell's poems (I do not often use it at mixed meetings of this kind when there are Republicans present, but I am sure that those who are here will forgive me) – the line, as I use it, says that the Republicans cannot sink and will not swim.

This is their problem in any case. But those that are here are prepared to swim, I want you to know. And I am glad that they have not sunk. So we are ready to go.

This meeting is the midcourse in my campaign here in Wisconsin, and as we have gone on through New Hampshire and into this state, I think everyone in this country has come to realize that this nation is coming much closer to a most important time of decision. In New Hampshire, we had to call upon the people of that state to anticipate what this nation should do, and the same is true here in Wisconsin. But I think events are helping us to form at least the pattern within which that decision and that judgment must be made.

What happened in Vietnam in the last two months had really been projected by some of us as long ago as late 1966. What was stated in the presidential commission's report on riots and the problems of the city was something which some of us knew to be true and what many said had to be recognized and had to be dealt with. These two sets of events – one a report simply describing a reality in this country and the other a set of events indicating clearly what the reality is in Southeast Asia – have helped to prepare the way and brought us closer to the moment, or at least the hour, of truth in this country.

I said early in my campaign, not, I suppose, being quite sure as to what it meant, that I did not know whether in the course of this campaign we could make many people any more honest than they were. But I said I thought we would make a lot more of them truthful. And I think that is the challenge, and I think that there is some indication that we may be accomplishing more with reference to honesty than I anticipated, but certainly we moved much closer to truth in this nation.

Last Tuesday, the President called on all Americans to join in a total national effort to win the war and to win the peace and to complete the job that must be done here at home. And then he asked all America to join in a program of national austerity. This was a proper appeal for him to make in pursuit of a cause to which he was committed. Yet in 1966 in the State of the Union message, he said, "The nation is might enough, its society is healthy enough, to pursue our goals in the rest of the world while still building a great society here at home." Then he went on to say, "There are men who cry out, 'We must sacrifice.'" Let us rather ask them, who will they sacrifice? Are they going to sacrifice the children of this nation who seek learning, or the sick who need medical care, or the families who dwell in squalor? Not long ago, he said we could fight two wars and win them both. But now the call is for an austerity program.

It is after all the poor and the sick and the distressed who are being called upon to pay the price of the war in Vietnam. Providing most of the manpower for that war, the poor of this nation are bearing the principal cost of it in inflation and higher interest rates and are being asked to submit to an across-the-board surtax, which gives no recognition to the progressive character of our taxes and the tradition that those who are best able to pay are to be called upon to pay for wars. The poor are again being denied the promise which has been held out to them year after year for at least fifteen years since the end of World War II.

With rather startling swiftness and without any adequate explanation, the Administration's position has gone from one extreme to the other. First the war was no strain on our economy and no strain on our budget. Now the strain is so great that the whole nation must embark on an austerity program. Although the explanations abut the war and the economy veer from extreme to extreme, the policy remains essentially the same: a continuing war which is no longer defensible even on military grounds, and has long since passed the point which was defensible on political or diplomatic or moral grounds. All of us here know that this nation, our people, are prepared and willing to make great sacrifices for the country. They have done so again and again. In two world wars and again in the Korean war, they submitted to wartime rules and restrictions, and they will always rally in support of a wise and just cause. But they will not or should not rally to support policies of proven failure.

In some countries, people may have no choice but to make a show of support for their government. In a free country such as ours, in an election year, people not only have an opportunity to demonstrate their position and to exercise choice, but they have a clear responsibility to pass judgment on existing programs and policies, to make decisions, and to indicate what they consider to be the priorities for this nation. It is to this end that I am, and have become by rather a strange way, your candidate for the presidency of the United States of America.

This movement of which you are a part, and which I, in a limited way, personify now by interaction of many circumstances, is not a movement which is carrying on a simple educational program in this country, as it was suggested we were going to do when we started. We are not really out trying to raise an issue for the attention of the people of this nation, because the issue has been raised and the people of this nation are aware of what that issue is. What we are doing is laying down a challenge to control the presidency of the United States of America. And I want to tell you that in pursuing this office I am not really fulfilling any boyhood dream of mine and not even a late adult dream. I could not say that the first time I looked at the White House I said, "I want to live there some time." In fact, I thought it should have been made into a museum the first time I saw it. And I am not seeking this office because party leaders sought me and urged me to run, or because I read most encouraging signs in the press of this nation. Nor could I say that I have any claim on it by way of succession.

I said in 1960 that power sometimes came to men who sought it, and I said I was not sure that the record of history showed that those who sought to gain power necessarily exercised it well or best in a democratic society. I prefer to support a man who has sought out to hold public office. The seeking of me as a candidate came like the dew in the night. It was rather gentle, I must say, soft, but there were signs in the morning that something had happened during the night, and so here I am. I can no longer say that I have not been supported by a single major American political figure, since I have the support of Henry Reuss. They cannot even say, as they did in New Hampshire, that not one United States Senator was supporting me. That, too, has changed.

I have not really become a candidate because a combination was put together in support of me. I saw a story today where one potential candidate has twenty-six separate committees of various kinds of Americans. I knew that Howard Johnson had twenty-eight varieties of ice cream, but did not know that there were twenty-six varieties of Americans who could be combined for political purposes. I have but one variety: a constituency that is a constituency of conscience. And, I believe, a constituency of hope and trust in the future. The only defectors who have come over to me are those who have defected from fear and from disillusionment and from defeatism and a kind of near despair in America; and those are most welcome defectors.

So we go on from here in this campaign for the presidency, and I think since you are so far committed perhaps I should not even tell you of my conception of the office, but let you wonder about it, and later discover me, like some are discovered.

I think that anyone who offers himself or permits himself to be offered or supported for the presidency must meet two or three conditions of character and experience and understanding. He must, I believe, be able to read with reasonable judgment the needs and the aspirations of the people of this nation. And I do hope that some twenty years in the Congress of the United States, in the House and the Senate, my travels around this land, and a limited amount of reading have brought me to the point where I have some comprehension of what this country is all about, what it needs, and what its people seek. I think a man who is presented for the presidency must also know the limitations of power and the limitations that must be placed upon the exercise of power in that office in which you do have the greatest power in any office in the modern world. He should understand that this country does not so much need leadership, because the potential for leadership in a free country must exist in every man and every woman. He must be prepared to be a kind of channel for those desires and those aspirations, perhaps giving some direction to the movement of the country largely by the way of setting people free.

The office of the presidency of the United States must never be a personal office. A President should not speak of "my country" but always of "our country"; not of "my cabinet" but of "the cabinet," because once the cabinet is appointed, it becomes something different from the man who may have nominated these persons, even from the Senate which confirms them in office; not of "my ambassador to the United Nations" but "the United States ambassador to the United Nations." This is the conception of an office which belongs not to the man who holds it but to the people of this nation: an office which must be exercised by the will of the majority who elect one to office; not in the sole interest of that majority, but by their determination for the good of the entire nation.

The role of the presidency – at all times, but particularly in 1968 – must be one of uniting this nation, not of adding it up some way, not of putting it together as a kind of odd-size jigsaw puzzle, for to unify this nation means to inspire it. Rather than to organize, we need to develop a sense of character in the nation with common purposes and shared ideals, and then move on as best we can to achieve limited or great progress toward establishing an order of justice in America.

The need now is not for division but rather for a great reconciliation: a reconciliation of the young and of the old, of labor and management, and farmers and businessmen, of the academic community with society as a whole; a reconciliation of race with race; a reconciliation of the Congress with the presidency, and, I hope, even of the Secretary of State with the Foreign Relations Committee; a reconciliation principally of the thought and the spirit and the best traditions of this nation with our most pressing need for action.

An ancient Celtic poet, called Cadoc the Wise, in one of his writings said that no man can love his country unless he loves justice, and no one can love justice unless he also has a love of learning, and no one can love learning unless has a love of poetry and song. You can reverse the order and say that no one who is insensitive to poetry and song can have respect for learning and no one who has no respect for learning can have real respect for justice, and that no one who does not respect justice can, in fact, manifest a true love for his country. We are called upon in our effort to be mindful of all of these considerations.

We call upon the people of this nation to pass judgment – a referendum on the war itself and our involvement in that war, upon the question of priorities for this nation, and more importantly on the very purpose and role we expect the United States to play in what remains of this century and, we would hope, in the century beyond.

This need not be a nation in anxiety and distress. This need not be a nation of mistrust and fear; we can return to what we have promised to be. I would conclude with lines from Walt Whitman which I think can describe the America of the very near future if we are prepared to do what it is indicated we must do: stop the war and proceed to deal with the problems of America and make our contribution to the needs of the world. He said:

I hear America singing, the varied carols I hear;
Those of mechanics – each one singing his, as it should be, blithe and
    strong;
The carpenter singing his, as he measures his plank or beam,
The mason singing his, as he makes ready for work, or leaves off work;

The boatman singing what belongs to him in his boat – the deck-hand
singing on the steamboat deck;
The shoemaker singing as he sits on his bench – the hatter singing as he
stands;
The wood-cutter's song – the ploughboy's on his way in the morning, or
at the noon intermission, or at sundown;
The delicious singing of the mother – or of the young wife at work – or of
the girl sewing or washing;
Each singing what belongs to him or her, and to none else.
And then he writes, speaking of the future, and speaking of all of us – and
we speak now to the youngest among us and to those who will come
after us –

Poets to come! Orators, singers, musicians to come!
Not to-day is to justify me, and answer what I am for;

He said:

But you, a new brood, native, athletic, continental, greater than
before known.

He was speaking of us. And then he said – and this must be our theme:

Arouse! Arouse – for you must justify me – you must answer.

Appendix 7

Speech by Senator Eugene J. McCarthy, Sargent Gymnasium, Boston University, Boston, Massachusetts, April 11, 1968

Professor Galbraith, students, faculty, and friends here at Boston University.

This has been in many ways a most unusual experiment in American politics. I hesitate to call it a campaign because it is just beginning to take on that character. It was said in the beginning that we could not accomplish what we set out to do because there was no precedent for what we were doing. That left the way open to all of us, particularly students, the academic profession, the more venturesome citizens of this country, and at least on politician who was prepared to take some chances. You have to be most careful of a politician who has no further ambitions, because he might run for President.

And so, by a coming together of judgment of confidence and a feeling of what had to be done in America, we did begin last November this effort which is continuing with such success. At least I thought it began last November after I had been on five or six college campuses around this country and found a demand that somehow the American political process be tested and that people of this country be given a chance to pass upon what that time obviously were the great national issues facing this nation.

I read Jimmy Breslin the other day and he said I decided to do it in Dublin at Easter time in 1966. I did not know it went back that far; he said it happened at three o'clock in the morning. Well, no one ought to dispute Breslin at three o'clock in the morning if he remembers something from Dublin, Ireland, and it might have been the right time because we were observing the fiftieth anniversary of the Easter Uprising. And for our movement in a kind of 1968 uprising, in which all of you have participated and are participating, I think that the colleges and the students of the colleges of this country deserve the principal credit for influencing me to move to the point at which I thought that something had to take place in this country, that something had to happen, that someone had to provide the leadership.

As to just what went into my making the decision to move as I did – well, that remains something of a political and personal secret, but I suppose that at some point I will have to explain it.

As of now I am reading all the columnists, all those who wrote about me in the early stages – the liberals who explained me in terms of some kind of psychological disturbance, and the conservatives who were more inclined to use traditional vices like anger or envy or jealousy or hatred. I got to a point where I almost favored the conservative columnists; they even attributed to me some vices that I thought had been forgotten in the modern world.

In any case, the campaign was moved along, mobilizing the general concern that was abroad in this country only four or five months ago that somehow the country had come apart, that it was unraveling, that instead of rather clear lines and threads we had become a nation of pulp in which no clear or positive decision would be made.

I think that it is quite clear now, by virtue of what has happened in two primaries and from other indications, that changes have taken place in this country, that this nation has made a decision with reference to the war in Vietnam. A public judgment has been passed.

And I do not say that this happened because of the particular arguments that any of us made (although I think that perhaps our presentation of the case helped some), but it did happen because we were prepared to put the issue before the public, to test their judgment and to test their will. Their response has been such that, in my opinion, this Administration or any administration that follows will have to dedicate itself and commit its powers to bringing that war to an end as quickly as possible.

The citizens of this country have taken it upon themselves to pass judgment, not leaving it to the executive branch of the government, not leaving it to the Congress, not leaving it to the national conventions, but in public forum, openly and clearly having said that they feel that this war cannot continue to be justified on a military basis or a diplomatic basis or an economic basis, but principally that the war must end because it is not morally justified. For the most part in the rest of this campaign, I think we can consider this mission if not altogether accomplished, at least half accomplished, and begin to deal with the other most pressing problems which face this country: the issue of civil rights and the needs of the people who live in poverty and suppression in our great cities.

I want to talk to you tonight principally about this problem and relate it at least in the beginning to the recent assassination of Dr. Martin Luther King. I sat on the steps of the Lincoln Memorial in 1963 when the first great march on Washington occurred. Martin Luther King was one of the speakers that day. The object of the march was to move the Congress of the United States to act on what we considered to be the basic or traditional civil rights, the limited civil rights – the right to vote, the right to equal protection under the law – those things which are very clearly defined in the Constitution of the United States and are as old as this country and even older in the history of the Western culture out of which our Constitution was drawn. The right to vote, the right of equality under the law – all of these in 1963 and 1964 were so accepted and so proved that there should not have been any necessity for a march on Washington and not even any need for special legislation. But the fact is that the march was necessary and the special legislation was also needed.

During the century which followed the Civil War, our country's Negro population had endured the system of discrimination and segregation which is totally incompatible with the Constitution of the United States and with the whole philosophy upon which we have been attempting to build this democracy for nearly two hundred years. For all those Americans traditionally classified as minorities, the elemental rights of American citizenship, were cleared away with the passage of the Civil Rights bills of 1964 and 1965. Yet as the National Advisory Commission on Civil Disorders pointed out and as Martin Luther King understood when he planned the Poor People's March this year, these legal victories did very little to alleviate the social and economic conditions which were at the root of the ghetto dweller's plight in America. Still remaining in this country is what the commission called the pervasive discrimination and segregation in employment, in education, and in housing which have resulted in the continued exclusion of Negroes from our current prosperity. What, in effect, we have is a kind of colonial nation living in our midst which is not allowed full participation in the good life of America – not very different, in fact, from the way in which some of the European countries were treating their colonial subjects, with the one difference that their subjects were separated by geography and ours are here in our own country.

Still remaining, as the commission also pointed out, is the pattern of Negro migration into the core areas of our cities, combined with a corresponding exodus of the white population, creating new ghettos. What we have is the convergence of all of these conditions – poor housing, limited educational opportunities, inadequate health care, low income, and dependency on welfare – a kind of handout state. Mired in the cycle of poverty, North Americans (especially the young ones) are presented through television with the constant reminder of the benefits of society, of the good life which is now enjoyed by the overwhelming majority of the white citizens of this country.

In many respects, the legislative gains of three and four years ago have heightened this frustration because there was implied in the passage of that basic civil rights legislation the promise that the people who were to be benefited by it would see a new America. The door, in a sense, was opened to them, but once it was opened, they found the other side was the same kind of dismal and disappointing life they had been suffering from before the passage of the Civil Rights bill. The expected new participation in the good life which so many Negro citizens had longed for and even anticipated simply did not materialize after we passed the 1964 and 1965 Civil Rights bills. This is the picture of disappointment and frustration which was drawn by the President's

Commission on Civil Disorders – a most responsible and perhaps the most significant political document to be published in this country in this century.

Some people have said that the picture which is painted in the report is overly grim and overly defensive. I do not think that this is a fair judgment. Th report, as I read it, was written with a kind of optimism, the optimism which I think is the only kind of honest optimism, the only kind we can accept, which comes when you see things to be as bad as in fact they are, when you take an honest look at the situation, but having done that, you still proceed in the belief and in the hope that something positive and constructive can be done about the circumstances. This must be our attitude, and certainly this is the only alternative to the kind of pessimism in which you see how bad things are and then despair and decide that nothing can be done about the situation.

Leaving aside all considerations of the past and all traditions and all history, there is sufficient moral burden upon us within the immediacy of this year itself to compel us to take action. And this is the significant conclusion of the President's commission's report: that we must begin immediately and on a massive scale to attack the causes of unrest and of dissent and of riots, and to proceed to bring within reach of all Americans all of those things which make up what we call the good life. This was the second dream and the object of Martin Luther King's most recent effort. Now that he has been assassinated in the pursuit of this cause, we can only resolve even more strongly to dedicate ourselves to the end that equality may become in America not a word, not a phrase, not a desirable objective, but a reality.

In addition to those traditional and constitutionally guaranteed legal civil rights, we must move on to establish a whole new set of civil rights which we consider to be the rights of every American citizen. First among these must be the right to a decent job, one which is becoming to the dignity of a man, a job which returns him satisfaction as an intelligent and creative person, and also an income with which he can support his family in dignity and in decency. This is not a simple declaration of a desirable objective, such as it was in 1946 when we passed the full-employment act, but rather an objective statement which must be realized within a period of two or three years. In order to secure it in the first instance, we must move on the question of income. The federal government must proceed to determine what a minimum income is and attempt to insure it for all Americans.

The second new citizen's right which we must pursue is the right to adequate health care without regard to income or without regard to race or without regard to habitation. This is a right which is not specifically guaranteed under the Constitution, but is very clearly implied in the concept of equality and in the search for happiness which is basic to the whole American way of life. To secure this right, we must have a federally subsidized insurance program to assure that no citizen will be deprived of health care because of lack of funds, because of income, or because of lack of facilities. This is not particularly revolutionary; most states now require automobile liability insurance, and it seems to me that we can take another step and say we ought to have some kind of insurance simply to protect the health of our people, whether they are hurt in automobile accidents or whether they just get sick.

Third, every American must now be accorded the right not simply to equal education or a kind of average education, but to that kind of education and that amount of education which is necessary to develop his full potential. This for the most talented among us, whose gifts, of course, must be brought to serve the whole society, but also for those of average gift, and those who are most handicapped and least gifted, but who have the potential to come to some knowledge of the truth no matter how limited that knowledge may be. In order to secure this right, we must have a massive program to upgrade the education of our adults who have been trapped in the poverty syndrome. This can be done through federally subsidized on-the-job training, through special vocational schools, and through adult literacy courses, and all of the other devices which are at hand for this purpose. For young Americans, projects such as Head Start, and late start, and even middle start must be established and perfected and expanded. Vocational training should come, as I see it, not in the form of some kind of public works program, but in on-the-job training programs provided largely within private industry itself.

This is a special problem for us today because the old more or less natural process by which men and women rose from being utterly unskilled to being somewhat skilled, to being semiskilled, to being skilled workers – a process which ran in this country for a hundred years, which was open to most immigrants but closed to the Negroes – no longer exists. Because of automation and the progress of technology, most of the middle steps of progress have been eliminated. What we must do is to take people who are unskilled by virtue of social pressures, which kept them from rising at a time when they might have risen through the normal steps to being skilled and even to being professional people, and move them over within one generation at least two steps, which have at the present been altogether removed from the process by which men rose in American industry and in American business in years past.

The final new citizen's right which I will speak of to you tonight is the right to a decent house – not a house in isolation, not a house in a ghetto, but a house in a neighborhood which is part of a community which must be a part of the United States of America.

There is no time for postponement, for the time is now. One of the witnesses who appeared before the commission noted that he had read the reports of the 1919 Chicago race riot and had found that what it recorded was essentially the same as that which was recorded after the Harlem riot of 1935, and even essentially the same as what the McCone Commission reported on the Watts riots of recent times. He said this a kind of Alice in Wonderland world with the same moving picture shown over and over again, the same analysis, the same recommendations, and, he said, the same inaction. So the time has come. The time has come to put an end to that kind of meaningless and purposeless and ineffective rerun of old reports.

I think the people of this country are ready for action and that this action – this readiness for action – is not limited to any racial minority or any single political interest group, but is shared almost universally by Americans, just as the sense of sorrow at the assassination and at the devastation which followed is also shared almost universally in this country of ours. It can be said, of course, that extremists and agitators exist on every side – on the white and on the black side. We cannot altogether eliminate the kind of wickedness of those who committed or participated in the assassination of the Reverend Martin Luther King and some who seem even to have applauded afterward and those who fomented the riots or applauded them after they occurred. These people are not even worthy of being considered, in my judgment, a minority in America, but are a deviation from the general pattern in this country.

The most important and profound causes of riots are rooted, we must accept, in the conditions of modern urban life, in poverty and, especially, in the ghettos of our great cities. Just as American Negroes are weary of the demeaning conditions and the racist attitudes which have brought rioting to our cities, so are all other Americans tired of the riots that these conditions cause. The country is longing for rational judgment and, on that basis, for a reconciliation which leads us to a new unity and to the strength of common purpose.

Throughout my campaign, whether it was in the somewhat cold and somewhat lonely towns and villages of northern New Hampshire or even in the more crowded streets of south Milwaukee, I have stressed the need for this kind of reconciliation, not a reconciliation of unreason, not a kind of unity for the sake of unity, not something which comes of our putting aside any kind of analysis of what our problems are or from refusing to consider the causes of division in this country, but, rather, a reconciliation which is based on reasoned judgment and moral commitment. This, I believe, is the great difference between the kind of political challenge which faces us in 1968 and that which faced us just a few years ago in 1948 and 1958 when the issues we were raising were relatively simple.

The need for medical care for the aged, for example, in 1948 was really not a great test of intelligence. It seemed a rather obvious thing. To see the need for federal aid to education in 1948, we did not require consultation with experts. The evidence was every place. To see the need for a housing program, particularly for public housing in the years after World War II, did not require any special kind of revelation or special insight. It was obvious that this need was present and the same was true of the basic civil rights bill, which we began to talk about as long ago as 1948. In addition to that, support for these programs did not require a great moral commitment, because almost everyone could see some personal benefit in it for himself, a kind of direct and almost selfish benefit. But the issues we are talking about today and the problems we are talking about today and the kinds of commitment we are calling for today – this does require something different. It requires a greater commitment of intellect to understand the problems of our cities, the problems of racial discrimination and racial antagonism, to understand the problems we face in international affairs. It requires a much greater commitment of intellect and much greater application of whatever knowledge we possess, but more important that that, a greater commitment of our moral strength, a greater commitment of will, than we have ever been called upon to commit in the past. This is the challenge.

I would say to you here tonight that I believe that this nation is prepared to make both of these commitments. We have passed a judgment on the war and we have also passed the point of no return with reference to our domestic problems, and somehow in these two steps the spirit of this country has been released. I sense a new flow of confidence in America, a new sense of understanding and of common purpose. Not that we are proceeding as though this were a new kind of dream world in which there would be no more war, one from which all potential for fault and failure had been eliminated – because this is certainly not the case; but this is an America which I think is not just on the edge but beyond the edge of repudiating the somewhat cynical criticism which some Europeans have been directing at us in recent years: that this would be the first great nation in the world that would decline before it had reached its peak. I do not think that will happen. Or the first nation that would grow old before it had reached maturity. We are repudiating that judgment upon us in this year of 1968.

We are demonstrating that we are not afraid to deal with differences in our own country as we have in the past (differences of nationality), as today we are prepared to deal significantly with racial differences and economic differences. We are not even afraid of the prospect of one billion Chinese by the year 2000 – even with nuclear weapons – as Secretary Rusk suggested a few months ago. We are not afraid of the future, and I would say we are proving that we have avoided that one fear against which Franklin Roosevelt warned us – that we are not even afraid of fear itself. We are not afraid of decision; we are not afraid of responsibility; and we have proved that we are not afraid, in this campaign, to test American democracy.

We are proving again, as we have in the past, when put to the test, that we, the people of the United States, deserve self-government, and deserve the democracy, but on the other hand, that democracy, self-government, and freedom are also being well served by the American people.

Appendix 8

Article by E. W. Kenworthy
The New York Times, May 5, 1968

Senator Eugene J. McCarthy accused the national office of Citizens for Kennedy today of distorting and even falsifying some parts of his voting record.

"I am surprised," Mr. McCarthy said in a telephone interview, "not only by the distortions of my voting record by the Citizens for Kennedy but also by the positively false statements about my record. If any such thing had been issued in my name, I would have repudiated it at once and set the record straight."

The accusation came two days before the Indiana primary. The polls will open at 6 A.M., Tuesday and close at 7 P.M. There are 4,361 precincts with 3,085 voting by machine. Party officials predict that about 700,000 votes will be cast in the Democratic primary.

Mr. McCarthy was referring to a press release and mimeographed brochure listing "issues" along with the votes of the two Senators. They were issued April 19 by the national office of Citizens for Kennedy at 39 West 96th Street, New York, and widely circulated.

Mr. McCarthy was also referring to a letter written March 30 on the stationary of the citizens headquarters by Roberta S. Feuerlicht to Mrs. Anita J. Greenbaum of Newton, Mass., in which Mrs. Feuerlicht accused Mr. McCarthy of having voted against many measures supported by "liberals" and having failed to vote on many others.

Pierre Salinger, one of Mr. Kennedy's press secretaries, said here today in response to a query: "I have not seen it, and it is not anything being organized by the national headquarters of the Kennedy campaign."

He was referring to the Kennedy for President headquarters in Washington.

Following are some of the statements in the citizens' brochure of the Feuerlicht letter which formed the basis of Mr. McCarthy's accusation, together with a description of the bill involved and the votes or announced positions of the two Senators as recorded by the Congressional Quarterly in Washington, an independent research organization that issues periodically a detailed record of all votes on important legislation.

1. MODEL CITIES.

The brochure and Mrs. Feuerlicht report Mr. McCarthy as not voting September 19, 1967, on an amendment to increase the Model Cities funds by $300 million. The Congressional Quarterly records both Mr. McCarthy and Mr. Kennedy as voting "yes."

2. MEDICARE AND SOCIAL SECURITY

The brochure and Mrs. Feuerlicht report Mr. McCarthy absent November 16, 1967, when the Senate defeated a motion to kill an amendment to expand Medicare to cover costs of drugs for the elderly. The Congressional Quarterly records Mr. Kennedy voting against the Motion to kill and Mr. McCarthy absent but "announced against" the motion.

The brochure and Mrs. Feuerlicht charge Mr. McCarthy with opposing regulation of the drug industry by his vote on November 21, 1967, to kill an amendment that would require the government to pay the generic rather than the trademark name price for drugs purchased for Federally aided programs.

Mr. McCarthy explained this vote by saying it was at the request of the Department of Health, Education and Welfare, which wanted to delay this legislation until a study that was being made on the whole question of drug prices had been completed. When the Senate rejected delay, he voted for the amendment because he favored it, he said.

The Congressional Quarterly records him and Mr. Kennedy as voting "yes" on the legislation itself. Neither the brochure nor Mrs. Feuerlicht mention this.

3. RENT SUPPLEMENTS

Mrs. Feuerlicht wrote that Mr. McCarthy had "managed not to vote" on funds for rent supplements, and the brochure says that he "missed" votes on them.

The Congressional Quarterly records that both Mr. Kennedy and Mr. McCarthy voted on September 19, 1967, for an amendment to the housing appropriation bill to provide $40 million in new rent supplement funds. On an amendment to cut the funds in half, Mr. Kennedy voted "no" and Mr. McCarthy was absent but "announced against."

4. OIL DEPLETION ALLOWANCE

Mrs. Feuerlicht wrote that "in the past Senator McCarthy has supported the oil depletion allowance" on tax returns of oil producers. The brochure said that the Senator on February 6, 1964, had voted against reducing the allowance.

Mr. McCarthy explains that vote by saying that the then Secretary of the Treasury, Douglas Dillon, had urged defeat of the amendment reducing the allowance from 27 1/5% to 20% so as not to jeopardize passage of the tax cut bill.

Senate Finance Committee records show that on June 24, 1959, June 9 and 15, 1960, and August 25, 1961, Mr. McCarthy voted for the amendment of Senator Paul Douglas to reduce the allowance to 15% for companies with a gross income above $5 million and to 21% for those with a gross income of $1 million to $5 million. It was defeated each time.

The Congressional Quarterly records that twice he supported this amendment when Mr. Douglas offered it on the floor – on June 20 and September 15, 1962.

As late as March 1966, he supported another Douglas reduction amendment in committee.

Neither the brochure nor Mrs. Feuerlicht mentions this support for reduction.

Los Angeles County Primary Election – 1968

(MEXICAN PRECINCTS)

Precinct	McCarthy	Lynch[47]	Kennedy
778	91	27	71
1189 combined with 1183 total	57	9	47
1849	39	11	217
50	46	10	209
51	51	7	235
52	40	17	228
53	34	3	283
54	38	11	256
55	38	18	245
56	34	9	240
57	26	14	167
58	53	11	202
59	58	8	208
60	39	8	232
1894	50	11	296

[47] Johnson-Humphrey stand-in

Los Angeles County General Election – 1968

Precinct	Nixon	Humphrey
778	217	190
1189	73	58
1849	58	244
50	43	241
51	49	284
52	36	261
53	26	312
54	35	308
55	38	283
56	32	283
57	62	211
58	51	229
59	66	260
60	82	261
1894	71	326

Excerpts of an Article by E. W. Kenworthy, The New York Times, August 30, 1968

Two days ago Senator Eugene J. McCarthy ended his forlorn and foredoomed trek among the delegations with a call on West Virginia's. At one point he reminded the delegates of the Biblical toilers who came into the field at the eleventh hour and those who had arrived in the chill of the morning.

"They also received a penny," he said. "Maybe that's what I'll get."

He sounded embittered. Actually he was not. After nine months of exhausting campaigning that took him into 40 states and through seven primaries at a cost of several millions of dollars, he had very much more to show than a penny's worth. And he knew it.

Campaign posters are not notable for either truth or understatement. But there was understated truth in the one showing Gene McCarthy in a cobbled square with the caption: "He stood up alone and something happened."

He had made the Vietnam war the issue of the campaign, driven Senator Robert F. Kennedy out of irresolution and into a rival challenge of President Johnson, and driven the President to modify his war policy and renounce renomination for fear of further dividing in the country.

The Senator was not depressed yesterday when the convention, by a 2-to-1 margin, rejected the dovish Vietnam plank. He was convinced that he, and the murdered Robert Kennedy, and the late-blooming Senator George S. McGovern had made such a telling case against the war that the next President would have to liquidate it.

Nor was he greatly concerned about the disillusioning effect of his defeat on his youthful followers. After midnight yesterday, he told reporters: "I think it's been worth it. We have opened up a new kind of politics in America."

He believed his young supporters, and Bobby Kennedy's and George McGovern's would carry on with it. "They have a deep sense of responsibility to their country," he told the West Virginia delegation.

At the heart of the mystery of how he had done what he had done lay the mystery of the man himself. For, after all the exposure on television, the daily news stories, the analytical articles, he remained hidden – from the public, the politicians whose favor he needed, the reporters who watched him and talked with him day after day.

Obviously, a very private man. But other private men in politics – Senator Mike Mansfield for one, Senator McGovern for another – make concessions to the ways and shibboleths of their trade. And so, as the campaign continued, so did the question: "Is he a serious candidate?"

The question should have been broken up. Is he a candidate for President? Is he serious about what he is doing?

The answer to the first question is that he did not so see himself at the outset. As late as April 1, after the President's withdrawal, he said he had agreed to run, "not aspiring to the Presidency directly" but because the issue of the war had to be personalized in a candidacy.

This candor appalled some of his advisers, and he later humorously alluded to his deficiencies in their eyes. They had come to him originally, he said, like the seven women in Isaiah (Chap. IV, 1), saying: "We will provide our own bread and our own apparel. Just lend us your name."

"But," he said, "pretty soon they were suing me for nonsupport."

There was never, however, any question among those who followed his campaign about the seriousness with which he took his cause.

Senator McCarthy is highly articulate but rarely eloquent. Strangely enough, in a man who loves poetry and writes it, he seems in his speeches to shun the concrete noun and the strong verb. He will smudge an otherwise telling sentence with meaningless qualifiers, with "in terms of" and "with reference to." He has developed the run-on sentence into the run-on paragraph.

Yet there have been occasions, usually before small crowds on Saturday night when it is too late to catch the Sunday editions, when something has moved him and he has lapsed – it seemed almost unconsciously – into an eloquence that revealed the fire burning beneath the cool surface.

It happened one Saturday night in New Hampshire before a rather small crowd in the gymnasium of the Bishop Guertin High School in Nashua. He said:

"We have supported a war which is contrary to our tradition, a tradition which is as old as this country. We would not proceed generally to war without some attention to what was called the respect for the decent opinion of mankind. In this war we do not have the support of the decent opinion of mankind.

"Nation after nation has indicated their disapproval, has suggested to us that we stop bombing, or that we negotiate. Most recently the terrible cry raised by the bishops of South Vietnam is one to which we must attend. They said collectively, 'In the name of God, let the killing to come an end!' and also other Vietnamese, poets and other spokesmen, have said that in the name of humanity this war should come to an end. I think the time has come for us as Americans and citizens of the United States to say, 'In the name of America and all that it stands for, this war must be brought to an end.'"

It happened again on a Saturday night in Milwaukee before a mixed group of Democratic and Republican businessmen.

"I have not really become a candidate because a combination was put together in support of me. I saw a story today where on potential candidate has 26 separate committees of various kinds of Americans. I knew that Howard Johnson had 28 varieties of ice cream, but did not know that there were 26 varieties of Americans who could be combined for political purposes. I do not really have but one variety: a constituency that is a constituency of conscience. And, I think, a constituency of hope and trust in the future. And the only defectors who have come over to me are those who have defected from fear and from disillusionment and from defeatism and a kind of near despair in America. And those are most welcome defectors."

Senator McCarthy does not believe truth is single and personal, but – with Cardinal Newman – that it may well be "the limit of converging probabilities," and therefore he advocates that Cabinet members have a constituency of their own, the better to speak out in meeting when they differ with the President.

There runs through the Senator's speeches a sense of history and continuity. And this is because he is basically a conservative, though his legislative record is liberal.

It is just because is a conservative that he set out to challenge the President within the party structure and to bring the disillusioned young dissidents into that structure, with the promise – somewhat nervous – that they could be effective there.

If this is so, it is asked repeatedly, then why will he not support Vice President Humphrey unless Mr. Humphrey turns himself around on Vietnam?

Because he sees a political party as an instrument and not as an end, or a good, in itself. There again, his approach is not political but moral and religious. The other day, when he offered his platform plank on Vietnam, he said he was not asking for "repentance" from the Administration and the party. Perhaps not, but he was asking for confession. Confession may be good for the soul, but politicians have never believed it is good for the party.

Senator McCarthy does. The first step to correcting error is to admit error. He told the North Carolina delegation that he knew this was hard. But, he said, the party had no other course "because we have a special responsibility for the war in Vietnam, since we said in 1964 that what has happened would not happen." The delegates listened with amazement to this application of Christian ethic to politics.

In a speech to the Fellowship of Reconciliation in New York last June, the Senator said:

"I think America stands at a critical point of decision...Never has a nation been so clearly confronted with the biblical saying that 'I put before you life and death and you must make the choice.' And I would hope that we as a nation, when facing that question, will choose life and demonstrate all of those virtues which have marked us in our best time."

The Senator may be right or wrong, or just impractical. But a man who thinks of the nation's troubles in those terms, who repeatedly tells his audience that the "highest level of patriotism" is to "to serve one's country not in submission but to serve it in truth," is not likely "to give up to party what was meant for mankind."

A strange candidate. A strange campaign.

In Fresno last May, after his defeat in Indiana and Nebraska, the Senator said to an airport crowd of mostly college students:

"The Secretary of Agriculture [Orville Freeman] has said we will be 'only a footnote in history.' But I think we can say with Churchill, 'But what a footnote!' And I think it could well be that we will become part of the main text."

236

Index

238

Acknowledgment is made to the following for kindly allowing use of their material:

Bly, Robert for "Counting Small-Boned Bodies" from Light Around the Body, ©1967 by Robert Bly.

Booth, Philip for "Maine" from The Islanders, ©1960 by Philip Booth, Viking Press.

Brown, Sue for the poem "For Gene," by Sue Brown.

Cather, Willa "Prairie Spring" from O Pioneers, © Willa Cather, Houghton Mifflin

Day-Lewis, C. "Sonnet for a Political Worker" from Short Is the Time, by permission Harold Matson Co., Inc.

Frost, Robert "New Hampshire" and "Stopping by Woods on a Snowy Evening," from Complete Poems of Robert Frost, ©1923 by permission of Holt, Rinehart and Winston, Inc., and Jonathan Cape Ltd.

Haag, John for "Kilroy"

Johnson, Gladys for "Convention,".

Kandler, Caroline for "The Candidates"

Kenworthy, E. W. articles by, 8/30/68, and 5/5/68. ©1968 by New York Times Company.

Lowell, Robert, for "Waking Early on Sunday Morning," from Near the Ocean, ©1965 by Robert Lowell.

Nhat Hanh, lines from "Our Green Garden" from Viet Nam Poems, Unicorn Press.

Orwell, George, "*Politics and the English Language*" from Shooting an Elephant and Other Essays, permission Harcourt, Brace & World, Inc., Martin Seeker & Warburg, Ltd., and Miss Sonia Brownell.

Stafford, William & The New Yorker for "An Oregon Message," ©1968 by The New Yorker Magazine

Yeats, William Butler for "An Irish Airman Foresees His Death" from Collected Poems ©1919 by Macmillan Co., renewed 1947 by Bertha Georgie Yeats, permission of Macmillan New York

About the Author

Eugene J. McCarthy was born in Watkins, Minnesota, in 1916, graduated from St. John's University in Collegeville, Minnesota, in 1935, and received a Master of Arts from the University of Minnesota in 1938.

During World War II, he served as a civilian technical assistant in military intelligence for the War Department. He was acting head of the sociology department at the College of St. Thomas in St. Paul at the time of his election to Congress in 1948.

Re-elected four more times, Mr. McCarthy represented Minnesota's 4th District in the House of Representatives for ten years, serving on Post Office & Civil Service, Agriculture, Interior & Insular Affairs, Banking & Currency, and Ways & Means committees.

McCarthy served two terms in the U.S. Senate from 1959 to 1971, serving on the Finance, Agriculture & Forestry, and Public Works committees, the Senate Special Committee on Unemployment Problems and from 1965 to 1969 he served on the Senate Foreign Relations Committee and chaired the special subcommittee on African Affairs. His run for the presidency in 1968, reported in this book, electrified the nation and forced a national political debate on issues fundamental to the operation of a deomocratic state. In 1976 and 1992 McCarthy again ran for the presidency to bring forward some discussion of these fundamentals, examined herein and in many of his other books which include:

America Revisited (Doubleday)
An American Bestiary (Lone Oak Press)
And Time Began (Lone Oak Press)
Challenge of Freedom (Avon)
Colony of the World (Hippocrene)
Complexities & Contraries (Harcourt)
Dictionary of American Politics (Macmillan)
Frontiers in American Democracy (World Publishing)
Ground Fog & Night (Harcourt)
Liberal Answer to the Conservative Challenge (Macfadden-Bartell)
Limits of Power (Holt)
Memories of a Native Son (Lone Oak Press)
Mr. Raccoon & His Friends (Academy Chicago)
No-Fault Politics (Times Books)
Nonfinancial Economic (Praeger)
Required Reading (Harcourt)
Selected Poems (Lone Oak Press)
Ultimate Tyranny (Harcourt)
Up 'Til Now (Harcourt)
View From Rappahannock (Lone Oak Press)